Wok Cookbook for Begi

CW01429127

300+ TRADITIONAL AND MODERN CHINESE RECIPES FOR STIR-FRYING, STEAMING, DEEP-FRYING, AND SMOKING WITH THE MOST VERSATILE TOOL IN THE KITCHEN

TABLE OF CONTENTS

Introduction 9

   How To Care For Your Wok.................... 9

   Chinese Cooking 10

     Stir-Frying............................10

     Blanching 10

     Poaching 11

     Deep-Frying 11

     Shallow Frying 11

     Slow-Simmering And Steeping...................11

     Braising And Red Braising 11

     Steaming 11

     Roasting 12

     Barbecuing 12

     Reheating Meals 12

     Twice Cooking 12

Chapter 1: Tools Needed 13

   Bamboo Steamer............................ 13

   Tongs Or Chopsticks 13

   Wide Spatula 13

   Strainer Or Slotted Spoon.................. 14

   Steamers 14

   Cleaver 14

   Chopping Board 14

Chapter 2: Techniques To Learn 15

   Horizontal Or Flat Slicing 15

   Roll Cutting 15

   Shredding............................ 16

   Dicing............................ 16

   Mincing............................ 16

   Marinating 16

   Thickening............................ 16

   Velveting............................ 16

Chapter 3: Dumplings Recipe 17

   1.   Chicken Arrabbiata Stew And Parmesan Dumplings 17

   2.   Oxtail Stew With Dumplings........ 17

   3.   Pork Goulash With Herby Dumplings . 18

   4.   Vegetable Stew With Herby Dumplings 19

   5.   Beef And Guinness Stew With Dumplings 20

   6.   Watercress Soup With Bacon Dumplings 20

   7.   Chipotle Sweet Potato And Cheddar Dumplings 21

   8.   Slow Cooker Vegetable Stew with Cheddar Dumplings 22

   9.   Clootie Dumplings...................... 22

   10.   Apple Dumpling Pudding Puddle .. 23

   11.   Lentil Dumplings In Yogurt 24

   12.   Delicious German Dumplings........ 24

   13.   Just Dumplings...................... 25

   14.   Chicken and Ham Casserole With Mustardy Dumplings 26

   15.   Chicken Casserole With Herby Dumplings 26

   16.   Pork and Apple Stew With Parsley And Thyme Dumplings 27

(eat with custard)

17. Tomato And Harissa Stew With Cheddar Dumplings 28

18. Golden Syrup Dumplings 28

19. Malfatti 29

20. Chinese Dumplings 29

21. Strawberries And Elderflower Cobbler................................... 30

22. Open Flower Dumplings.............. 30

23. Ricotta Gnudi With Sage Butter 31

24. Cheat's Gnudi 31

25. Gnocchi with Pancetta, Spinach & Parmesan Cream 32

26. Creamy Gnocchi With Smoked Trout & Dill   32

27. Muffin Topped Winter Beef Stew... 33

28. Gulab Jamun 33

Chapter 4: *Chinese Egg Recipes*..................... 35

29. Apple Pie Egg Roll 35

30. ~~The Nigerian Egg Roll~~ 35

31. Chinese Chives And Ginger Breakfast Egg Roll.................................... 36

32. Cookie Dough Egg Rolls.............. 36

33. Chicken Curry Egg Rolls.............. 36

34. Cheesecake Egg Rolls 37

35. Beefy Egg Rolls........................ 37

36. Corned Beef Filled Egg Rolls 38

37. Scrambled Bread Egg Roll........... 39

38. Supreme Pizza Egg Rolls 39

39. Sloppy Joe Egg Rolls 39

40. Mashed Potatoes Egg Roll 40

41. Crab Rangoon Egg Rolls 40

42. Breakfast Egg Rolls 41

43. Pork Filled Egg Roll 41

44. Mac And Cheese Egg Rolls 42

45. Vegetarian Egg Roll 42

46. Chinese Styled Egg Roll 43

47. Nadiya's Egg Rolls..................... 43

48. Egg Rolls 43

49. Vietnamese Fresh Spring Rolls 44

50. Chicken Filled Egg Roll............... 45

51. Coconut Flavored Egg Roll 45

52. Flavorful Egg Roll In A Bowl......46 Salad

53. Easy Pork Egg Rolls 46

54. Oven-Baked Breakfast Egg Roll......46

55. Buffalo Chicken Egg Roll............. 47

56. Pan-Fried Egg Roll 47

57. Deconstructed Egg Roll 48

Chapter 5: *Vegetarian Recipes* 49

58. Tofu Veggie Stir-Fry 49

59. Chinese Style Eggs and Tomatoes...49

60. Sweet & Spicy Kimchi Jars 50

61. Vegetarian Sweet And Sour Compliment...................................... 50

62. Chinese Vegetarian Pancakes 50

63. Tofu and Veggies Stir Fry............. 51

64. Watercress Oyster Sauce 51

65. Potato and Veggies Hot Pot 52

66. Simple Warm Tofu & Veggies Winter Bowl   52

67. Cabbage & Black Bean Bowl 52

68. Simple Cabbage And Carrot Salad In Rice Wine-Oyster Sauce 53

69. Spicy Sweet Vegetable Lo Mein 53

70. It's Tofu And Vegetable 54

71. Homemade Chinese crepe 54

72. Steamed-Stir-Fried Iceberg Lettuce In Soy Sauce 54

73. Hot Roasted Bok Choy 55

74. Buttery Snap Peas & Mushrooms ... 55

75. Stir-Fry Summer Veggies With Honey 56

76. Simple Garlic And Spinach Side 56

77. Cucumber Salad 57

78. Cauliflower And Oyster Sauce 57

79. Sweet & Sour Braised Mushroom ... 57

80. Steamed Shitake Mushroom With Spicy Sweet Sauce 58

81. Cucumber Stir-Fry With Spicy Cashew Nuts 58

82. Fried Seaweed (Napa Cabbage) 59

83. Mung Bean Sprout Salad 59

84. Spicy Fried Aubergines 59

85. Chinese Steamed Veggies 60

Chapter 6: Chinese Fish Recipe 61

86. Pan-Fried Fish Fillets In Ginger Sauce 61

87. Fried Fish Cakes 61

88. Fried whole Fish 62

89. Steamed Aromatic Fish In Soy 62

90. Oven Ginger And Scallion Steamed Fish 62

91. Potato Fish Soup. 63

92. Spicy Sweet Braised Fish 63

93. Ginger-Soy Fried Fish Fillets 64

94. Cantonese Simple Winter Fish Soup 64

95. Shallow Fried Fish With Soy Veggies Relish 65

96. Milky Way Mushroom And Fish Soup 65

97. Steamed Fish In Banana Leaves 66

98. Simple Homemade Fish Soup 66

99. Creamy Fish Bowl 66

100. Spicy Fish Stew 67

101. Ginger Scallion Steamed Fish Fillets 67

102. Fish and Summer Veggies 68

103. Simple Spicy Fish Bites 68

104. Chinese Fish Cheeks Tomato Stew. 68

105. Sweet & Sour Fried Fish on the Bone 69

106. Sweet & Spicy Baked Salmon Steak 69

107. Lemon Honey-Ginger Glazed Baked Salmon 70

108. Extra Spicy Fish head................. 70

109. Sweet Fish Balls 70

110. Braised Fish Head And Bean Curd.. 71

Chapter 7: Chicken and Duck Recipes 72

111. Sweet Chicken Popcorn 72

112. The Best Chinese Chicken Broth .. 72

113. Chicken Noodle Bowl 73

114. Chinese White Cut Chicken 73

115. Chinese Chicken And Cashew Dish. 73

116. Baked Sweet And Sour Chicken 74

117. Traditional Soy Seared Duck Breast 74

118. Spicy Sweet Chicken Cubes 75

119. Chicken Skin And Shrimp Pasta Soup 75

120. Chicken Feet With Healthy Nuts ... 76

121. Coca-Cola Ginger Sticky Chicken Wings 76

122. Asian BBQ Chicken Drumstick 76

123. Simple Chicken And Mushroom Soup 77

124. Crisp Roast Duck 77

125. Duck Breast Stir-Fry 78

126. Homemade Duck Sauce 78

127. Easy Chinese Pan Seared Duck Breast 78

128. Chicken And Veggies Wrap 79

129. Dried Chili Stir-Fry Chicken 79

130. Chicken And Wild Shitake Mushroom 80

131. Teriyaki Marinated Pan-Seared Duck 80

132. Simple Duck Salad 80

133. Modern Take On Ginger Duck 81

134. Seared Duck Breast 81

135. Lemon & Ginger Duck 81

Chapter 8: Beef Recipes 83

136. Braised Beef 83

137. Crispy Chili Beef 83

138. Beef, Scallion, And Ginger Stir-Fry .84

139. Beef, Pineapple, And Ginger Stir-Fry 84

140. Beef And Broccoli Noodles 85

141. Sticky Green Stir-fry And Beef 85

142. Sugar Snap Noodles And Beef 85

143. Beef Noodles Cake 86

144. Chili Beef, Broccoli, and Oyster Sauce 86

145. Honey Beef Noodles 87

146. Chili And Lime Steak Salad 87

147. Beef And Bok Choy 88

148. Spicy Beef, Shiitake, And Aubergine Stir-Fry 88

149. Beef Curry 88

150. Beef And Aubergine Sauce 89

151. Beef, Mangetout, And Peanuts 89

152. Mongolian Beef 90

153. Beef And Broccoli 90

154. Beef In Oyster Sauce 90

155. Chinese Pepper Steak 91

156. Beef Stew And Potatoes 91

157. Sweet And Sticky Crispy Beef 92

158. Panda Express Beijing Beef 92

159. Big Batch Chinese Beef 93

160. Beef Teriyaki Skillet 93

161. Low Syn Sweet Chili Beef 94

162. Hunan Beef 94

163. Beef And Tomato 95

Chapter 9: Pork Recipes 96

164. Sweet And Sour Pork.................. 96
165. Char Siu BBQ Pork ..... ✓............. 96
166. Garlic Ginger Pork 97
167. Mongolian Pork...................... 97
168. Braised Pork Belly 98
169. Pork And Pepper Stir-Fry ✓ 98
170. Chinese Stir-Fry Pork .... ✓........... 99
171. Pork Fried Rice.... ✓................. 99
172. Hunan Pork Stir-Fry 99
173. Sticky Chinese Pork 100
174. Pork And Mushroom Stir-Fry ✓ 100
175. Peking Pork Chops................... 101
176. Barbequed Roast Pork .. ✓.......... 101
177. Asian Noodles Bowl With Pork 102
178. Grilled Chinese Pork 102
179. Sweet Glazed Pork 102
180. Sticky Honey Ginger Pork 103
181. Chinese Pork Ribs ......✓.......... 103
182. Chinese Pork Chops Steak 104
183. Chinese Pork Curry.................. 104
184. Fruity Pork Steak 104
185. Spiced Pineapple Pork 105
186. Pork And Noodle Stir-Fry.. ✓........ 105
187. Spiced Honey Soy Pork 106
188. Twice Cooked Pork.................. 106
189. Pork And Tomatoes 107
190. Fish Flavored Shredded Pork...... 107

191. Pork Medallions...................... 108

Chapter 10: Lamb Recipes......................... 109

192. Cumin Lamb Stir-Fry... ✓ ✳....... 109
193. Shredded Lamb 109
194. Lamb And Sesame Fried Rice .. ✓...110
195. Chinese Spiced Lamb 110
196. Braised Lamb........................ 111
197. Mongolian Lamb .... ✓........... 111
198. Lamb Cutlets .... ✓............. 111
199. Hoisin Lamb Chops 112
200. Hunan Lamb... ✓ nice recipe 112
201. Lamb Stew...... ✓ nice recipe 113
202. Lamb Curry ... ✓................... 113
203. Sticky Lamb 114
204. Salt And Pepper Lamb 114
205. Roast Lamb .. ✓................... 115
206. Spiced Orange Lamb 115
207. Pak Choy BBQ Lamb 116
208. 5-Spice Lamb......................... 116
209. Pepper Lamb Stir-Fry............... 116
210. Sesame Lamb, Ginger, And Garlic.117
211. Chinese Lamb Noddle Soup... ✓....117
212. Chinese Lamb Ribs 118
213. Lamb and Veggies 118
214. Grilled Lamb Chops 118
215. Lamb Chuanr........................ 119
216. Scallion Lamb 119
217. Spicy, Sweet, And Sour Lamb Chops 120

Beef marinade – 95/91

218. Herbal Lamb Soup....................120

219. Chilies And Cumin Lamb 120

220. Toothpick Lamb 121

Chapter 11: Chinese Noodles Recipes *122*

221. Pan-Fried Noodles....................122

222. Chinese Noodles Salad 122

223. Noodles With Fried Bean-Paste Sauce 123

224. Hot And Spicy Meat Sauce Noodles 124

225. Cold Noodles With Sesame Sauce .124

226. Spicy Pork Noodles.................125

227. Stir-Fry Hokkien Noodles With Chicken 126

228. Chicken Chow Mein Noodles 126

229. Szechuan Spicy Cold Noodles 127

230. Spicy Beef Noodle Soup 128

231. Stir-Fried Noodles With Steamed Dried Scallops................................129

232. One-Wok Fried Veggie Noodles....130

233. Spinach, Shrimp, And Bean Thread Noodle Soup.......................130

234. Noodle Soup With Chicken And Mushrooms 131

235. Sweet And Spicy Chicken Noodles 131

236. Spicy Cold Skin Noodles............132

237. Sesame Peanut Butter Noodles Recipe 133

238. Noodles With Gravy 133

239. Simple Crispy Noodles..............134

240. Fried Eggs With Chinese Noodles..135

241. Stir-Fried Rice Noodles With Eggs And Greens 135

242. Crispy Pan-Fried Noodles With Gravy 136

243. Spicy Sichuan Noodles With Eggplant 137

244. Shrimp Noodle Soup 138

245. Parmesan Chicken Noodles 138

246. Lemon Chow Cheddar Noodle 139

247. Mutton Fry Noodles.................. 139

248. White Scallop Noodles 140

249. Mushroom-Peanut Butter Noodle . 140

Chapter 12: Chinese Rice Recipes...................*142*

250. Chinese Chicken Fried Rice........ 142

251. Chinese Fried Rice................. 142

252. Chinese Pineapple Rice............ 143

253. Chinese Mushroom Soup With Brown Rice 144

254. Chinese Lentil Rice 145

255. Chinese Aubergine Rice Dish And Potatoes 145

256. Pilaf With Pineapple And Cashew Nuts 146

257. Asian Tomato Rice 147

258. Chinese Rice In Green Tea With Salmon 148

259. Chinese Seafood Fried Rice........ 148

260. Chinese Fish Soup With Rice....... 149

261. Chinese Steamed Glutinous Rice.. 150

262. Chicken Congee 151

263. Chinese Rice With Egg And Chicken 152

Custard Tarts—179

264. Yeung Chow Fried Rice 153

265. Chinese Diced Pork On Crackling Rice 153

266. Lamb And Apricot Pilaf 154

267. Asian Mango And Sticky Rice 155

268. Asian Black Rice Dessert 156

269. Date And Rice Pudding 157

270. Middle Eastern Rice With Meat And Chickpeas 158

271. Chinese Braised Saffron Rice 158

272. Capsicum Stuffed With Lamb And Rice   159

273. Asian Veal And Rice Casserole 160

274. Pork Congee 161

275. Chinese Rice Pudding With Peas And Bacon 162

276. Braised Rice With Bolognese Sauce 163

277. Riz Melba (Rice And Peach Dessert) 164

Chapter 13: Chinese Sweet Recipes 164

278. Ginger And Pumpkin Torta......... 164

279. Creamy Strawberry Torta.......... 165

280. Vanilla Durazno 166

281. Rice-Water Sesame Balls 166

282. Red Pâte De Haricots 167

283. Vanilla-Coated Walnuts............. 167

284. Golden Sesame....................... 168

285. Walnut Frito En Aceite 168

286. Pineapple-Banana Cake 169

287. Fruity Gelatin 169

288. Fortune Vanilla 169

289. Vanilla Galleta De Avena........... 170

290. Buttery Vanilla...................... 170

291. Chinese Tarta De Crema Pastelera 171

292. Vanilla Peanut Butter Fudge 171

293. Vanilla Oatmeal Cookies 172

294. Vanilla Fortune Cookies........... 172

295. Fruit Gelatin 173

296. Baked Pineapple And Banana 174

297. Deep-Fried Walnut.................. 174

298. Sweetened Sesamum-Seed 175

299. Vanilla Walnut Cookies........... 175

300. Red Beans Paste 176

301. Sweetened Sesame Seed Balls 176

302. Vanilla Peach Cobbler 177

303. Creamy Strawberry Pie 178

304. Ginger Pumpkin Pie................. 178

305. Chinese Milk Custard Tarts 179

Conclusion 180

"The art of CHINESE COOKING," *says Master James Wei*

When the word WOK cooking is mentioned, most people always visualize a big WOK wielded above an intense flame by a chef. One also envisions Chinese comfort food when the Wok is mentioned, and you don't blame them because the Chinese and the Asians are known for using Wok to prepare healthy meals.

It is believed that people suffer various health conditions due to their lack of eating clean and healthy, so one of the best ways to correctly manage your health is by eating good stir-fry meals from Wok.

WOK was used in the olden days by our aged parents and if you can recall the taste of the food prepared then and now are very different. When you think about those comfort foods you ate in time past, some images accompany your thoughts, including the picture of you and your family sitting and eating together in the comfort of your home.

While it is true that it is a mystery how the Asian chefs prepare all their ingredients with ease, some of the chefs today don't have the time to craft their meals with Wok meticulously. However, WOK stir-frying happens to be one of the best and easiest ways of preparing your meal, and the best part is, the taste you get from meals prepared with a wok is heavenly. Furthermore, meals prepared using a wok has their Nutritional Information: intact. Maybe that is why our parents lived longer without any complicated health issues.

In recent times, you get to see people suffering from obesity, heart diseases, etc. and when you ask the cause of such illness, what you get most of the time is cholesterol. Most people try to keep fit by skipping meals, which becomes detrimental to their health at the end of the day. However, you can be confident that you will begin to eat healthily and stay healthy with a wok.

If this is your first time wanting to use a wok, you can start with the Chinese Wok because it is deep and comes in a bowl-like shape, and it makes sure that your ingredients remain in the middle, which is at the point where the heat is more concentrated.

This WOK cookbook for beginners introduces you to healthy, nutritious, and easy-to-prepare wok recipes, especially if your first time using a WOK. However, before we jump into the tools needed to prepare meals with a wok, let us show you how to care for your Wok as a beginner.

HOW TO CARE FOR YOUR WOK

To keep your Wok in good condition and ready for use all the time, you need to put some simple and essential tips into practice. As a beginner, you need to get a new wok, and every new Wok will need oil to develop continuously until they get to their seasoned layer. So instead of doing a lot of poaching, it will be better to do more stir-frying.

Ensure your Wok is well heated before adding oil, so your food doesn't stick to the Wok. You can start by making some excellent popcorn with your peanut oil. Also, ensure you don't wash your Wok with soap; use warm water to rinse it when you are done using it and use a soft sponge or brush to wipe it.

You should never scrub your wok with any abrasive or hard object, but you can wash the outer layer if it is dirty? As a beginner, after rinsing your WOK, you can place it on it to dry up, but if your WOK isn't new, you can wipe it, but be sure that water isn't left in it, so it doesn't rust.

Cooking with a WOK isn't as difficult as you think and caring for it is also not difficult. You need to use it often so that the seasoned layer can be developed and if you can't use it often, then rub some peanut oil in it before storing it. This cookbook will bring lots of cooking pleasure to you and various recipes that you can enjoy preparing with your WOK. With the recipes in this book, you can never get tired of using your WOK, so keep reading further while we bring you many exciting recipes.

CHINESE COOKING

As time passes, Chinese cooking becomes even better and tastier, and everyone is eager to learn the tricks and tips of their cooking style. If you grew up in America and have always loved the various Chinese meals you eat there, then chances are, you night nit find such tasty Chinese meal in China itself.

In the 80s, some Chinese workers moved over to California for some work or, let's say, greener pastures, and most of them came from the rural area where they loved to cook. In the spirit of making money, some of them decided to open Chinese restaurants to provide their colleagues with their meals' same taste and flavor.

These immigrants were not trained, they only used their little knowledge to provide good food to their counterparts, but that little act of theirs has given birth to the rise of so many other Chinese restaurants in America and all over the world today.

However, due to the recent happenings around the world, most people dread going out to have their meals, which is why we have decided not to bring you recipes but to let you in on the techniques and tips you can use while cooking your favorite Chinese meal. Cooking a Chinese meal in the comfort of your own comes with different styles, which will be listed below.

STIR-FRYING

Stir-frying is one of the most important and famous Chinese cooking techniques, and it is safe to say it is also very tricky to master because being successful in it means you have to have all the ingredients ready and measured out as a good source of heat. One of the advantages of the stir-fried meal is the fact that it can be cooked within a space of a few minutes.

Furthermore, you get to stir-fry your meals with just a little oil, and its flavors will be retained. You also need to ensure that any stir-fried meal is not greasy or overcooked. Once your ingredients for stir-frying are ready, the next thing you need to do is heat your Wok until it is scorching, then add your oil. This way, your food will not stick, and it will heat up evenly. The best oil for your Wok is vegetable oil because it absorbs heat properly without burning.

Once you heat the oil, use a spatula to spread it over the surface of the Wok, and you need to ensure your work is well heated to the point that it is almost smoky before you put in your other ingredients. However, if you wish to flavor your oil, when it is smoky hot, add your garlic, onions, or any different flavor to the heated oil, toss for a few seconds before removing it and putting in your ingredients.

Once you have added your ingredients, begin to stir-fry using your spatula, move the food in the Wok and be careful not to let it stick too much in the Wok. You can also add your cornflour to make a thick sauce, but before this is done, you can bring your Wok down from heat to avoid getting lumps. Stir-frying makes cooking more uncomplicated than you think.

BLANCHING

Blanching is also another way the Chinese prepare their meals. Blanching is the process of putting your food into a bowl of hot water or into oil that is moderate for just a few minutes and cooks very briefly. You can call it a process of softening meals to prepare your meals for the final cooking.

For example, you can blanch your chicken after it has been velveted in either oil or water; even your meat can be blanched to get rid of the unwanted Fat: and gristle to get the clean taste and appearance you need. It is prevalent to blanch vegetables in water in most cases, especially those hard veggies like carrots and broccoli.

To blanch the veggies, you need to put the veggies inside a pot of boiling water for just a few minutes, then you remove it, drain and place in cold water for another few minutes. However, when blanching, be careful not to overcook your meals, and trust the process; it will make your cooking less stressful and timely.

POACHING

Poaching has to do with gently simmering your food until it is half cooked. Once you are done poaching, you can now place your poached meals into the soup or meal and complete your cooking process. In most cases, foods such as chicken and eggs are always simmered.

DEEP-FRYING

Another way of Chinese cooking is deep-frying. Asides from the Chinese, most individuals use the deep-frying technique, which is a crucial cooking technique. The trick about deep-frying is regulating the heat to seal the surface of the food but ensure it is not quickly brown because there is every tendency that it might not be adequately cooked inside. Deep-fried meals should not be greasy even though the process has to do with oil. The

Chinese use a wok for deep-frying, and it doesn't need too much oil like the regular deep fryer. However, as a beginner, it might be challenging for you to use the Wok to deep-fry; however, if you do insist on using it, you should be on standby to monitor it. To deep-fry, ensure the oil is hot enough, and you can throw a slice of onion into the oil to be sure it is hot, and then reduce the heat before deep-frying so it doesn't smoke or overheat. Understandably, oil could splatter on you while frying, so to avoid such, ensure you dry the food you are about to fry appropriately with a paper towel. If you had to marinate the food, remove it from the marinade and drain it before frying. Ensure the batter drips off before you fry if you are frying batter. Furthermore, the oil you used in deep-frying can be kept to be used again, just put it in a jar and seal until when next you are ready to use it again. But note that you can only use the oil about twice before it loses its potency.

SHALLOW FRYING

This is sautéing but with a little more oil than stir-frying. It requires a little oil, and whatever you are frying in is first fried on one side before turning to the other side. In most cases of shallow frying, the excess oil is drained, and then you can decide to fry your sauce in the same pan—however, shallow-frying needs a frying pan and not a wok. After shallow-frying in your pan, you can then transfer whatever you fried to your Wok to complete your cooking process.

SLOW-SIMMERING AND STEEPING

When it comes to slow-simmering, food is absorbed in liquid, cooked until it is almost boiling, then the heat is reduced, and the food is allowed to simmer until it gets to your desired degree of doneness. This technique is used mostly when you want to prepare your stock. While steeping, you let the food absorb the liquid while it simmers for a certain time; then, you turn off the heat and allow the heat in the pan to finish the cooking for you.

BRAISING AND RED BRAISING

This method is most commonly used on challenging meat pieces and some veggies. Typically, the food is browned before being placed in a stock that has been prepared with seasonings and spices. Simply said, red braising is the process of braising food in a dark liquid, like your soy sauce.

This imparts a flavor to food that has been cooked in a dark liquid, such as soy sauce. As a result, the meal turns a reddish-brown color, hence the method's name. This form of braising sauce can be frozen and used again. It may be re-used many times and gets better with each usage.

STEAMING

Another Chinese cooking technique is steaming your food. Steaming food means you have to cook the meal in a moist heat that will circulate freely and let your food cook carefully. If you want to bring out the flavors in your meal, then steaming the meal is the best way. Most people steam things like meat and fish to absorb the taste. The Chinese chefs mainly use bamboo steamers in a wok, but in the absence of bamboo steamers, you could use any other type of steamer you have. If you are using a bamboo steamer in a wok, put water in the Wok and let it boil, then place your food item in the steamer and place the steamer in the Wok with boiling water, cover the steamer and let the food steam until it is cooked.

You can also use your Wok as a steamer by placing a rack in the Wok with boiling water, placing your food on a plate, and place on the shelf in the Wok and steam. You can also use a roasting pan as a steamer, so you don't need to worry too much if you don't have a bamboo steamer.

ROASTING

Since most Chinese homes lack an oven, they mostly roast, which is done in commercial premises. Food is roasted in enormous metal drum-shaped ovens about 5ft tall and uses charcoal as fuel. Inside the oven, the food is hung on hooks. The objective is to heat all of the food's surface area, resulting in a crisp exterior coating with a moist interior. By placing food on a rack in a roasting pan and allowing the hot air from the oven to circulate it, you can emulate the Chinese method.

BARBECUING

Barbeque is not common among the Chinese, but it is another roasting method. Meats and marinated fish are placed on the barbeque and roasted over your charcoal fire. However, there are new types of barbeque stand everywhere in recent times, and barbequed meals are always delicious.

REHEATING MEALS

Steaming is one of the most significant ways to reheat food since it warms it without overcooking it or drying it out. For example, you get to reheat your soups and braise your foods by bringing the liquid to a simmer but not boiling. Please remove it from the stove as soon as it reaches a high temperature to avoid overcooking.

TWICE COOKING

As the name implies, you get to stir-fry and simmer simultaneously. Twice-cooking is always done if the texture of the food needs to be changed and flavor infused into the meal. It is also used to ensure meals that are difficult to cook are adequately managed.

Besides the fact that you need a WOK, there are other cooking tools that you also need to make your daily Chinese cooking easier than you envisioned. Of course, if you are an expert in cooking already, you might already have these tools, but for beginners' sake, below is a list of the essential tools you will need to prepare a fantastic Chinese recipe using your WOK.

Let us start with the rice cooker: a rice cooker is necessary, especially if you want to cook any grain or Chinese food. A rice cooker makes your cooking faster and easier, and it also ensures your food stays warm for a more extended period. A combination of a wok and a rice cooker will make a sumptuous meal within a few minutes.

BAMBOO STEAMER

Do you wish to make some lovely dumpling recipes, steamed fish, or any other fantastic dish with your WOK? If so, it would be best if you got a bamboo steamer. The bamboo steamer will enable you to steam your foods according to the amount of time it needs to be steamed and if possible, get a multilayered steamer to steam whatever you want to steam in layers. Bamboo steamers come in different sizes, so you should consider your needs before getting one.

TONGS OR CHOPSTICKS

Cooking a Chinese meal cannot be complete without tongs or chopsticks. Chopsticks or tongs ensure you can move things around with ease. In addition, these cooking chopsticks are long and resistant to heat. However, you can only use chopsticks if you are used to it, but if not, you can decide to use tongs. But the bottom line is, using any of these tools will make your cooking process more accessible.

WIDE SPATULA

A spatula is being used all the time, but your wide metal spatula is the best with a wok, mainly when used for fried rice. With the metal spatula, you can comfortably scrape anything from sticking in your WOK while cooking. However, you can also use the regular spatula for any other meal that doesn't need too much scraping.

STRAINER OR SLOTTED SPOON

Two types of filters are handy for Chinese cooking. One is the steel mesh strainer which comes with a long split bamboo handle, and it ranges from about 4 inches to 14 inches to get the perfect size for you. Then the second type of strainer is a combination of a long metal and hollow handle with a large shallow, sturdy stainless-steel bowl. It also comes with perforated holes and in different sizes as well. With these strainers in your kitchen, cooking will be easier because you can drain quickly and confidently.

STEAMERS

There are a lot of steamers in the market, but if you can get bamboo steamers, you are good to go. The bamboo steamers are traditional, and they consist of a woven bamboo mesh base, a circular frame, and a shallow bamboo cover. The bamboo steamers also come in various sizes, and you could choose the size that is perfect for you and can comfortably fit into your standard Wok. Do you know you could also stack about 2 or 3 steamers simultaneously? Yes, it makes your cooking easier and faster. Furthermore, if you don't want to get a bamboo steamer, you can choose a stainless-steel steamer that will fit perfectly into your work. However, some stainless-steel steamers also come with a bamboo mesh.

CLEAVER

Your Chinese cooking tool cannot be complete without a cleaver. It could be small or big, and it could also be heavy or light with either a carbon-steel blade or a stainless-steel blade and a wooden or metal handle.

Most chefs will always recommend the cleaver with a wooden handle and a stainless-steel blade that is balanced because it can be used for chopping, cutting, mincing, and slicing. The cleaver is a professional knife perfect for almost everything cutting and chopping, thereby making your cutting task more uncomplicated than you think.

CHOPPING BOARD

Your kitchen is incomplete without a chopping board. There are a lot of chopping boards in the market that sometimes, one gets confused about the perfect fit for their kitchen.

But among various Chinese cooks, the rubber-like chopping board is ideal for them, and it comes in different sizes and shapes, so you will undoubtedly see the right size for your kitchen and needs. It is more important than making your knife dull, unlike the white plastic chopping board. Of course, you can also go for the wooden cutting board or the laminated bamboo chopping boards; they are also perfect.

In time past, Chinese cooks have always relied on ingredients to make their meals taste great and various cooking and chopping techniques to give their meals that unique taste and flavor. The cutting and cooking technique has to do with multiple steps, including chopping your meats and veggies from different angles, marinating your meats or fish, slicing, shredding, and preheating the wok and oil. They also tactically prepare their meals by removing it from the hot oil almost immediately it touches the oil and keeps it to rest while preparing other meals. This may look like an easy task, but it sure isn't. You need to put in a little more effort to get your desired result. However, once you can master the cooking techniques, you will become a Chinese chef in your home. Below are some nice techniques that happen to be an important part of Chinese cooking. You can consider the techniques to be various ways of amazing cooking dishes passed down to you from generation to generation. Every technique you see here needs to be experimented with, and you will certainly love them.

The first on our list is slicing: Slicing is a standard way of slicing your veggies and other foods that need slicing. How do you get to slice swiftly? You just need to hold down the food you are about to slice with one hand on your chopping board and chop them into thin slices. You can decide to slice your meat to make it more tender and break up the fiber for easy cooking. You can decide to use a cleaver to slice, and with a cleaver, you need to guide the cleaver with your index finger to slice properly.

HORIZONTAL OR FLAT SLICING

The horizontal or flat slicing is more like you slicing a kidney. The technique breaks down your food into smaller bits and pieces while also preserving the shape of the meal. You need to keep whatever you are using a blade to slice at a parallel angle on your chopping board. Place your hand on the meal you are about to slice and slice sideways smoothly to get a good cut. You might need to chop whatever you are slicing in half to cook faster, but that also depends on the kind of meal you are slicing.

ROLL CUTTING

The roll cutting is like diagonal slicing, but it is mostly used to cut large and thick veggies like courgettes, aubergines, or even large carrots. This method allows more of your vegetable surface to be exposed while cooking. With this technique, you need to slice your veggies diagonally at one end and turn it around to make the next diagonal cut; you need to continue this way until you are done chopping your vegetables.

SHREDDING

The shredding technique is also equivalent to the French julienne technique, and this has to do with slicing your meat or any other meal into some tiny little shreds. You can start by first slicing your meat or veggies, then stack the slices on each other, and then chop them into strips. To get better and nice shreds, you can decide to freeze like your meat first, then shred afterward.

DICING

Dicing is easy and very straightforward, and it is also something you do almost every day while you cook. You can decide to dice your meals in cubes or any shape you want. You need to start by slicing your meals like vegetables, then stack them together and dice them to equal cube sizes. This is always lovely when you choose to dice your carrots.

MINCING

When you mince, it simply means you are nicely chopping your meals. Most chefs get to use two cleavers to chop their meals quickly and swiftly for an amazing result. However, using a single cleaver will be better, or even a knife as a beginner. You start by slicing your meal first and then chop it with a sharp knife or even a cleaver and be careful not to hurt yourself in the process. When you finish chopping for the first time, you scrape whatever you have sliced into a mound and then go ahead to chop it again and again until it is well minced and consistent. You can decide to grip your knife with both hands to get the desired texture you need.

MARINATING

Marinating your meal is another way of getting the ingredients to seep into the meal properly. Liquids that your raw meat or fish can be marinated in are soy sauce, rice wine, or corn flour for a while or for a few hours to improve the taste and flavor of your meat. You can include things like ginger, garlic, salt, pepper, or any other seasoning of your choice.

THICKENING

Most people use corn flour as a thickener to make a nice sauce and glaze their meals. You get to find most Chinese chefs using it, and it is always mixed with water to get the kind of texture you desire.

VELVETING

Chicken breast is one of the things that is always velvet, and it is done to keep it from overcooking. To velvet your meal, you will use egg white, salt, and corn flour. Place your meat in the mixture and cover it for about 30 minutes so the mixture sticks to your meat so that when you fry it, it will come out firm.

"I am the emperor, and I want Dumplings" – Emperor Ferdinand 1

Dumpling is a vast category of dishes made up of pieces of dough, and they are made from different starch sources. For example, the dough could be based on bread, potatoes, meat, fish, cheese, or whatever you prefer. In addition, dumplings have other preparation directions, including baking, frying, cooking, simmering, or string; they can all be discovered in different cuisines worldwide.

1. CHICKEN ARRABBIATA STEW AND PARMESAN DUMPLINGS

Preparation Time: 30 minutes

Servings: 6

Ingredients:

- 2 tbsp. of oil
- 1 medium-sized diced onion
- 8 boneless chicken thighs
- 2 large cloves of minced garlic
- 1 tsp. of chili flakes
- 4 tbsp. of sun-dried tomato pesto
- 250ml of chicken stock
- 400g can chopped tomatoes
- 5 thyme sprigs
- 1 tbsp. of sugar
- ½ bunch of parsley
- 80g of cold unsalted butter
- 150g of self-rising flour
- 80g of parmesan
- 60ml milk

Directions:

- Heat the oil in a big deep pan, fry the onion for about 7 minutes, add the chicken and fry for another 5 minutes. Add the garlic and chili into the pan and fry for 1 minute. Stir in the pesto, turn the stock, tomatoes, thyme, sugar, and seasoning to taste. Cover with a lid and simmer for 40minutes.

- To make the dumplings, add the butter and flour in a container, put ½ tsp. of the salt, then brush the butter into the flour with your fingertips till it looks like fine breadcrumbs. Combine the 50g of cheese and turn in the 50ml of the milk; slowly mix with a knife until everything is well allocated, and you have a soft dough. Bring the dough together on a plain surface and divide it into eight balls.

- Organize the dumplings over the stew, then sprinkle each with the balance cheese. Place it in the oven and bake for 25 minutes uncovered. Sprinkle the parsley over it and serve.

Nutritional Information:

Calories: 512

Protein: 24 g

Fat: 33 g

Carbs: 29 g

2. OXTAIL STEW WITH DUMPLINGS

Preparation Time: 20 minutes

Servings: 6

Ingredients:

- 2 tbsp. of plain flour
- 2 oxtails
- 4 tbsp. of sunflower oil
- 2 diced onions
- 3 sliced carrots
- 2 celery sticks
- 2 cloves of minced garlic
- 2 tbsp. of tomato purée
- 2 bay leaves and thyme sprigs
- 1 bottle of red wine
- 1 c. of beef stock
- 300g of flour
- 1 bunch basil leaves
- 75g of butter
- 3 egg whites

Directions:

- Put salt and pepper in the flour and turn the oxtail until equally garnished. Heat the oil in a big saucepan, and doing it in batches, fry the meat very well. Discard the meat from the pan, add the vegetables and garlic and fry for 3minutes.

- Add the tomato purée and herbs. Turn the meat back in the pan, pour the wine on it, and add the stock cube. Season it properly, and cook for 3 hours

- To prepare the dumplings, pour the flour and basil inside a food processor with a large pinch of salt, then blend until the basil is finely crushed. Add the butter and mixture until the texture seems like it's breadcrumbs, then slowly add the egg whites until they all mix. On a flat surface, wrap the dumplings into small size balls, cover with a tea towel until they are ready to be cooked.

- When it is time to serve, take a big pan of saltwater and boil, cook the dumplings for 15 minutes and remove with a wooden spoon. While they cook, slowly heat the meat in the sauce, serve a few pieces of meat in a soup bowl with dumplings, sprinkled with olive oil, and drizzled with basil leaves.

Nutritional Information:

Carbs: 50

Calories: 812 g

Fat: 41 g

Protein: 53 g

3. PORK GOULASH WITH HERBY DUMPLINGS

Preparation Time: 25 minutes

Servings: 10

Ingredients:

- 2 tbsp. of olive oil
- 1kg of pork tenderloin
- 2 medium-sized diced onions
- 2 cloves of minced garlic
- 2 tbsp. of smoked paprika
- 500ml of beef stock
- 500g of tomato
- 1 tbsp. of sugar
- 3 red bell peppers, diced
- 250g of flour
- 140g of suet

- 1 tsp. of baking powder
- 1 bunch oregano

Directions:

- Warm half the oil in a deep saucepan, fry the pork for 4minutes, and set aside. Use the balance oil to fry the onion for 10 minutes, add garlic and paprika and cook for a minute. After that, put the pork back in the pan and turn the stocks, sugar, and tomatoes. Boil for about 25 minutes or until your sauce is thick enough.

- To prepare the dumplings, mix all the ingredients, asides from the oregano leaves, with cold water to make a dough. Wrap into 30 ball size, add the pepper in the goulash. Put the dumplings, cover the saucepan, and allow it to cook for 2minutes, and serve hot.

Nutritional Information:

Calories: 476

Fat: 25 g

Carbs: 27 g

Protein: 38 g

4. VEGETABLE STEW WITH HERBY DUMPLINGS

Preparation Time: 40 minutes

Servings: 6

Ingredients:

- 1 tbsp. of oil
- 350g of shallot
- 2 leeks
- ½ swede
- 2 parsnips
- 350g of carrot
- 175g of pearl barley
- 225ml of white wine
- 400ml of vegetable stock
- 1 bay leaf
- 3 sprigs thyme
- 1 bunch parsley
- 100g of flour
- 50g of unsalted butter
- 50g of cheddar cheese
- 2 tsp. of finely chopped fresh rosemary
- 1 tsp. of fresh thyme leaves

Directions:

- Heat oil in a big saucepan, add shallots, and simmer for 5 minutes until it begins to get soft. Next, stir the leeks, swede, parsnips, and carrots together.

- Turn in the barley and wine and cook until the wine has reduced. Add the stock, bay, thyme, parsley, and any other seasoning. Cover pan with a lid, boil, cook for 45 mins until they become soft.

- Prepare the dumplings. While heating the oven, rub the flour and butter together to create breadcrumbs. Add the remaining ingredients and mix properly. Drizzle over 2 tablespoons of water, combine to create a soft dough. Share it into 6 and wrap it into balls. Cook, for 20 minutes until dumplings turn golden.

Nutritional Information:

Calories: 391

Fat: 14 g

Carbs: 57 g

Protein: 10 g

5. BEEF AND GUINNESS STEW WITH DUMPLINGS

Preparation Time: 40 minutes

Servings: 4

Ingredients:

- 2 tbsp. of oil
- 1kg of boneless beef shin
- 200g of diced onions
- 4 medium carrots
- 3 celery sticks
- 3 tbsp. of flour
- 500ml of beef stock
- 500ml of Guinness
- 1 large thyme sprig
- 4-star anise
- 1 head of cabbage
- 100g of smoked bacon
- ½ tbsp. of oil
- 1 tsp. of thyme leaves
- 125g of flour
- 60g of beef suet
- 1 egg yolk
- 50g of parsley

Directions:

- First, make your dumplings. Gradually fry the bacon until crisp in a big, covered frying pan. Add the thyme, turn and allow to cool for a while. Add the flour and suet to the bacon and stir everything together. Make a well in the middle, add the egg yolk, parsley, pepper, and 2 tbsp. icy water, and start mixing into a dough. Continue adding water until you have a firm but pliable dough. Share the combination into eight balls and chill till needed.

- Instantly clean the pan with some kitchen paper and heat the oil. Fry the meat properly in batches, then keep aside. Next, turn the onions, carrots and celery, flour, and meat into the pan. After that, turn in the stock and Guinness and stir properly. Cover with a lid and cook for 2 hours.

- Remove the stew from heat and organize the dumplings equally on the top. Cover the lid and take it back to the oven for 20 minutes. Put the dish on the table and add cabbage if desired.

Nutritional Information:

Calories: 800

Fat: 41 g

Carbs: 43 g

Protein: 57 g

6. WATERCRESS SOUP WITH BACON DUMPLINGS

Preparation Time: 30 minutes

Servings: 6

Ingredients:

- 25g of butter
- 2 cloves of minced garlic
- 2 small, diced onions
- 4 big floury potatoes
- 200g of watercress

- 2 tbsp. of fresh horseradish

- 200ml of vegetable stock

- 50ml of oil

- 8 streaky bacon rashers

- 3 tbsp. of fresh breadcrumbs

- 50g of flat-leaf parsley

Directions:

- To make the dumplings, combine the bacon with breadcrumbs and parsley, roll them into balls; the Fat: from the bacon will hold the dumplings together. Cover and put in the refrigerator.

- Dissolve the butter in a big saucepan, add the garlic, onion, potatoes, watercress stalks, and horseradish and cook for 10 minutes. Add the stock and cook properly. When the potatoes get soft, stir the watercress leaves, place the dumplings into the soup and let them cook for 3 minutes.

- Slowly take out the dumplings with a spoon and put them on one side. Turn the soup in a blender and add spices. Split between 6 bowls and top each of them with 3 dumplings. Sprinkle with oil, if desired, and serve with the remaining watercress leaves on top of it.

Nutritional Information:

Calories: 306

Fat: 12 g

Carbs: 34 g

Protein: 12 g

7. CHIPOTLE SWEET POTATO AND CHEDDAR DUMPLINGS

Preparation Time: 10 minutes

Servings: 4

Ingredients:

- 1 c. of oil

- 1 big red diced onion

- 250g bag of diced butternut squash and sweet potato

- 400g can chopped tomatoes

- 400g cans of black chili beans

- 3 tbsp. of chipotle chili paste

- 125g of self-flour

- 60g of unsalted butter

- 70g of cheddar

- 1 big green jalapeño

- ½ tsp. of salt

Directions:

- Heat a tiny amount of vegetable oil in a big saucepan, add the onion, and 1 tsp. of salt and cook for 5 minutes till it is soft. Turn in the squash and sweet potato and fry for 2 minutes before putting the tomatoes, beans, and 250ml of water. Place the chipotle paste and add spices to taste—cover and cook for 25 minutes.

- Mix the flour in salt, add butter, and rub it with your fingers until the combination looks like fine breadcrumbs. Add the grated cheddar and rapidly mix in 4 tbsp of cold water. Wrap the mixture into 8 balls. Place the dumplings on top of the stew, uncovered, in the oven for about 20 minutes. And serve.

Nutritional Information:

Calories: 547

Fat: 23 g

Carbs: 69 g

Protein: 18 g

8. SLOW COOKER VEGETABLE STEW WITH CHEDDAR DUMPLINGS

Preparation Time: 20 minutes

Servings: 6

Ingredients:

- 2 tbsp. of oil
- 200g of baby carrots.
- 3 leeks
- 2 cloves of minced garlic
- 2 tbsp. of plain flour
- 400ml of vegetable stock
- 2 courgettes
- 400g cans of butter
- 1 bay leaf
- 2 thymes
- 200ml of crème Fraiche
- 1 tbsp. of wholegrain mustard
- 200g of broad beans
- 200g of spinach
- ½ little bunch of parsley
- 100g of flour
- 50g of vegetarian suet
- 100g of shredded cheddar
- ½ bunch of parsley

Directions:

- Heat parts of the oil in a pan, fry the carrots for 5 minutes and then turn it into the slow cooker.

- Heat the balance oil in the frying pan and fry the leeks with 1 tsp. of salt for 5 minutes. Add the garlic and the flour. Slowly add the stock, stirring continuously until the flour dissolves properly. Boil and turn in the slow cooker, add the courgettes, beans, and herbs, top it up with water, cover with a lid and cook for 4 hours.

- Turn the flour inside a bowl, add the suet, and mix until equally distributed to prepare the dumplings. Add cheese, parsley, ½ tsp. of black pepper, and 1 tsp of salt. Combine in 3 tbsp. cold water using your hands to make a soft and sticky dough. Share into six and wrap into balls.

- Put the crème fraîche, mustard, and spinach in the slow cooker, arrange the dumplings on the stew, cover with a lid and cook for 1 hour. Sprinkle with parsley and serve.

Nutritional Information:

Calories: 544

Fat: 33 g

Carbs: 40 g

Protein: 18 g

9. CLOOTIE DUMPLINGS

Preparation Time: 25 minutes

Servings: 8

Ingredients:

- 1 tbsp. of sunflower oil
- 175g of white breadcrumbs
- 175g of flour
- 150g of beef suet
- 100g of dark soft brown sugar

- ½ tsp. of salt
- 1 tsp. of mixed spice
- 2 tsp. of ground cinnamon
- 1 tsp. of ground ginger
- 1 tsp. of bicarbonate of soda
- 100g of currants
- 175g of sultanas
- 2 tbsp. of black treacle
- 150ml of milk
- 1 big egg
- 2 long baking parchment
- 1 big tea towel

Directions:

- Make your tea towel wet, and place the baking parchment beneath the tap, then drain out the surplus moisture. Spread the towel on your work surface, keep the parchment on top, and drizzle with oil. Put a big pan of water and boil.

- Put the breadcrumbs, student, sugar, flour, salt, dried fruits, and bicarbonate of soda in a big bowl and mix. Mix the treacle in the milk and egg using a fork. When properly blended, stir the mixture and turn it into the dried ingredients.

- Brush the paper charitably with flour, then put the dough in the center of the cross and shape with your hands. Bring the paper around the pudding and tie it with a string at the top. Cut off any excesses and wrap in a cloth and tie. Place it in the pan, cover, and boil for about 3 hours.

- Dip the pudding into a colander to soak, gradually removing the cloth and the paper. Keep the pudding in the oven and bake for 15 minutes. Serve chopped with custard.

Nutritional Information:

Calories: 499

Fat: 21 g

Carbs: 60 g

Protein: 7 g

10. APPLE DUMPLING PUDDING PUDDLE

Preparation Time: 20 minutes

Servings: 6

Ingredients:

- 75g of butter
- 250g of light brown sugar
- 3 tbsp. of golden syrup
- 6 apples
- 50ml of double cream
- 200g of flour
- 1 tsp. of baking powder
- 2 tbsp. of caster sugar
- ⅓ tsp. of ground cinnamon
- 100g of cold butter
- 4 tbsp. of milk

Directions:

- Dissolve the butter, sugar, and golden syrup in a saucepan, adding 100ml water. Simmer, add apples, and salt, cook for 10 minutes. Pour the flour into a bowl, combine with the baking powder, cinnamon, sugar, and ½ tsp. of salt.

- Brush the butter into the combination using your fingertips until it looks like damp sand. Pour the milk, mix with a knife till it begins to clump together, then make use of your hands to join the dough together. Share into 12 pieces and wrap into dumplings. Organize the apples and sprinkle with a little extra sugar and bake for 25 minutes. Allow it to rest for a few minutes and serve with cold cream.

Nutritional Information:

Calories: 763

Fat: 26 g

Carbs: 127 g

Protein: 5 g

11. LENTIL DUMPLINGS IN YOGURT

Preparation Time: 40 minutes

Servings: 6

Ingredients:

- 65g of skinned white urad dal

- 65g of yellow mung dal

- ¾ tsp. of ground cumin

- ¼ tsp. of coarsely ground black peppercorns

- 40g of peeled ginger

- 2 green chilies

- ½ tsp. of bicarbonate of soda

- 100ml of Sunflower oil

- 250ml of buttermilk

- 300ml of Greek or yogurt

- 1 tsp. of caster sugar

- 3 tbsp. of milk

- 1 tsp. of ground cumin

- ¼ tsp. of Kashmiri chili powder

- 2 tbsp. of coriander relish

- 4 tbsp. of date & tamarind sauce

- Small coriander leaves

Directions:

- Remove both lentils using a basket and toss out the moistening water. Dip it into a food processor, add the ground cumin, peppercorns, ginger, and green chilies together, blend till it is soft enough and add 2 tablespoons of water.

- Use a spoon to dip the lentil mixture into a bowl and whisk energetically for 7 minutes. Heat the oil in a karahi, add the bicarbonate of soda inside the lentil combination, use a spoon to scoop and carve the dumplings. Place the dumplings in the oil using a spoon. After that, fry the dumplings for 4 minutes tossing each side with a spoon. Remove and drain on kitchen paper.

- Mix the butter and milk with water in a deep pan, garnish the dumplings in the buttermilk mixture and allow to soften overnight.

- Squeeze the dumplings to discard excess buttermilk and organize them on a plate. To serve, mix the yogurt with sugar and milk, garnish the dumplings, and drizzle with ground cumin and chili powder. Sprinkle with coriander leaves if needed.

Nutritional Information:

Calories: 763

Fat: 26 g

Carbs: 127 g

Protein: 5 g

12. DELICIOUS GERMAN DUMPLINGS

Preparation Time: 30 minutes

Servings: 8

Ingredients:

- 150ml of milk
- 90g of caster sugar
- 7g of sachet instant dried yeast
- 400g of plain flour
- 1 big egg
- 70g of unsalted butter
- 500ml of whole milk
- 1 tbsp. of seeds from a vanilla pod
- 4 big egg yolks
- 100g of sugar
- 2 tsp. of corn flour

Directions:

- To prepare your dumplings, heat the milk to be warm. Be gentle not to let it get hotter or destroy the yeast. Add 1 teaspoon of sugar and yeast and allow to warm up for 10 minutes.

- In a big mixing bowl, join the flour, the balance sugar, egg, dissolved butter, and the yeast combination. Mix them with a spoon and use your hand when the dough begins to form a ball. Dip it is a floured surface and knead for 4 minutes.

- Place the dough in an oiled bowl, cover with a lid and allow it to rise for an hour. Prepare the vanilla sauce, join the milk and vanilla seeds in a pan and warm, in another bowl, mix the egg yolks and sugar, pour the milk on the egg combination, and combine everything, return the combination to the pan and heat, stirring continuously until the combination is thick enough.

- When the dough rises, make ready the poaching liquid, add the milk, sugar, and butter in a big pan, cover with a lid, and heat till the butter and sugar have dissolved.

- Share the dough into 8 places, carve them into a ball shape, put the dumplings into the poaching liquid, make sure to give a little space between each dumpling, and cook for about 25 minutes. Remove the cover and cook for another 5 minutes. Add vanilla over the top of the dumplings to serve.

Nutritional Information:

Calories: 528

Fat: 20 g

Carbs: 74 g

Protein: 11 g

13. JUST DUMPLINGS ✓

Preparation Time: 5 minutes

Servings: 4

Ingredients:

- 150g of flour
- 70g of suet
- 1 tsp. of crushed parsley

Directions:

- While your stew is bubbles, prepare the dumplings, weigh the flour in a bowl and add ½ tsp. of salt, suet, and parsley. Make a hole in the middle and include 3 tablespoons of cold water, mix the dough, and add water till it is firm. Share into 8 pieces and wrap in more flour.

- Bake for 10 minutes or till they are brown. Remove from oven and serve warm.

Nutritional Information:

Calories: 281

Fat: 16 g

Carbs: 30 g

Protein: 4 g

14. CHICKEN AND HAM CASSEROLE WITH MUSTARDY DUMPLINGS

Preparation Time: 20 minutes

Servings: 4

Ingredients:

- 1 tbsp. of sunflower oil
- 1 tbsp. of butter ✓
- 1 onion, diced
- 2 leeks
- 2 chopped carrots
- 6 boneless chicken thighs
- 200ml of cider
- 800ml of hot chicken stock
- ½ bunch of tied thyme
- 1 tbsp. of corn flour
- 150g of ham hock or cooked gammon
- 100g of frozen peas
- 1 tbsp. of English
- 200g of flour ✓
- ¼ tsp. of baking powder ✓

- 2 tbsp. of English mustard powder ✓
- 100g of suet ✓
- ½ bunch of parsley

Directions:

- Heat the butter and oil in a pan, add the onion, carrots, leeks, and little salt, fry slowly for 10 minutes. After that, add the chicken, fry for 5 minutes, add the cider, pour in the chicken stock and the thyme, and cook for 30 minutes.

- Prepare the dumplings by joining the flour, baking powder, suet, butter, mustard powder, butter, parsley, and a pinch of salt. Add 10 tablespoons of water and mix with your hands. Share into 8 pieces.

- Discard the thyme from the stew and toss it off. Add a little corn flour, stir the mixture into the casserole. Put in the ham hock, mustard, and peas, organize the dumplings over the top of the stew, place in the oven, cover with a lot and leave for 30 minutes. Discard the old and cook for another 10 minutes. And serve in bowls.

Dumplings

Nutritional Information:

Calories: 517

Fat: 26 g

Carbs: 39 g

Protein: 27 g

15. CHICKEN CASSEROLE WITH HERBY DUMPLINGS

Preparation Time: 30 minutes

Servings: 6

Ingredients:

- 12 skinless chicken pieces
- 3 tbsp. of flour
- 2 tbsp. of sunflower oil

50g – ¼ cup + 1 tbsp

100g – ½ cup + 2 tbsp

200g – 1¼ cups

- 3 small-sized diced onions

- 3 carrots, diced

- 200g of bacon lardons

- 2 bay leaves

- 2 sprigs thyme

- 250ml of red wine

- 3 tbsp. of tomato paste

- 2 chicken stock cubes

- 140g of cold butter

- 250g of flour

- 2 tbsp. of chopped mixed herb

Directions:

- Throw the chicken pieces with the flour, add a little salt and pepper to garnish them. Heat the oil in a covered casserole and fry the chicken in batches. Discard off the pieces on a plate and dip the carrot, onions, bay, lardons, and thyme in the pan. Cook for about 10 minutes, or until the onion is soft.

- Take the chicken pieces back in the pan, pour the red wine, tomato, and add the stock cube. Cover with the help of life and bake for 20 minutes. Discard off the cover and bake for 10 minutes again while preparing your dumplings.

- Brush the butter in the flour and use your fingertips till it feels like breadcrumbs. Springer 150ml of water and stir with a knife. Use your hand to carve it into a ping pong ball. Put the dumplings over the top of the stew and bake for 20 minutes. When the dumplings are properly cooked, serve.

Nutritional Information:

Calories: 744

Fat: 38.3 g

Carbs: 43.9 g

Protein: 34.9 g

16. PORK AND APPLE STEW WITH PARSLEY AND THYME DUMPLINGS

Preparation Time: 25 minutes

Servings: 4

Ingredients:

- 1 tbsp. of rapeseed oil

- 3 onions, diced

- 4 celery sticks

- 2 bay leaves

- 2 tbsp. of thyme leaves

- 500g of lean pork fillet

- 1 tbsp. of English mustard powder

- 3 large cloves of minced garlic

- 2 tbsp. of flour

- 4 tbsp. of cider vinegar

- 800ml of chicken stock

- 2 Granny Smith apple

- 3 leeks

- 5 carrots, diced

- 140g of flour

- 1 tsp. of baking powder

- 1 tsp. of English mustard powder

- 2 tbsp. of flat-leaf parsley

- 1 tbsp. of picked thyme leaves

- 2 tbsp. of yogurt

- 2 tbsp. of rapeseed oil

Directions:

- Heat the oil in a saucepan, put the onions, celery, thyme, and bay, and fry for 9 minutes. Place the pork in the pan and cook for 4 minutes. Add the mustard powder, flour, garlic, vinegar, and chicken stock, occasionally stir to avoid lumps forming.

- Put the apple, carrots, and leeks, and boil. Cover the pan and cook for 1 hour, stirring occasionally.

- Make your dumplings by dipping the baking powder, flour, mustard powder, parsley, and thyme in a bowl and mix properly. Pour the yogurt in a bowl with water and oil to soft. Share the dough into 8 and shape like a ball, dip them on the top of the stew, sprinkle with the remaining oil, and bake for 29 minutes and sprinkle the remaining thyme on it if you like before serving.

Nutritional Information:

Calories: 526

Fat: 17 g

Carbs: 50 g

Protein: 36 g

17. TOMATO AND HARISSA STEW WITH CHEDDAR DUMPLINGS

Preparation Time: 10 minutes

Servings: 4

Ingredients:

- 1 tbsp. of sunflower oil

- 2 diced onions

- 2 celery sticks

- 400g can of plum tomato

- 1 tbsp. of harissa

- 2 big courgettes

- 400g can of chickpea

- 2 vegetable stock cubes

- 25g of butter

- 200g of flour

- 1 tsp. of baking powder

- 75g of extra mature cheddar

- 100ml of milk

Directions:

- Heat the oil in a big pan, fry the onions and celery for 7 minutes, dip the tomatoes in a can of water, add the harissa, chickpeas, courgettes, and the stock cube. Cover with a lid and cook for 18 minutes.

- Brush the butter and baking powder in the flour, add a pinch of salt, and mix the cheese. Before the stew gets ready, turn the milk in the dumpling and mix with the life. Use a flat surface to shape the dough into a sausage and cut it into 8 pieces.

- Place the dumplings over the top of the stew and bake for 20 minutes. When cooked enough, take it out, allow it to cool, and serve.

Nutritional Information:

Calories: 444

Fat: 17 g

Carbs: 54 g

Protein: 16 g

18. GOLDEN SYRUP DUMPLINGS

Preparation Time: 15 minutes

Servings: 8

Ingredients:

- 200g of butter

- 225g of brown sugar

- 100g of golden syrup
- 400ml of milk
- 500g of flour

Directions:

- In a big pan, turn in 450ml of water, divide the butter, sugar, and golden syrup and boil them together. After that, warm the milk, turn the flour and butter in a food processor, and blend till it looks like breadcrumbs. Add 2 tablespoons of golden strip and milk, and mix till it blends

- Boil the combination and drop the pieces of dough in it. Cook for 10 minutes, flipping up and down. You can do it in batches, so they do not stick together, use a spoon to scoop the first set and cover with a foil.

Nutritional Information:

Calories: 560

Fat: 22 g

Carbs: 88 g

Protein: 8 g

19. MALFATTI

Preparation Time: 20 minutes

Servings: 4

Ingredients:

- 1 tbsp. of oil
- 500g of frozen spinach
- 250g of ricotta
- 50g of breadcrumbs
- 50g of parmesan
- 2 big eggs, whisked
- 1 tbsp. of semolina

- 1 nutmeg
- 60g of butter
- 25g of sage leaves

Directions:

- Heat oil in a big pan, dip the Spanish inside a colander, and squeeze out excesses. Take the diced spinach, place it in a bowl with the ricotta, parmesan, and breadcrumbs, add egg, flour, nutmeg, and stir to mix evenly

- Put 3 tablespoons of flour in a big tray and move gently to spread the flour. Take ½ spoon of the spinach combination, sprinkle it on the tray and wrap it into balls. Heat the oven, take a big pan of salted water, and boil. Dip the malfatti and cook for 2 minutes, scoop it out with a spoon and drain with kitchen paper. Move it to the oven and keep warm.

- Prepare the sage butter by dissolving it in a little pan, add the sage leaves and fry slowly. Stir continuously until it becomes crispy. Turn the sage butter into the malfatti and top it up with cheese if you desire.

Nutritional Information:

Calories: 395

Fat: 30 g

Carbs: 11 g

Protein: 19 g

20. CHINESE DUMPLINGS

Preparation Time: 15 minutes

Servings: 10

Ingredients:

- 1 tbsp. of chives
- 250g of pack pork mince
- 100g of raw prawn

- 100g can of water chestnut

- 1 tbsp. of soy sauce

- 2 gingers, crushed

- 15 wonton wrappers

Directions:

- Combine part of the chives and all the ingredients. Spread 1 tablespoon of the ingredients into each wonton skin. Take the wrapper up and round it with the pork until you have a dumpling.

- Grill the dumplings for about 10 minutes, top it up with the remaining chives, and serve with sauce.

Nutritional Information:

Calories: 141

Fat: 3 g

Carbs: 15 g

Protein: 16 g

21. STRAWBERRIES AND ELDERFLOWER COBBLER

Preparation Time: 15 minutes

Servings: 6

Ingredients:

- 2 kg of strawberries

- 2 vanilla pods

- 1 tbsp. of lemon juice

- 40g of soft brown sugar

- 70ml of elderflower cordial

- 1½ tbsp. of corn flour

- 1 c. of vanilla ice cream

- 1 c. of flour

- 50g of golden caster sugar

- 100g of unsalted butter

- 100ml of buttermilk

- 20g of demerara sugar

Directions:

- Throw the strawberries in an ovenproof plate with vanilla, sugar, lemon, and cordial. Leave in the oven for about 10 minutes. Discard the vanilla pod and mix a little strawberry juice in the corn flour. Add the mixture to the strawberries and mix well.

- To top the cobbler, mix the flour with sugar and salt. Brush the butter inside the flour combination with your fingertips, then slowly stir in 100ml of buttermilk. Drizzle demerara sugar and bake for 30 minutes. Allow to rest for 10 minutes and serve with ice cream.

Nutritional Information:

Calories: 290

Fat: 11 g

Carbs: 41 g

Protein: 3 g

22. OPEN FLOWER DUMPLINGS

Preparation Time: 30 minutes

Servings: 10

Ingredients:

- 5 big filo pastry sheets

- 4 tbsp. of dissolved butter

- 1 tbsp. of oil

- 2 cloves of minced garlic

- 1 diced carrot

- ½ sprig of thyme, chopped

- 220g can of bamboo shoot

- 100g of chestnut mushroom

- 3 tbsp. of oyster sauce

- 2 tbsp. of light soy sauce

- 1 bunch of chives

Directions:

- Sandwich 4 sheets of filo, rubbing them with dissolved butter. With a cutter, cut 25 circles, brush the holes with butter and hold the circles and create holes. Bake for 10 minutes.

- To serve, take the full-back and warm. Heat oil in a pan, fry the garlic, carrot, bamboo shoots, cabbage, and fry for 2 minutes. Add the mushrooms, soy sauce, and oyster for a minute. Toss off from the ear, add chives, season with pepper, and serve.

Nutritional Information:

Calories: 47

Fat: 3 g

Carbs: 5 g

Protein: 1 g

23. RICOTTA GNUDI WITH SAGE BUTTER

Preparation Time: 10 minutes

Servings: 4

Ingredients:

- 350g of ricotta

- 25g of parmesan

- 2 egg yolk

- 1 small, grated Nutmeg

- 225g of semolina

- 50g of butter

- 15 sage leaves

- 1 tbsp. of pine nuts

Directions:

- Place a sieve with muslin over a bowl, dip the ricotta inside the cloth and gently gather the ends, securing with an elastic band. Leave to drain for 3 hours

- Move the soaked-out ricotta in a neat bowl, whisk in cheese, egg yolk, nutmeg, and good seasoning. Dip the semolina flour inside a baking dish, make your hands wet, scoop 1 teaspoon of the ricotta mixture, and roll into the size of a ball. You are expected to make about 20 balls. After that, cover them with baking parchment, put them in the fridge, and allow them to cool for 24 hours.

- When ready to serve, take a big pan of salted water and boil for 2 minutes. Scoop slowly with a spoon and move to a sieve. Gently melt butter in a pan, add the sage, and fry until crispy. Move it to a plate with kitchen paper, share the gnudi between warm plates, sprinkle on top of the browned butter, and serve with cheese, pepper, and onion salad.

Nutritional Information:

Calories: 501

Fat: 28 g

Carbs: 44 g

Protein: 19 g

24. CHEAT'S GNUDI

Preparation Time: 20 minutes

Servings: 2

Ingredients:

- 200g bag of spinach

- 130g of garlic & herb Boursin

- 100g of breadcrumbs

- 2 tbsp. of parmesan cheese

Directions:

- Place the spinach in a big colander ser, our hot water on it and allow to cool. After that, drain out the excess steam and blend in a food processor with breadcrumbs, cheese, and seasoning.

- Brush oil on your palms and shape the combination into 15 balls. Cook in a saucepan of boiling salted water for 5 minutes. Scoop, add spices sprinkle some oil parmesan.

Nutritional Information:

Calories: 502

Fat: 36 g

Carbs: 24 g

Protein: 19 g

25. GNOCCHI WITH PANCETTA, SPINACH & PARMESAN CREAM

Preparation Time: 15 minutes

Servings: 4

Ingredients:

- 500g pack of gnocchi

- 1 clove of minced garlic

- 2 tbsp. of oil

- 100ml of double cream

- 1 tsp. of grated nutmeg

- 130g pack of pancetta cubes

- 100g of spinach

- ½ lemon zest

- 25g of parmesan cheese

- 25g of toasted pine nuts

Directions:

- Prepare the gnocchi following the instructions on the pack. Heat part of your oil in a little pan and fry the garlic, add cream, and nutmeg and set aside.

- Heat the remaining oil in a pan and cook the pancetta until crispy. Turn the gnocchi in and fry for 5 minutes. Add the spinach, lemon zest, and other seasonings.

- Place the parmesan inside the cream sauce, put the gnocchi on a plate, sprinkle over with sauce and add the pine nuts.

Nutritional Information:

Calories: 500

Fat: 32 g

Carbs: 37 g

Protein: 13 g

26. CREAMY GNOCCHI WITH SMOKED TROUT & DILL

Preparation Time: 5 minutes

Servings: 2

Ingredients:

- 300g pack of gnocchi

- 100ml pot of double cream

- 1 big courgette

- 3 hot smoked trout fillets

- 1 small pack of dill

Directions:

- Place a big pan of water to cook the gnocchi. Make sure to follow the instructions on the pack. Heat the cream in a pan, mix in the courgette and cook for 2 minutes. Add the trout, dill, a pinch of salt, and seasoning.

- Squeeze the gnocchi out and stir in the sauce. Drizzle with the balance dill fronds, add black pepper to serve if desired.

Nutritional Information:

Calories: 704

Fat: 44 g

Carbs: 52 g

Protein: 21 g

27. MUFFIN TOPPED WINTER BEEF STEW

Preparation Time: 20 minutes

Servings: 4

Ingredients:

- 500g of braising steak

- 2 tbsp. of plain flour

- 2 tbsp. of oil

- 2 big onions, diced

- 450g of carrot

- 3 big parsnips

- 1 bay leaf

- 2 tbsp. of sundried tomato paste

- 300ml of red wine

- 450ml of vegetable stock

- 225g of plain flour

- 2 tsp. of baking powder

- 140g of cheddar

- 150ml of milk

Directions:

- Flip the beef in flour, heat the oil in a big pan and fry the beef until brown. Remove with a spoon and keep aside. Add 3 tablespoons water and onion in the pan, occasionally stir until the onions get soft.

- Add the parsnips, carrots, and bay leaf and fry for 5 minutes. Take the beef back to the pan and mix in the tomato paste, stocks, wine, and boil. Cook covered in the oven for 1 hour.

- Sieve flour and baking powder in a bowl together and put half cheese to prepare toppings. Combine the milk and oil and turn it into flour to make it fluffy and sticky. Use a spoon to make the dough, drizzle with cheese, and bale for 10 minutes. Serve hot.

Nutritional Information:

Calories: 847

Fat: 39 g

Carbs: 82 g

Protein: 46 g

28. GULAB JAMUN

Preparation Time: 35 minutes

Servings: 6

Ingredients:

- 3 green cardamom pods

- 600g of caster sugar

- 1 tsp. of rosewater

- ¼ tsp. of saffron strands

- 2 tsp. of chopped pistachios

- 7 green cardamom pods
- 100g of full-cream milk powder
- 40g of plain flour
- ½ tsp. of baking powder
- 40g of unsalted butter
- 1 tbsp. of natural yogurt
- 1 tbsp. of lemon juice
- 4 tbsp. of whole milk
- 1 tbsp. of sunflower oil

Fat: 22 g

Carbs: 85 g

Protein: 5 g

Directions:

- To prepare the syrup, slowly heat the cardamom, water, and sugar in a pan, do not allow the water to boil. Add sugar and water to a pan. Do not let the water boil before the sugar melts. Cook for 10 minutes and allow to cool.

- Slowly add the rosewater and saffron and keep aside. To prepare the gulab jamun, use a little and mortar to lb. the cardamom and sugar together. Sieve the milk, baking powder, and flour into a bowl and stir the mixture together. Rub the 50g of ghee, use your fingertips to mix until it looks like coarse crumbs

- Add lemon juice, yogurt, and milk to form a dough, then oil your hands with a little oil and carve small parts of the dough into a ball size. Ensure that the dumplings are very smooth. Reheat the syrup till it boils, turn off the heat and cover properly with a lid.

- Heat the ghee, share into small pieces, and fry the balls in batches for 5 minutes. Discard from the pan with a spoon and drain on a kitchen paper, add the syrup to it and allow it to soak for 2 hours.

- When ready to eat, re-heat the Gulab jam in a pan, and serve hot with pistachios sprinkled around.

Nutritional Information:

Calories: 599

"Everyone loves egg rolls, but what makes it tastier is the various ways of preparing it as well as eating a very healthy egg roll snack."

29. Apple Pie Egg Roll

Preparation Time: 35 min.

Servings: 10

Ingredients:

- 2 tbsp. of butter
- ¼ c. of sugar
- ½ tsp. of cinnamon
- 10 egg roll wrappers
- 1 tbsp. of sugar
- 1 tbsp. of Caramel sauce
- 3 c. peeled and chopped apples
- 1 c. of oil

Directions:

- Melt the butter in a pan over medium heat, add the brown sugar, apples, and cinnamon. Cook till the apples are tender. Bring it down and let it cool for 30 minutes. Into each egg roll wrapper, place 2 tablespoons of apple filling. Fold edges of the wrappers. Seal the edges with wet fingers and make sure it is firm.
- Heat your oil and add 3 or 4 egg rolls each until golden brown using a big pot. Transfer the egg rolls to a tray or baking sheet and sprinkle the sugar on it and serve with caramel sauce

Nutritional Information:

Calories: 151.2

Fat: 2.6 g

Carbohydrates: 29.2 g

Protein: 3.2 g

30. The Nigerian Egg Roll

Preparation Time: 50 min.

Servings: 8

Ingredients:

- 8 big, boiled eggs
- 600 grams of flour
- ½ tsp. of salt
- 1 tsp. of baking powder
- 3 tbsp. of sugar
- 1 tsp. of nutmeg
- 200 grams of butter
- 1 c. of cold milk
- 2 raw eggs
- 200ml c. of oil

Directions:

- In a bowl, thoroughly mix the flour, salt, baking powder, sugar, nutmeg, then add the butter into the mixture and rub together till it looks crumbly. Break eggs and beat them before adding them to the mixture.
- Pour the milk into the mixture bit by bit till it forms a dough. Mold the dough like a ball and show it relax for 20 minutes. Divide the dough equally into 8 parts, put one dough in your palm, or use a flat surface to wrap the dough about the egg and roll it into a ball. Do the same for all other eggs.
- Preheat a deep-frying pot for about 3 minutes over high-medium heat. Heat oil in the pan and deep-fry your egg rolls until golden brown. Then remove the egg rolls and place on a sieve allow to cool before serving

Nutritional Information:

Calories: 305

Carbohydrates: 35 g

Protein: 5.5 g

Fat: 15 g

Sugar: 11 g

31. CHINESE CHIVES AND GINGER BREAKFAST EGG ROLL

Servings: 2

Cook Time: 15 minutes

Ingredients:

- 4 eggs beaten
- ⅛ tsp. sugar
- 1 tsp.'s sake
- 1 tbsp. chives chopped
- 1 tsp. smashed ginger
- 1 tbsp. water
- 2 tbsp. vegetable oil
- Salt to taste
- 1 tsp. Chopped chili
- ¼ tsp. white pepper ground
- 1 tsp. sesame oil

Directions:

- To the beaten eggs, add sugar, salt, sake, white pepper, water, and sesame oil and beat well
- Add the chives, chili, and mix again
- Heat the wok and add the oil a little at a time
- Pour a portion of the egg and swirl it around the wok
- Using a spatula, roll it halfway and add some of the egg mixtures again
- Keep the roll and pour action until the egg is exhausted
- Allow to brown, then serve with soy-chili sauce

Nutritional Information:

Calories: 169

Protein: 12.8 g

Fat: 12.0 g

Carbs: 0.9 g

32. COOKIE DOUGH EGG ROLLS

Preparation Time: 20 min

Servings: 6

Ingredients:

- 1 c. of flour
- ¼ c. of sugar
- ½ c. of butter
- ½ c. of brown sugar
- ½ of tsp. of salt
- ½ c. of pure vanilla extract
- ¾ c. of chocolate chips
- 6 egg roll wrappers
- 200ml of Vegetable oil

Directions:

- Mix your sugar and butter in a large bowl, then add your flour, salt, and vanilla into the mixture and mix properly. Add your chocolate chips and combine. Place your egg roll wrappers on a flat surface, spread your cookie mixture on them, and rub the wrapper's edges with your water, and fold.
- Heat oil in a pan or wok, then place your rolls in it and deep-fry on each side for a few minutes or until golden brown.
- Remove from oil and drain on a paper towel before serving.

33. CHICKEN CURRY EGG ROLLS

Preparation Time: 50 min.

Servings: 10

Ingredients:

- ¼ c. of oil
- 3 tbsp. of soy sauce
- 5 oz. of chopped chicken breast, boneless
- ½ c. of red cabbage, chopped
- ¼ c. of red chopped onion
- ¼ c. of mayonnaise
- 1 tbsp. of red curry paste
- 1 tsp. of minced garlic
- 16 oz. of egg roll wrappers
- ¼ c. of chopped carrot
- 3 tbsp. of curry powder

Directions:

- Heat a large saucepan over medium-high heat and add 1 tbsp. olive oil and soy sauce, cook for 2 minutes before adding the chicken. Cook till it turns white. Add carrot, onion, and cabbage until they get soft.
- In a bowl, mix your soy sauce, curry paste, garlic, mayonnaise, curry powder and turn into the saucepan where you have the chicken. Preheat your oven to about 220F. Brush your baking sheet with oil and set it aside.
- Spread all the egg roll wrappers with the chicken mixture, roll up the wrappers and brush the tops with oil. Place them on the baking sheet, put them in your oven, and bake for 10 minutes flipping each side while cooking. Remove from oven when it is golden brown.

Nutritional Information:

Calories: 163

Carbs: 16.3 g

Fat: 9.2 g

Protein: 6.4 g

Cholesterol: 12.1 mg

34. CHEESECAKE EGG ROLLS

Preparation Time: 30 min.

Servings: 12

Ingredients:

- 2 c. of chopped strawberries
- 50ml of water
- 2 tbsp. of granulated sugar
- 2 blocks of cream cheese, softened
- 100g of granulated sugar
- ½ c. of sour cream
- 1 tbsp. of vanilla extract
- 12 eggroll wrappers
- 100ml of oil
- 1 tbsp. of sugar

Directions:

- To make the strawberry sauce, cook the strawberry, sugar, and water in a saucepan for about 4 minutes over medium heat and

occasionally stir till it becomes thick. Pour it into a small bowl and keep it aside.
- Put the cream cheese, sugar, vanilla, salt, sour cream in a bowl and beat them together using an electric mixer. Spread out the egg roll wrappers and apply 3 tablespoons of the mixture just at the center.
- Roll the wrappers from a diagonal position, make sure you shut it properly, and then fry the egg rolls over medium heat until it turns golden brown. Sprinkle the powdered sugar and serve with the sauce.

Nutritional Information:

Calories: 195

Carbs: 26.4 g

Fat: 9.8 g

Protein: 4.3 g

35. BEEFY EGG ROLLS

Preparation Time: 45 min.

Servings: 10

Ingredients:

- 1 lb. ground beef, lean
- 1 finely sliced onion
- ½ tsp. of dried minced garlic
- ½ tsp. of salt
- ½ tsp. of crushed black pepper
- 2 tsp. of sherry
- 1 tsp. of ginger powder
- 200ml c. of water
- 1 large head cabbage, finely shredded
- 1 tbsp. oil
- 1 tsp. sugar
- 2 quarts deep-frying vegetable oil
- Egg roll wrappers (16 oz.)

Directions:

- Brown the beef in a large skillet over medium heat, then add the onion, garlic, soy sauce, salt, pepper, 2 tablespoons sherry, and ginger. Just until the onions are tender, continue to sauté. Place the mixture in a mixing dish and put it aside.

- Sauté the cabbage with water, add your oil, sugar, remaining soy sauce, sherry, salt, and pepper in the same skillet. Continue to sauté for another 5 minutes, or until cabbage is tender and crispy. Return the meat mixture to the pan and stir in the cabbage until it is heated through. Remove the pan from the heat.
- Heat the oil in a large pan. Fill each egg roll wrapper with about ¼ c. of filling and roll up as directed on the package. Fry till golden brown in hot oil. Serve immediately after draining on paper towels.

Nutritional Information:

Calories: 267

Protein: 9 g

Carbs: 22.1 g

Fat: 15.8 g

36. CORNED BEEF FILLED EGG ROLLS

Preparation Time: 90 minutes

Servings: 10

Ingredients:

- 1 tbsp. of unsalted butter
- 1 medium-sized well-chopped onion
- 2 cloves of minced garlic
- 1 c. of well-chopped cabbage
- 1 c. of frozen and thawed hash brown potatoes
- 1 c. of well chopped corned beef
- 2 tbsp. of Dijon mustard
- ½ tsp. of salt
- ½ tsp. of freshly ground black pepper
- 8 (7 8-inch square) egg roll wrappers
- 2 tbsp. of oil
- 2 tbsp. of Thousand Island dressing, for garnish

Directions:

- Dissolve your butter in a small pan over medium heat, then add your onion and garlic to it and let it simmer for about 5 minutes. Add your cabbage and cook for another 2 minutes while stir-frying. Then add your potatoes, cook for another 10 minutes or until your potatoes and cabbage are soft.
- Then add your corned beef and mustard, simmer a little and remove the pan from heat. Season it with your salt and pepper, then transfer the mixture from the pan to a bowl and set aside to cool for about 20 minutes.
- Preheat your oven to about 200F, place your egg roll wrap on a flat surface, then divide your mixture among the wrappers, brush the edges of the wrappers with a little water and fold.
- Brush the egg rolls with oil, place them on a cookie sheet, and bake for about 20 minutes or until it is crispy and golden brown. Remove from oven and serve with your thousand island dressing. Enjoy!

Nutritional Information:

Calories: 450

Protein: 14 g

Carbs: 38 g

Fat: 27 g

37. SCRAMBLED BREAD EGG ROLL

Preparation Time: 30 minutes

Servings: 3

Ingredients:

- 6 slices of bread
- 4 big eggs
- 2 medium-sized diced onions
- 1 c. of oil
- ⅓ tsp. of salt
- 1 tsp. of crushed thyme
- 1 tsp. of garlic powder
- 200g of flour

Directions:

- Break eggs into a clean bowl, add your onions and spices into it, whisk properly. Add your oil to a pan, pour your whisked eggs, cover, and simmer for a few minutes. Stir-fry the eggs until it is properly scrambled.
- Cut the edges of your bread, then add your scrambled egg on each slice and roll it. Mix your flour with a little water so the batter can be thick, and then use your brush to spread the batter on the bread.
- Heat your oil in a pan and deep fry your bread egg rolls for just a few minutes, remove from heat, and allow draining before serving.

Nutritional Information:

Calories: 257

Protein: 9 g

Fat: 18 g

Carbs: 14 g

38. SUPREME PIZZA EGG ROLLS

Preparation Time: 15 min

Servings: 10

Ingredients:

- 40 pieces of pepperoni
- 5 pieces of string cheese
- 1 small diced green pepper
- 1 small, sliced mushroom
- Egg roll wrappers
- ⅓ c. of marinara sauce
- 3 cooked Italian sausage
- 1 small, sliced olive

Directions:

- Cut the string cheese into halves
- Place the egg roll wrappers on a flat surface as usual and put 4 pieces of pepperoni, some olives, mushrooms, pepper, sausage, and cheese.
- Fold the egg roll wrappers, and make sure you shut them by brushing the edges with water.
- Deep fry the egg rolls using a pot for about 3 minutes until they turn golden brown.
- Turn occasionally and serve with marinara sauce.

Nutritional Information:

Calories: 178

Carbs: 8 g

Protein: 7 g

Fat: 12 g

39. SLOPPY JOE EGG ROLLS

Preparation Time: 20 min

Servings: 8

Ingredients:

- 1 lb. of ground beef
- ⅛ c. of mustard
- 2 tbsp. of brown sugar
- ¾ of ketchup
- ½ c. of diced onion
- 8 egg roll wrappers
- 4 c. of vegetable oil

Directions:

- In a pot, cook the ground beef and onions till they are done,

- Combine the beef, brown sugar, onion, ketchup, mustard, and mix thoroughly in a large bowl
- Add the ingredients to suit your taste.
- Fill all the egg roll wrappers with the mixture and fold it firmly.
- Preheat the vegetable oil and fry the egg rolls for about 4 minutes until golden brown.
- Serve with any sauce

Nutritional Information:

Calories: 1055

Fat: 94 g

Carbohydrates: 45 g

Protein: 15 g

40. MASHED POTATOES EGG ROLL

Preparation Time: 15 min.

Servings: 8

Ingredients:

- 2 c. of mashed potatoes
- 2 green sliced onions
- ¼ c. of crumbled bacon
- 1 egg
- ½ tsp. of garlic powder
- ½ tsp. of onion powder
- 8 sticks of cheese
- Egg roll wrappers
- Vegetable oil

Directions:

- Mix the mashed potatoes, bacon, egg, garlic powder, and onion powder in a bowl. Stir and mix properly. On each cheese stick, apply 3 tablespoons of the mashed potatoes filling. Be sure it is well coated.

- Place the egg roll wrappers on a flat surface, making sure one angle points to you. Place the egg roll filling at the centre of the wrapper and roll up the sides. Make sure it is firm by applying a little water to the tip of the wrapper.

- Pour the vegetable oil into a pot and heat up before frying the egg rolls. Fry for about 5 minutes on each side until golden brown, remove from oil and drain.

- Serve hot!

Nutritional Information:

Calories: 208

Fat: 8 g

Carbohydrates: 23 g

Protein: 12 g

41. CRAB RANGOON EGG ROLLS

Preparation Time: 35 min.

Servings: 12

Ingredients:

- 2 oz. of drained crab meat
- 2 c. of vegetable oil
- 1 minced garlic
- 8 oz. of cream cheese
- 1 sliced green onion
- 1 tbsp. of Worcestershire sauce
- ½ tbsp. of salt
- 1 tsp. of lemon juice
- Egg roll wrappers

Directions:

- Thoroughly mix the Worcestershire sauce, garlic, onion, lemon juice, salt, and cream cheese in a large bowl, then add the crab meat and mix thoroughly. Spread the egg roll wrapper on a flat surface and place the crab filling in it.

- Fold the egg roll wrappers and fry in a pan or wok of heated oil. Fry for about 3 minutes till they are golden brown. Remove from heat, drain on a paper towel and serve.

- Serve with any dipping sauce

Nutritional Information:

Calories: 208

Fat: 8 g

Carbohydrates: 23 g

Protein: 12 g

42. BREAKFAST EGG ROLLS

Preparation Time: 20 min.

Servings: 4

Ingredients:

- 1 tsp. of butter

- ½ tsp. of salt

- ½ c. of shredded cheddar cheese

- 4 eggs

- 4 slices of crumbled bacon

- 4 Egg roll wrappers

- ½ tsp. of pepper

- 1 c. of oil

Directions:

- Break the egg into a bowl and add salt and pepper. Whisk well and keep aside. Preheat the vegetable oil in a pan, add the butter to a pan over low heat, and add the cheddar cheese and crumbled bacon to the egg and stir thoroughly. Cook the mixture into the pan and stir till the egg is done.

- Spread the egg roll wrapper on a flat surface and put the egg mixture at the centre of the egg roll wrapper. Fold up the wrapper and seal edges with little water, and deep fry in a pot for 3 minutes until it turns golden. Remove, drain, and serve hot!

Nutritional Information:

Calories: 258

Carbohydrates: 8 g

Protein: 13 g

Fat: 19 g

43. PORK FILLED EGG ROLL

Preparation Time:

Servings: 6

Ingredients:

- 1 lb. of pork, grounded
- 1 tsp. of crushed ginger
- 1 tsp. of garlic powder
- 200ml c. of peanut oil
- 2 tbsp. of flour
- ¼ c. of water
- 2 c. of cabbage, shredded
- 2 c. of carrot, shredded
- Egg roll wrappers

Directions:

- Place your pork in a bowl and season with your ginger and garlic. Place pork in a pan and heat until it is not pink anymore. Remove from heat and set aside. Then in another pan, heat your oil and while your oil is heating, mix your flour and water in a bowl until it becomes a batter.

- Then in another bowl, mix your cabbage, carrots, and pork, then mix it with your flour mixture. Place your egg roll wrapper on a flat surface and scoop the mixture in the center. Brush water on the edges and fold.
- Place rolls in your heated oil and deep fry for a few minutes. Remove from oil, drain and serve. Enjoy!

Nutritional Information:

Calories: 330

Protein: 14.2 g

Carbs: 22.6 g

Fat: 20.5 g

44. MAC AND CHEESE EGG ROLLS

Preparation Time: 20 minutes

Servings: 6

Ingredients:

- 6 wrappers of egg rolls
- 2 c. of mac and cheese, leftover
- 1 c. of short ribs, leftover
- 2 chopped scallions
- 1 tbsp. of lime juice
- ½ c. of oil
- 1 bowl of water

Directions:

- Heat your leftover Mac and cheese in a microwave so you can mix with ease. Then transfer the heated Mac and cheese to a bowl, add your short ribs, scallion, and lime juice, and mix properly.
- Place the egg roll wrapper on a flat surface, place mixture in the middle, and fold the edges, using water to seal the edges. Heat your oil in a pan or wok and deep fry your rolls for a few minutes on both sides.
- Remove from oil, drain, and serve.
- Enjoy!

Nutritional Information:

Calories: 400

Protein: 12 g

Carbs: 30 g

Fat: 29 g

45. VEGETARIAN EGG ROLL

Preparation Time: 50 minutes

Servings: 10

Ingredients:

- 1 tbsp. of oil
- 2 c. of shiitake mushrooms, thickly sliced
- 1 c. of shredded carrots
- 2 c. of sliced napa cabbage
- 1 c. of bean sprouts
- ¼ c. of sliced green onions
- 1 tsp. of garlic, minced
- 1 tsp. of crushed ginger
- 2 tbsp. of soy sauce
- ½ tsp. of sesame oil
- ½ c. of water
- 10 egg roll wrappers
- 4 c. of peanut oil

Directions:

- Heat your wok or pan over high heat, then add your oil, and once it begins to smoke, add your mushrooms and simmer for just a minute. Add your carrot, sauté for another minute, then the cabbage and sauté for one minute before adding your bean sprouts, green onions, and sesame oil, then stir properly for just a minute.
- Transfer the mixture to a pan and spread evenly, place in your fridge, and chill for about 10 to 15 minutes. Place your wrappers on a flat surface, fill with your mixture, brush the edges of the wrapper with water and fold properly.
- Heat your peanut oil in your pan and deep fry your rolls for a few minutes on both sides. Remove from heat, transfer to a rack, and drain.
- Serve hot!

Nutritional Information:

Protein: 3 g

Calories: 78

Carbs: 13 g

Fat: 1 g

46. CHINESE STYLED EGG ROLL ✓

Preparation Time: 2 hours

Servings: 20

Ingredients:

- 4 c. of shredded cabbage
- 2 c. of shredded carrots
- 2 c. of shredded celery
- 2 chopped scallions
- 1 tbsp. of salt
- 1 tbsp. of sugar
- 2 tsp. of sesame oil
- 1 c. of peanut oil
- ¼ tsp. of white pepper
- 2 c. of shredded roast pork
- 2 c. of chopped and cooked shrimp
- 1 pack of egg roll wrappers
- 1 big egg, whisked

Directions:

- In a pot of boiling water, add your cabbage, celery, and carrots and blanch for just 2 minutes. Remove from water, transfer to running cold water, drain with a kitchen towel, and dry more.
- Once dried, transfer to a bowl and add your scallions, salt, sugar, sesame oil, white pepper, pork, a little sesame oil, and shrimp. Mix properly and set aside. Place your wrappers on a flat surface and scoop mixture in them.
- Heat your peanut oil in a pan, then deep fry your rolls for a few minutes, or until it is golden brown and crispy. Remove from oil, drain, and serve.

Nutritional Information:

Calories: 180

Carbs: 15 g

Protein: 13 g

Fat: 8 g

47. NADIYA'S EGG ROLLS

Preparation Time: 40 min.

Servings: 6

Ingredients:

- 6 eggs
- 1 tbsp. of dried parsley
- ½ tsp. of salt
- ½ tsp. of black pepper
- 1 tsp. of garlic, ground
- 1 c. of vegetable oil
- 5 Tortilla wraps
- 85g of sliced black olives
- 6 tsp. of sun-dried tomato paste

Directions:

- Break the eggs into a medium-sized bowl. Add the pepper, salt, garlic, and parsley into the same bowl and mix thoroughly. Preheat a frying pan with a little vegetable oil. In another bowl, place the olive and mushroom. Just mix them.
- Put 3 tablespoons of the egg mixture in the frying pan alongside the olive and mushrooms. Sprinkle mixture on the eggs. Spread the tortilla wraps with tomato paste and add the fried egg. Roll up the tortilla wrapper and cook for 1 minute or until the eggs get attached. Turn each side of the tortilla while cooking.
- Serve immediately or refrigerate.

Nutritional Information:

Calories: 105

Carbohydrates: 10.5 g

Fat: 7.77 g

Protein: 5 g

48. EGG ROLLS

Preparation Time: 50 min.

Servings: 6

Ingredients:

- 1 c. of steamed cabbage
- 1 c. of diced potatoes
- 1 c. of shredded carrot
- ½ c. of sliced onion
- 1 c. of vegetable oil
- ½ tsp. of Salt
- ½ tsp. of pepper
- 6 Egg roll wrappers

Directions:

- Heat the vegetable oil over medium heat in a pot
- Combine the cabbage, potatoes, onion, carrot, corned beef, some pepper, and salt, mix them well in a large bowl.
- Place the egg roll wrappers on a flat surface and put ½ c. of the mixture at the centre. Wet edges of the wrappers, and seal firmly.
- Fry the egg rolls for 3 minutes. Turn occasionally and remove when it's golden brown.

Nutritional Information:

Calories: 286

Protein: 7 g

Carbohydrates: 25.2 g

Fat: 18.4 g

49. VIETNAMESE FRESH SPRING ROLLS

Preparation Time: 50 min.

Servings: 8

Ingredients:

- 1 ⅓ tbsp. of fresh Thai basil (chopped)
- 3 tbsp. of mint leaves (chopped)
- 2 oz. of rice vermicelli
- 2 c. of cooked shrimps, halved
- 3 tbsp. of cilantro, chopped
- 2 chopped lettuce leaves
- 4 tsp. of fish sauce
- ¼ c. of water
- 2 tbsp. of sugar
- 1 clove of minced garlic
- ½ tsp. of garlic sauce
- 2 tbsp. of lime juice
- 3 tbsp. of Hoisin sauce
- 1 tsp. of peanuts, chopped

Directions:

- Boil the rice in a small pot till it's done. Get a bowl and fill it with water. Drop the wrapper in it for a second to soften. Place the wrapper on a flat surface; add the shrimps, basil, mint, lettuces, cilantro, and rice.

- Fold the wrappers and set them aside. Mix the lime juice, fish sauce, water, garlic, sugar, chili sauce in a small bowl and set aside. Mix the peanut and hoisin sauce in a small bowl and mix well. Serve the spring rolls with your hoisin and fish sauce.

Nutritional Information:

Calories: 84

Protein: 4 g

Carbohydrates: 16 g

Fat: 0.8 g

50. CHICKEN FILLED EGG ROLL

Preparation Time: 30 minutes

Servings: 4

Ingredients:

- 1 lb. of shredded chicken, skinless and boneless,
- 1 tsp. of crushed ginger
- 1 tsp. of garlic powder
- 200ml c. of peanut oil
- 2 tbsp. of flour
- ¼ c. of water
- 2 c. of cabbage, shredded
- 2 c. of carrot, shredded
- Egg roll wrappers

Direction:

- Place your chicken in a bowl and season with your ginger and garlic. Pour a little oil in your wok, heat up properly, and stir-fry your chicken until it is a bit brown. Remove from heat and set aside. Then in another pan, heat your oil and while your oil is heating, mix your flour and water in a bowl until it becomes a batter.
- Then in another bowl, mix your cabbage, carrots, and chicken, then mix it with your flour mixture. Place your egg roll wrapper on a flat surface and

scoop the mixture in the middle of your wrapper. Brush water on the edges and fold.

- Place rolls in your heated oil and deep fry for a few minutes. Remove from oil, drain and serve. Enjoy!

Nutritional Information:

Calories: 330

Protein: 14.2 g

Carbs: 22.6 g

Fat: 20.5 g

51. COCONUT FLAVORED EGG ROLL

Preparation Time: 30 minutes

Servings: 6

Ingredients:

- ⅓ c. of coconut amino
- 2 tbsp. of sesame oil, toasted
- 2 tbsp. of rice vinegar
- 4 cloves of minced garlic
- 1 tbsp. of grated ginger
- ½ tsp. of Chinese five-spice powder
- 2 tsp. of coconut oil
- 6 sliced green onions
- 1 lb. of lean turkey
- 2 oz. of coleslaw mix

Directions:

- Mix your coconut amino, vinegar, sesame oil, ginger, garlic, and five-spice powder in a small bowl. Mix properly and set aside. Place a large pan on fire. When it is hot, add your oil, coat the pan, and add your green onions and simmer for a few minutes or until it is soft.
- Add your turkey and cook until it is cooked through. Add your coleslaw mix and simmer until it is crispy while you keep stirring. After a while, remove from heat and serve in your serving bowls.
- Enjoy!

Nutritional Information:

Calories: 229

Protein: 23 g

Carbs: 15 g

Fat: 16 g

52. FLAVORFUL EGG ROLL IN A BOWL

Preparation Time: 30 minutes

Servings: 4

Ingredients:

- 3 tsp. of sesame oil
- 4 sliced green onions with the white and green parts separated
- 1 medium-sized red onion, diced
- 2 cloves of minced garlic
- 1 lb. of pork, grounded
- 1 tsp. of fresh ground ginger
- 200g of chopped water chestnuts
- 2 tbsp. of hot sauce
- 250g bag of coleslaw mix
- 2 tbsp. of coconut amino
- 2 tsp. of rice wine vinegar
- ¼ tsp. of white pepper
- 1 tsp. of salt
- ⅓ c. of mayonnaise

Directions:

- Heat your sesame oil in a pan, add your red onions, the white of your green onions, garlic, and sauté while stir-frying for about 5 minutes. Add your pork, ginger, water chestnuts, and part of your hot sauce, and cook until your pork is brown.
- Add your coleslaw mixture, coconut amino, vinegar, white pepper, and salt, mix properly and stir-fry until it is soft.
- Mix your mayonnaise, remaining hot sauce, and salt mix in another bowl until it becomes creamy. Scoop your pork mixture in a bowl, and drizzle your creamy sauce on it and garnish with the green part of your green onions. Serve and enjoy!

Nutritional Information:

Calories: 416

Protein: 21 g

Fat: 31 g

Carbs: 12 g

53. EASY PORK EGG ROLLS

Preparation Time: 35 minutes

Servings: 10

Ingredients:

- 1 lb. of ground pork
- 1 tsp. of grounded ginger
- ½ tsp. of garlic powder
- 1 c. of oil
- 2 tbsp. of water
- 2 c. of coleslaw mix
- 10 egg roll wrappers

Direction:

- Heat your pork and keep breaking it until it is well cooked in a wok. Sprinkle your ginger and garlic on it and stir properly, remove pork and set aside. In another pan, heat your oil, and while heating, mix your flour and water in a small bowl.
- In another bowl, mix your coleslaw and pork mixture, then transfer to the flour mixture and mix properly. Place your egg roll wrappers on a flat surface and scoop pork mixture on it.
- Brush edges with water, fold, and then deep fry in your hot oil. Fry until it is brown, remove from oil, and drain.
- Serve hot!

Nutritional Information:

Calories: 271

Protein: 9 g

Carbs: 18 g

Fat: 7 g

54. OVEN-BAKED BREAKFAST EGG ROLL

Preparation Time: 35 minutes

Servings: 8

Ingredients:

- 5 big eggs
- 2 tsp. of water
- ⅓ tsp. of salt
- ¼ tsp. of black pepper
- ½ lb. of chicken sausage
- 2 tbsp. of green onions, chopped
- 2 tbsp. of red bell pepper, diced
- 1 tbsp. of oil
- 8 egg roll wrappers

Directions:

- Mix your eggs with water, salt, and pepper, whisk properly. In a medium pan, simmer your sausage until it is cooked, break it up and drain. Add your scallions and bell peppers, cook for a few minutes, and set aside.
- Heat your pan or wok, spray your oil in it, pour your egg mixture and cook and stir until your eggs are fluffy. Add your sausage mixture. Place your egg roll wrapper on a flat surface, then scoop your mixture on it, brush edges with water, fold properly.
- Preheat your oven to about 260F, place your egg rolls in a baking pan and bake for about 20 minutes.
- Turn often until it is well baked and crispy. Remove from oven and serve.

Nutritional Information:

Calories: 240

Protein: 17 g

Carbs: 24 g

Fat: 8 g

55. BUFFALO CHICKEN EGG ROLL

Preparation Time: 25 minutes

Servings: 8

Ingredients:

- 2 tbsp. of oil
- ½ c. of sliced red onions
- 3 c. of shredded cabbage
- 2 c. of shredded and cooked chicken
- ½ c. of buffalo sauce
- 8 egg roll wrappers

Directions:

- Preheat your oven to about 260F. Heat oil in a large pan, add your red onions and cabbage and stir-fry until the onions are soft and brown. Add your chicken and sauce and cook for another 4 minutes while stirring.
- Place your egg roll wrap on a board, add your buffalo mixture to it and carefully fold on both sides. Lay them on a parchment paper-lined on your baking sheet. Brush the rolls with oil and bake for about 15 minutes.
- Remove from the oven and serve with your buffalo dressing.

Nutritional Information:

Calories: 315

Protein: 29 g

Carbs: 13 g

Fat: 10 g

56. PAN-FRIED EGG ROLL

Preparation Time: 40 minutes

Servings: 8

Ingredients:

- ½ c. of chili sauce
- 10 oz. of chopped bean sprouts
- 10 wrappers of egg roll
- 10 cooked and peeled jumbo shrimps
- 5 tbsp. of fresh cilantro
- ½ c. of peanut oil
- ½ tbsp. of rice vinegar
- 1 tsp. of soy sauce
- ½ tsp. of ginger, grated
- ½ tsp. of black pepper

Directions:

- Mix 2 tablespoons of bean sprouts and chili sauce together, mixing well to garnish

- Using 1 egg roll wrapper per time, keep the wrappers on a flat surface with one part facing towards your direction. Take 2 spoons of the mixture and place it in the center of the wrapper, top it up with 2 shrimps divided into half, part of your cilantro, and fold inside corners. Add water to moisten the wrapper, roll it in a jelly-like fashion, and keep the egg roll on a baking sheet.
- Heat 1 tbsp. of oil in a big pan, add 6 egg rolls, and simmer for 10 minutes, endeavor to flip occasionally, and keep on a wire rack.
- Mix the balance ½ tablespoons of vinegar, chili sauce, and the balance ingredients. Serve the sauce with the egg roll.

Nutritional Information:

Calories: 103

Carbs: 8.7 g

Fat: 4 g

Protein: 7.9 g

57. DECONSTRUCTED EGG ROLL

Preparation Time: 30 minutes

Servings: 4

Ingredients:

- 2 tbsp. of sesame oil
- ½ onion
- 1 lb. of beef
- ½ tsp. of ground black pepper
- 1 tsp. of garlic powder
- 1 tsp. of salt
- 1 tbsp. of sriracha
- 15 oz. of coleslaw mixture
- 2 tbsp. of coconut aminos
- 1 tbsp. of rice wine vinegar
- 15 oz. of cauliflower rice

Directions:

- In a big pan, heat the sesame oil
- Put in the onion and sauté. Add the black pepper, meat, salt, garlic, and sriracha and simmer until the meat is properly cooked.
- Add the coleslaw mixture, soy sauce, rice vinegar, and cook until the cabbage becomes soft.

- Before you serve, make the cauliflower rice using the instructions on the package.

Nutritional Information:

Calories: 400

Protein: 26 g

Carbs: 36 g

Fat: 19 g

58. TOFU VEGGIE STIR-FRY

Servings: 4

Cook Time: 30 mins

Ingredients:

- 500g extra firm tofu cubes marinated and baked
- 2 tbsp. sesame oil
- 1 red bell pepper
- 1 small onion
- 1-inch ginger grated
- 1 small Bok Choy chopped
- 2 c. red cabbage chopped
- 1 tsp. lemon juice
- 1 tbsp. sweet chili sauce
- ½ c. edamame beans
- ½ tsp. pepper flakes
- 2 tbsp. vegetable broth

Directions:

- In a hot wok, add the oil and sauté the onion, ginger, onion, and pepper to soften
- Add the Boy Choy and cabbage to cook for 2 minutes, and then pour the rest of the ingredients
- Allow it to cook for 2 – 5 minutes, then serve

Nutritional Information:

Calories: 854

Protein: 56.17 g

Fat: 57.37 g

Carbs: 45.87 g

59. CHINESE STYLE EGGS AND TOMATOES

Servings: 4

Cook Time: 25 minutes

Ingredients:

- 2 large tomatoes cut in wedges
- 3 duck eggs whisked
- 2 tbsp. scallion
- 1 tbsp. oil
- 1 tsp. sesame oil
- 4 tbsp. water
- Salt and pepper to taste

For the Ketchup Slurry:

- ¼ c. ketchup
- 1 tbsp. corn flour
- 1 tsp. lemon juice
- 1 tbsp. brown sugar
- ½ c. water
- 1 tsp. ginger paste
- Salt and pepper

Directions:

- Combine the ingredients for the slurry and set aside
- Sauté the scallion until fragrant, then add the tomatoes to soften and pour in the water to cook down
- Meanwhile, mix the eggs with the sesame oil
- Into the cooking tomatoes, pour the ketchup slurry and cook for another 2 -3 minutes
- Then add the eggs, stir gently until creamy and glossy
- Serve as desired

Nutritional Information:

Calories: 761

Protein: 34.57 g

Fat: 48.6 g

Carbs: 51.85 g

60. SWEET & SPICY KIMCHI JARS

Servings: 4

Preparation Time: 12 minutes

Ingredients:

- 500g shredded cabbage
- ½ c. white vinegar
- 2 red chili peppers chopped
- 2 tbsp. ginger
- 1 tsp. whole peppercorn
- 4 stalk green scallions cut
- 6 cloves garlic smashed
- 1 tbsp. sugar
- 1 tbsp. Soy sauce
- ½ tbsp. Salt

Directions:

- Mix all the ingredients and squeeze into a jar
- Keep it for 6 days before use

Nutritional Information:

Calories: 43

Protein: 1.5 g

Fat: 0.53 g

Carbs: 8.62 g

61. VEGETARIAN SWEET AND SOUR COMPLIMENT

Servings: Makes a jar

Preparation Time: 15 minutes

Ingredients:

- 1 c. cane sugar
- ½ c. ketchup or sweetened tomato paste
- ½ c. white wine vinegar
- ½ c. water
- 2 tbsp. tamari soy sauce
- ½ tbsp. garlic paste
- 1 sweet yellow bell pepper thinly diced

- 1 small onion diced
- 1 tbsp. chopped scallion
- Salt and pepper

Directions:

- In a med sized wok, cook the onion and bell peppers for about 5 minutes
- Meanwhile, whisk the sugar, tomato paste, vinegar, water, tamari sauces, garlic, and pepper in a bowl
- Pour it into the wok with the onion and pepper and stir to combine
- Let it come to a gently simmer for 6 minutes until thickened
- Drop and add the scallion. Use it in any vegetarian dishes as it stores well.

Nutritional Information:

Calories: 1080

Protein: 12.9 g

Fat: 1.19 g

Carbs: 264.8 g

62. CHINESE VEGETARIAN PANCAKES

Servings: 2

Cook Time: 20 minutes

Ingredients:

- ¾ c. flour
- Salt
- 1 large egg
- ¾ c. water
- 1 c. bean sprouts
- 3 oz. zucchini strips
- 2 stalks scallions strip
- 1 large carrot strips
- 1 red bell pepper strips
- 1 yellow bell pepper strips
- 1 portabella mushroom in strips
- ¼ tsp. pepper flakes
- 1 tbsp. oil

Directions:

- Sauté all the veggies in oil to soften
- Meanwhile, mix the flour, water, and egg in a bowl to form a batter
- Pour it over the veggies and allow it to set before flipping it to cook on the other side
- Serve as desired

Nutritional Information:

Calories: 91

Protein: 3.2 g

Fat: 2.9 g

Carbs: 13.4 g

63. TOFU AND VEGGIES STIR FRY

Servings: 4

Cook Time: 30 minutes

Ingredients:

- 14 oz. extra firm tofu cut into cubes
- 3 tbsp. oyster sauce
- 1 tbsp. oil
- ½ c. vegetable broth
- 12 oz. Brussels sprouts
- 1 yellow pepper strips
- 1 tsp. rice flour
- 1 tbsp. Minced ginger
- ½ tbsp. ginger
- 1 red chili chopped
- 2 tbsp. toasted sesame seed
- ¼ tsp. Chinese five-spice powder

Directions:

- Sprinkle the five-spice powder over the tofu and set aside
- Shallow fry the tofu until brown for about 10 minutes and set aside
- Whisk the oyster sauce, rice flour, and vegetable broth with part of the five-spice powder in a bowl
- In this wok, add the Brussels sprout, peppers, and spices to cook for about 5 minutes
- Add the oyster mixture, cook for 30 to 60 seconds, then pour the tofu and allow the sauce to coat it.

- Serve with the toasted sesame seeds

Nutritional Information:

Calories: 71

Protein: 4.9 g

Fat: 3.9 g

Carbs: 5.9 g

64. WATERCRESS OYSTER SAUCE

Servings: 4

Cook Time: 15 minutes

Ingredients:

- 1 tbsp. sake
- 2 tsp. vegetarian oyster sauce
- ¼ tsp., cane sugar
- 350g watercress
- 1 tsp. garlic
- 1 tsp. minced ginger
- 1 red chili chopped
- 1 tsp. sesame oil

Directions:

- In a small saucepan, add the sake, oyster, cane sugar and gently simmer
- In another pan, heat the sesame oil and cook the ginger, garlic, and chili until fragrant
- Add the watercress and sauté until wilted
- Pour the sauce over and toss to coat
- Serve

Nutritional Information:

Calories: 30

Protein: 2.2 g

Fat: 1.2 g

Carbs: 2.8 g

65. POTATO AND VEGGIES HOT POT

Servings: 4

Cook Time: 50 minutes

Ingredients:

- 2 c. baby carrot
- 2 c. turnips
- 4 c. potatoes
- 1 c. bone marrow broth
- 1 celery stalk chunks
- 2 stalk scallions
- ½ c. low sodium soy sauce
- 3 tbsp. sake
- 1 tbsp. sugar
- 2 tbsp. freshly grated ginger
- 1 tbsp. minced garlic
- 1 tsp. nutmeg
- ¼ c. cornstarch slurry

Directions:

- Toss all the ingredients into the slow cooker except the slurry
- Allow it to cook slow and long to enable all the ingredients to release their flavors
- Just before serving, add the slurry and cook for 5 minutes
- Serve

Nutritional Information:

Calories: 191

Protein: 3.5 g

Fat: 14.03 g

Carbs: 12.1 g

66. SIMPLE WARM TOFU & VEGGIES WINTER BOWL

Servings: 6

Cook Time: 35 minutes

Ingredients:

- 450g extra firm tofu, in cubes
- ¼ c. tamari sauce
- 1 tbsp. garlic minced
- 2 tbsp. peanut oil
- 1 tbsp. cane sugar/brown sugar
- 1 tbsp. sweet chili sauce
- 4 c. fresh spinach
- ½ c. short brown grain rice cooked
- 3 c. vegetable broth
- 120g shitake mushroom
- 1-inch ginger knob
- 1 stalk scallion

Directions:

- In a deep wok, heat the oil and make the ginger and garlic fragrant for about 45 seconds
- On low heat, add the shitake and cook for 2 minutes
- Add the broth cane sugar, soy sauce, sweet chili sauce and bring it to a gentle simmer
- Add the tofu, spinach and cook until spinach is wilted but still bright green
- Taste for seasoning and cover for two more minutes
- Serve the soup in a bowl garnished with scallions

Nutritional Information:

Calories: 93

Protein: 4.5 g

Fat: 3.4 g

Carbs: 12.8 g

67. CABBAGE & BLACK BEAN BOWL

Servings: 6

Cook Time: 10 minutes

Ingredients:

- 1 small head cabbage
- 2 c. black bean rinsed and drained
- 1 tsp. black garlic paste
- ½ c. vegetable broth
- 1 tsp. sake
- 1 tsp. cornstarch

- 2 tsp. canola oil
- 1 tsp. garlic minced
- 2 c. Bok Choy or Swiss chard or Broccoli
- 2 tbsp. sesame seed

Directions:

- Toast the sesame seeds in a wok for 2 minutes or toasty enough for you and transfer it to a bowl
- In a small bowl, mix the broth, sake, and cornstarch and stir in the black garlic paste until smooth
- In the same wok, add the oil and sauté the garlic for 30 seconds, and then add the vegetable of choice, black beans and stir until the vegetable starts to wilt.
- Pour the slurry mix into the wok and coat the veggies until thickened
- Serve and sprinkle with sesame seeds.

Nutritional Information:

Calories: 67

Protein: 3.7 g

Fat: 1.08 g

Carbs: 11.6 g

68. SIMPLE CABBAGE AND CARROT SALAD IN RICE WINE-OYSTER SAUCE

Servings: 2

Preparation Time: 10 minutes

Ingredients:

- 2 tbsp. rice wine-oyster sauce homemade or store-bought
- 2 shallots thinly sliced
- 2 cloves of garlic sliced
- 2 oz. extra firm tofu cubes
- 8 oz. Napa cabbage chopped
- 4 oz. baby carrots grated
- 2 tbsp. coconut oil
- 1 tsp. sesame oil

Directions:

- Heat the wok to a smoky point, and then add the coconut oil
- Add the shallot and garlic; it should take 10 seconds to sauté
- Add the tofu to crisp up, still stirring
- Pour the cabbage and carrot, then the rice wine oyster sauce
- Toss and serve with a drizzle with sesame oil

Nutritional Information:

Calories: 95

Protein: 2.25 g

Fat: 8.01 g

Carbs: 4.9 g

69. SPICY SWEET VEGETABLE LO MEIN

Servings: 4

Cook Time: 35 minutes

Ingredients:

- 250g rice noodles
- 2 tbsp. low-sodium soy sauce
- 1 tbsp. rice wine
- 1 tsp. sesame oil
- 1 tsp. chopped red chili no seeds
- 1 tbsp. minced garlic
- 1 tbsp. minced ginger
- 10 oz. baby broccoli
- 2 tbsp. oil divided
- 1 tsp. honey
- 4 oz. white mushroom, cleaned and sliced

Directions:

- Cook the rice noodles as instructed and rinse in cold water
- Toss the noodles in sesame oil and set them aside
- In a bowl, combine the soy sauce, rice wine, and chili a bowl
- Meanwhile, clean the broccoli and set it aside
- In a large hot wok, add half the oil with the ginger and garlic for 30 seconds
- Next goes the mushrooms, broccoli for another 30 seconds

- Add the remaining oil, toss in the noodles and pour the sauce over and honey
- Allow it to heat for 2 minutes
- Serve.

Nutritional Information:

Calories: 94

Protein: 2.55 g

Fat: 4.4 g

Carbs: 11.4 g

70. IT'S TOFU AND VEGETABLE

Servings: 4

Cook Time: 40 minutes

Ingredients:

- 10 oz. extra firm tofu cubes
- 5 oz. carrots
- 5 oz. potatoes quartered
- 1 small head Napa cabbage
- 2 tbsp. sesame oil
- 2 tbsp. black bean garlic sauce
- 2 tsp. Tabasco hot sauce
- 2 tbsp. sake
- Scallions for garnish

Directions:

- Preheat the oven to 350F
- Mix the black bean garlic sauce and 1 tbsp. sesame oil in a bowl and toss the tofu in it
- Arrange on the baking tray and bake
- Meanwhile
- Toss the remaining vegetable rest of the ingredients and add them to the tofu in the oven
- Allow it to cook, soft but firm, and then serve

Nutritional Information:

Calories: 73

Protein: 3.3 g

Fat: 3.7 g

Carbs: 7.21 g

71. HOMEMADE CHINESE CREPE

Servings: 2

Cook Time: 20 minutes

Ingredients:

- 1 duck egg
- 2 tbsp. liquid coconut milk
- ¼ c. flour
- 2 tbsp. water
- ¼ c. bean sprout
- ¼ c. par boiled cabbage
- ¼ c. spinach chopped
- ¼ c. shallot diced
- 1 tsp. Garlic minced
- ½ tsp. ginger minced
- 1 small red chili chopped
- 1 tbsp. oil
- 1 tbsp. soy sauce
- 1 tsp. oyster sauce

Directions:

- In a large flat wok, add the oil, sauté the shallots, ginger, and garlic until fragrant
- Add the chili and all veggies to cook for a minute with the soy and oyster sauce
- Meanwhile, whisk the flour, milk, egg, and add a little water if needed to make a batter
- Pour this batter over the veggies in the pan and allow it to set as a pancake would
- Flip and cook the other side.
- Serve.

Nutritional Information:

Calories: 182

Protein: 6.08 g

Fat: 11.5 g

Carbs: 14.5 g

72. STEAMED-STIR-FRIED ICEBERG LETTUCE IN SOY SAUCE

Servings: 4

Cook Time: 10 minutes

Ingredients:

- One med head of iceberg lettuce
- ½ tbsp. garlic
- 1 tsp. ginger
- 1 small red chili chopped
- 1 tbsp. rice wine
- 1 tbsp. soy sauce
- 1 tsp. sugar
- Salt to taste
- 2 tbsp. oil

Directions:

- In a large wok with water, place a bamboo steamer over it and layer in leaves of the lettuce for about a minute to soften them
- In another wok, sauté the garlic, ginger, and chili
- Mix the sauces with the sugar until dissolved, pour into the wok to mix with the spices
- Remove the steamed lettuce and toss in the mixture.
- Serve.

Nutritional Information:

Calories: 51

Protein: 1.05 g

Fat: 3.6 g

Carbs: 4.1 g

73. HOT ROASTED BOK CHOY

Servings: 4

Cook Time: 15 minutes

Ingredients:

- 2 large Bok Choy, cleaned and slit down the middle
- 1 tsp. garlic powder
- 1 tsp. Ginger powder
- ½ tsp. chili flakes
- 1 tbsp. sesame oil
- 2 tbsp. soy sauce
- 2 tbsp. olive oil

- 1 tsp. cane syrup
- A dash of salt

Directions:

- Preheat the oven to 400F
- Mix all the ingredients except the Bok Choy in a bowl
- Arrange the veggie on a baking tray, center side facing up
- Douse the entire surface with the mix
- Allow it to roast until slightly wilted and drench in the sauce
- Serve

Nutritional Information:

Calories: 117

Protein: 2.1 g

Fat: 10.1 g

Carbs: 6.2 g

74. BUTTERY SNAP PEAS & MUSHROOMS

Servings: 2

Cook Time: 15 minutes

Ingredients:

- 1 tbsp. oyster sauce
- 1 tbsp. unsalted butter
- 1 tbsp. oil
- 2 c. sliced button mushrooms
- 4 c. sugar snap peas
- 1 clove garlic, thinly sliced
- A dash of cumin powder
- ¼ tsp. Szechuan pepper
- Salt to taste

Directions:

- Add the butter and oil to the pan
- Sauté the mushroom, garlic with pepper and cumin until soft
- Add the snap peas and a tbsp. of water, oyster sauce and replace the lid with cooking for 2 minutes at least
- Adjust the seasoning and serve

Nutritional Information:

Calories: 71

Protein: 1.9 g

Fat: 4.7 g

Carbs: 6.9 g

75. STIR-FRY SUMMER VEGGIES WITH HONEY

Servings: 4

Cook Time: 10 minutes

Ingredients:

- 1 tbsp. sesame oil
- 5 oz. baby corn
- 5 oz. Green beans
- 5 oz. baby carrot
- 1 small red pepper chopped
- 1 tbsp. oyster
- 1 tbsp. soy sauce
- 1 tbsp. slice garlic
- 1 tbsp. honey
- 1 tsp. toasted sesame seed
- 2 tbsp. plain broth

Directions:

- Into an oiled wok, add the veggies in a hot wok with the broth to steam the veggies
- Add the garlic and chili, and pour in the soy and oyster sauce
- Allow it to cook for 2 minutes, then drizzle the honey over
- Serve with the sesame seed

Nutritional Information:

Calories: 87

Protein: 2 g

Fat: 3.6 g

Carbs: 13.5 g

76. SIMPLE GARLIC AND SPINACH SIDE

Servings: 4

Cook Time: 10 minutes

Ingredients:

- 2 tbsp. oil
- 1 tsp. minced garlic
- 1 small red pepper
- 1 sweet bell pepper strips
- 300g spinach
- 1 tbsp. Soy sauce
- ¼ tsp. sugar
- A drizzle of sesame oil
- Salt and black pepper to taste

Directions:

- Add the oil to a wok and bring it to a smoky point
- Sauté the garlic, chili, and bell pepper
- Toss in the spinach and cook until wilted
- Add the soy sauce, sugar, and stir-fry for a minute
- Serve with a drizzle of sesame oil

Nutritional Information:

Calories: 95

Protein: 2.5 g

Fat: 7.6 g

Carbs: 5.6 g

77. CUCUMBER SALAD ✓

Servings: 4

Preparation Time: 10 minutes

Ingredients:

- 8 cucumbers
- 2 tbsp. honey
- 1 tsp. garlic
- 1 tbsp. toasted sesame oil
- 1 tsp. sweet chili oil
- 1 tbsp. lemon juice
- 1 tbsp. oyster sauce

Directions:

- Divide the cucumbers into two and cut diagonally
- Towel-dry the piece to extract excess water
- Warm the ingredients for the sauce in a saucepan just until it simmers
- Pour over the cucumber and serve

Nutritional Information:

Calories: 27

Protein: 0.61 g

Fat: 0.98 g

Carb 4.38 g

78. CAULIFLOWER AND OYSTER SAUCE

Servings: 2

Cook Time: 10 minutes

Ingredients:

- 100g cauliflower florets
- 1 sweet red pepper strips
- 1 sweet yellow pepper strips
- 1 med. onion cut diagonally
- 1 tbsp. oyster sauce
- 1 tbsp. + 1tsp. oil
- 1 tsp. minced garlic
- 1 tsp. minced ginger
- 1 tsp. chopped red chili
- Salt to taste
- 2 tbsp. water

Directions:

- In a large wok, sauté the chili, ginger, and garlic with the onion until soft
- Add the peppers and cook for 2 minutes
- Add in the cauliflower and mix the oyster sauce with water
- Pour over the ingredients and stir-fry for 5 – 7 minutes
- Serve

Nutritional Information:

Calories: 54

Protein: 1.06 g

Fat: 2.88 g

Carbs: 6.73 g

79. SWEET & SOUR BRAISED MUSHROOM

Servings: 4

Cook Time: 30 minutes

Ingredients:

- ¼ c. sake
- 1 tbsp. honey
- 1 lime
- 2 tbsp. vegetable oil
- 1 lb. button mushroom cleaned and sliced in twos
- One large chili chopped
- ½ tbsp. minced garlic
- ½ tbsp. minced ginger
- 1 tbsp. corn flour slurry
- 2 tbsp. soy sauce
- ½ c. fish stock
- Cilantro to garnish

Directions:

- Sauté the garlic, ginger, and chili in a wok, then remove and set aside

- In the same wok, add the mushrooms and stir continuously until they begin to release their juices
- Add the fish stock, soy sauce, honey, and sake, stir well and return sautéed garlic-ginger and chili
- Allow it to cook for 15 minutes, and then add the slurry until thickened
- Serve with cilantro garnish

Nutritional Information:

Calories: 83

Protein: 2.6 g

Fat: 4.6 g

Carbs: 7.5 g

80. STEAMED SHITAKE MUSHROOM WITH SPICY SWEET SAUCE

Servings: 4

Cook Time: 20 minutes

Ingredients:

- 20 Fresh shitake mushrooms cleaned
- 1 large lemon
- Sauce
- 1 tbsp. dry sherry
- 1 tbsp. sesame oil
- 1 tsp. Sugar or 2 tbsp. Honey
- ¼ tsp. white pepper
- 1 tbsp. rice flour slurry
- A dash of salt

Directions:

- In a large wok, add water and then place the sliced lemon in it
- Place a bamboo steamer over the wok, arrange the shitake mushroom, do not press together
- Mix the ingredients for the sauce and brush over the mushrooms
- Cover to cook for about 7 – 10 minutes
- Serve with a drizzle of the sauce

Nutritional Information:

Calories: 257

Protein: 4.7 g

Fat: 8.8 g

Carbs: 44.1 g

81. CUCUMBER STIR-FRY WITH SPICY CASHEW NUTS

Servings: 4

Cook Time: 12 minutes

Ingredients:

- 2 lb. cucumber, cut diagonally
- 1 tbsp. salt

For the Sauce:

- 1 tsp. Water
- ½ tbsp. sauce
- 1 tsp. toasted sesame oil
- 1 tbsp. oil
- 1 tsp. chili flakes
- 1 tsp. ginger
- ¼ c. spicy cashew nuts chopped

Directions:

- Place the cucumber in a colander and sprinkle with salt
- Allow it to sit for about two minutes to drain off excess water
- Meanwhile, add the sesame oil and oil to a pan, sauté the garlic until fragrant
- Add the cucumber and toss in the rest of the ingredients except the cashew nuts
- Stir-fry for 3 minutes
- Serve with the cashew nuts

Nutritional Information:

Calories: 48

Protein: 1.1 g

Fat: 3.6 g

Carbs: 3.3 g

82. FRIED SEAWEED (NAPA CABBAGE)

Servings: 1

Cook Time: 10 minutes

Ingredients:

- 6 large Napa leaves julienned
- Oil for frying
- 2 tsp. sugar

Directions:

- In a wok of boiling water
- Boil the leaves for 60 seconds to 2 minutes
- Remove and rinse with cold water
- Squeeze out excess water and flash fry until crisp in hot oil
- Sprinkle sugar all over and serve

Nutritional Information:

Calories: 87

Protein: 1.2 g

Fat: 6.4 g

Carbs: 7.6 g

83. MUNG BEAN SPROUT SALAD

Servings: 2

Cook Time: 10 minutes

Ingredients:

- 300g bean sprout
- ½ tbsp. soy sauce
- 1 tsp. toasted sesame seed
- Salt to taste
- 1 small chili chopped
- 1 tsp. sugar
- 1 tbsp. oil

Directions:

- Heat the oil and sauté the chili and sprouts

- Add the soy sauce with tbsp. water and allow it to cook for 2 minutes
- Remove from heat and add the rest of the ingredients
- Servings

Nutritional Information:

Calories: 73

Protein: 3.9 g

Fat: 4.8 g

Carbs: 5.8 g

84. SPICY FRIED AUBERGINES

Servings: 2

Cook Time: 45 minutes

Ingredients:

- 2 Chinese eggplants, sliced thinly
- 1 tsp. chili red
- 1 tbsp. honey
- 1 tsp. minced garlic
- ¼ c. soy sauce
- 2 tbsp. sake
- 1 tsp. sugar
- Oil
- ½ c. rice flour

Directions:

- Mix all the ingredients in a bowl and add the aubergine slices to marinate for 30 minutes
- Remove from the marinade and dust with rice flour
- Immediately fry in hot oil until crisp
- Serve

Nutritional Information:

Calories: 51

Protein: 1.3 g

Fat: 1.1 g

Carbs: 8.4 g

85.CHINESE STEAMED VEGGIES

Servings: 2

Cook Time: 15 minutes

Ingredients:

- 5 oz. frozen carrots
- 5 oz. broccoli frozen
- 5 oz. frozen cauliflower
- 4 garlic cloves
- 2-inch ginger knob
- 1 red chili sliced
- 2 tbsp. soy sauce
- 2 tbsp. sake
- 1 tsp. whole pepper corns
- 1 tsp. toasted sesame oil

Directions:

- Throw all the ingredients in a slow cooker and set to steam
- Allow it to cook for 5 – 7 minutes
- Open and serve as a side

Nutritional Information:

Calories: 62

Protein: 2.3 g

Fat: 2.2 g

Carbs: 8.1 g

"You give a poor man a fish, and you feed him for a day. You teach him to fish, and you give him an occasion that will feed him for a lifetime." – Chinese proverb

86. PAN-FRIED FISH FILLETS IN GINGER SAUCE

Servings: 2

Cook Time: 20 minutes

Ingredients:

- 2 large white fish fillets
- ½ tsp. Salt
- ½ tsp. black pepper ground
- ⅓ c. rice flour
- 3 tbsp. oil

For the Sauce:

- 2 tbsp. ginger
- 1 tbsp. Red chili
- ½ tbsp. garlic minced
- 2 tbsp. tamari sauce
- 2 tsp. sugar
- 4 tbsp. water
- 1 tbsp. scallions

Directions:

- Dry the fish with a kitchen towel and season generously with salt and pepper
- Using a Ziploc, dust the fillets with rice flour and set them aside
- Heat the oil in a wok and allow it to get to a smoky point

- Fry the fish until crisp and flakes easily
- Set aside on a kitchen towel to remove excess oil
- Using the same pan, sauté the ginger, garlic, and chili on low heat
- Add the water, sugar, and tamari sauce
- Allow it to cook down until it thickens
- Serve over the fish

Nutritional Information:

Calories: 222

Protein: 11.2 g

Fat: 14.4 g

Carbs: 12.3 g

87. FRIED FISH CAKES

Servings: 4

Cook Time: 20 minutes

Ingredients:

- 300g fish fillets, skinless & bone-free
- 3 scallion stalk green part
- ½ tsp. Ginger minced
- ¼ tsp. Garlic minced
- ¼ tsp. chopped red pepper
- 1 tsp. mirin
- 1 tsp. cider vinegar
- 1 duck egg white
- ¼ c. wheat flour
- Oil for frying
- Salt to taste

Directions:

- Add the fillets, salt, pepper, cider, mirin, and egg white to a food processor
- Gradually add in a tbsp. of flour at a time until it just comes together and can be shaped
- Using wet hands make into balls or patties
- Fry the fish patties, three minutes or until brown on each side
- Serve as desires

Nutritional Information:

Calories: 202

Protein: 12.27 g

Fat: 8.85 g

Carbs: 18.75 g

88. FRIED WHOLE FISH

Servings: 2

Cooking Time: 15 minutes

Ingredients:

- 1 whole fish about 500g
- 1 tsp. ginger minced
- 1 tsp. garlic minced
- 1 tsp. chili paste
- 1 lemongrass stalk smashed
- ¼ c. corn starch
- 2 tbsp. Soy
- ½ tbsp. sugar
- Oil for deep frying

Directions:

- Clean the fish and score it a bit
- Mix the ginger, garlic, chili paste, soy, and sugar in a bowl
- Using a large Ziploc bag, place the fish in it, add the lemongrass and pour the sauce mix into it.
- Allow it to marinate for 10 minutes
- Remove after 10 minutes and dust with corn starch, then into the frying oil until crisp
- Enjoy

Nutritional Information:

Calories: 103

Protein: 17.8 g

Fat: 1 g

Carbs: 4.76 g

89. STEAMED AROMATIC FISH IN SOY

Servings: 2

Cook Time: 30 minutes

Ingredients:

- 4 large white fish fillets skinless
- 1 long chili sliced
- ¼ c. scallion, white only diagonally cut
- The sauce
- 2 tbsp. ginger
- ½ c. light soy sauce
- 1 tbsp. garlic slice
- 2 tbsp. brown sugar
- ¼ c. oyster sauce
- 2 tbsp. Cider vinegar
- ½ tsp. sesame oil
- 1 sprig of cilantro to garnish

Directions:

- Pat the fish, fillets dry and arrange them on a plate large enough to fit in the steamer
- Mix the ingredients for the sauce in a bowl and add the chili to it
- Place water in the steamer and pour the sauce over the fish
- Cover the steamer and allow it to cook until flaky and white
- Serve with the cilantro as garnish

Nutritional Information:

Calories: 73

Protein: 10.5 g

Fat: 0.66 g

Carbs: 6.2 g

90. OVEN GINGER AND SCALLION STEAMED FISH

Servings: 4

Cook Time: 30 minutes

Ingredients:

- 2 * 700g whole fish cod or grouper cleaned
- 8 scallion stalks
- 3 tbsp. ginger in strips
- 4 tbsp. vegetable oil

- ¼ c. soy sauce
- 1 large red chili pepper slices
- Salt
- ½ c. sake

Directions:

- Stuff the fish with the scallions, ginger, chili and arrange them on a baking tray
- Pour the remaining ingredients over the fish and cover with a foil sheet
- Place into the oven at 350F to steam covered for the first 15 minutes
- Remove the foil sheet and allow to cook for 5 minutes more
- Serve

Nutritional Information:

Calories: 79

Protein: 9.5 g

Fat: 2.9 g

Carbs: 2.9 g

91. POTATO FISH SOUP

Servings: 4

Cook Time: 75 minutes

Ingredients:

- 1 lb. sea bass cleaned and cut into cubes
- 3 c. diced potatoes
- 5 slices ginger
- 3 liters vegetable stock
- 1 tsp. chili pepper

- 1 tbsp. soy sauce
- 1 tbsp. oyster sauce
- 1 tsp. tomato paste
- 1 c. chopped tomato
- ¼ c. shallot
- salt and pepper
- 1 chicken cubes
- 1 tbsp. oil

Directions:

- Mix the soy, oyster, and chili in a bowl
- Add the fish cubes and allow them to marinate
- Meanwhile, add the oil in a pan and sauté the shallot and ginger until fragrant
- Add the tomato and tomato paste cooking for 2 minutes
- Add the potatoes and stock until the potatoes are partially done
- Pour in the fish and all the marinade, stir and cover to cook for about 10 minutes
- Stir and adjust for seasoning using the chicken cubes
- Serve with a sprinkle of scallions

Nutritional Information:

Calories: 40

Protein: 3.48 g

Fat: 0.95 g

Carbs: 4.38 g

92. SPICY SWEET BRAISED FISH

Servings: 4

Cook Time: 40 minutes

Ingredients:

- 2 ½ lb. tilapia about 2 large or 3 med scaled and cleaned
- 2 tbsp. ginger diced
- ¼ c. oil
- ¾ c. rice wine
- 1 large chili
- ¾ c. balsamic vinegar
- 1 tbsp. sugar
- 2 scallion stalk big cuts

- 1 tbsp. dark soy sauce
- 1 tbsp. fish sauce
- 1 tsp. light soy
- 1 tbsp. corn starch

Directions:

- Score the fish giving it diagonal markings over the skin (you need a large wok for this recipe)
- Using a sieve of Ziploc bag, coat the fish with dust the corn starch
- Add the oil to the hot wok and sauté the chili and ginger. Once it is fragrant, remove and set aside (do not discard, it will be used again)
- Place the fish into wok and do not be tempted to turn until when you shake the wok and the fish moves, then it is ready to turn
- Add the pepper and ginger back to the pan and pour the rest of the ingredients and allow it to cook until the sauce is sticky and delicious
- Serve

Nutritional Information:

Calories: 136

Protein: 15.6 g

Fat: 5.94 g

Carbs: 6.3 g

93. GINGER-SOY FRIED FISH FILLETS

Servings: 4

Cook Time: 20 minutes

Ingredients:

- 12 oz. fish chunks
- 1 tbsp. corn starch
- 1 tbsp. ginger
- ¼ c. cooking oil
- 1 tbsp. scallions
- ¼ c. slice shallots

For the Sauce:

- 2 tbsp. Tamari sauce
- 1 tsp. pepper flakes
- 1 tsp. Sugar

- ¼ tsp. black pepper

Directions:

- Dust the fillets with corn starch and set them aside
- In a wok, fry the shallots, scallions, and ginger until crisp but not burnt
- Set aside and place the fish in the oil to crisp up
- Add the ingredients of the sauce to the wok and allow it to bubble away, and give it that golden sticky look
- Serve with the fried shallots, scallions, and ginger

Nutritional Information:

Calories: 227

Protein: 13.7 g

Fat: 17.3 g

Carbs: 4.23 g

94. CANTONESE SIMPLE WINTER FISH SOUP

Servings: 4

Cook Time: 40 minutes

Ingredients:

- 500g White fish fillets cut into strips
- 2 tbsp. light soy sauce
- 2 tbsp. Chinese wine
- ½ c. white onion diced
- 1 celery stalk diced
- 4 -6 c. chicken stock
- salt and pepper
- 4 sliced of ginger
- 1 red chili pepper diced
- 1 lemongrass chopped and smashed
- 1 tbsp. oil
- cilantro to garnish

Directions:

- Add the soy sauce, wine, and salt & pepper to the fish and allow it to marinate for about 30 minutes
- In a pan, sauté the onion, celery, and ginger with the chili pepper for 3 to 5 minutes

- Add the stock and bring it to a boil, pour in the fish, and cook until fish is cooked
- Serve with a garnish of cilantro

Nutritional Information:

Calories: 58

Protein: 2.58 g

Fat: 1.83 g

Carbs: 8.8 g

95. SHALLOW FRIED FISH WITH SOY VEGGIES RELISH

Servings: 4

Cook Time: 30 minutes

Ingredients:

- 2 garlic cloves sliced
- ¼ c. ginger strips
- 1 sweet yellow bell pepper in strips
- 1 sweet red bell pepper in strip
- 1 large shallot thinly sliced
- 1 tbsp. sweet chili sauce
- 1 tsp. lemon zest
- 1 tsp. lemon juice
- 1 tbsp. light soy sauce
- 1 tsp. honey
- One lb. fish fillet
- ½ tbsp. rice flour
- 1 tsp. white pepper ground
- ¼ c. vegetable oil

Directions:

- Dust the fish with a mix of rice flour and white pepper
- Shallow fry the fish fillets until crisp and set aside
- In the same wok, sauté the garlic, ginger, shallots, and bell peppers until soft
- Add in the sweet chili sauce, lemon zest, juice, soy, and stir while it simmers down gentle
- Add the fish and honey, toss and serve

Nutritional Information:

Calories: 196

Protein: 12.37 g

Fat: 14.11 g

Carbs: 5.2 g

96. MILKY WAY MUSHROOM AND FISH SOUP

Servings: 3

Cook Time: 30 minutes

Ingredients:

- 8 white button Mushrooms, cleaned and sliced
- 1 lb. carp tail cut into bite-sized pieces
- 4 ginger slices, finely diced
- 250g soft tofu
- ½ tsp. white pepper
- 1 red chili pepper
- 4 – 6 c. water
- 1 tbsp. rice or potato flour
- Salt and pepper to taste
- 2 tbsp. oil

Directions:

- Add the oil to the hot wok and cook the ginger for a minute, add the chili and then fry the fish in this aromatic oil
- Remove with all the pieces of chili and ginger and set aside
- When cool, pick the flesh from the bones
- Place the bones back into the wok and fry until crisp
- Add the stock and simmer for 20 minutes for flavor
- Sieve the bones out of the liquid, add the rest of the ingredients, and return the fish
- Mix the rice flour with water and pour over, cook for 2 to 5 minutes until thick and white
- Serve

Nutritional Information:

Calories: 46

Protein: 5.6 g

Fat: 1.95 g

Carbs: 1.6 g

97. STEAMED FISH IN BANANA LEAVES

Servings: 2

Cook Time: 20 minutes

Ingredients:

- 225g cod
- 2 tbsp. butter unsalted
- 2 tbsp. chicken stock
- 1 tsp. garlic minced
- 1 tsp. ginger minced
- 3 tbsp. Chinese rice wine
- 1 red chili chopped
- 2 tbsp. soy sauce
- 2 tsp. sesame oil
- 2 tbsp. cilantro
- 2 large banana leaves

Directions:

- Whisk all ingredients in a bowl
- Place the fish fillet on the banana leaf like a pocket
- Pour the sauce in the fish and fold
- Place in a steamer to cook until flaky
- Serve in the leaves with scallions as garnish

Nutritional Information:

Calories: 142

Protein: 10.54 g

Fat: 9.04 g

Carbs: 6.3 g

98. SIMPLE HOMEMADE FISH SOUP

Servings: 4

Cook Time: 60 minutes

Ingredients:

- 500g white firm fish
- 2 tbsp. peanut oil
- 2 tbsp. scallions

- shallot fine dice
- 1 tsp. garlic
- 1 tsp. ginger
- 1 tbsp. Lemongrass or lemon peel
- ½ tsp. red chili pepper diced
- 3 c. fish stock
- 1 tsp. cane sugar
- 2 tbsp. light soy sauce
- 1 tbsp. dark soy sauce
- 1 lime juiced
- Salt and pepper
- Scallions to garnish

Directions:

- Heat the oil in a smoky wok and cook the shallot, garlic, ginger, chili, and lemongrass for 3 minutes
- Add the stock, lime juice, soy sauces, sugar, and fish with the stock
- Cook for 3 to 5 minutes, then remove from heat and sprinkle the scallions to garnish
- Taste for seasoning before serving

Nutritional Information:

Calories: 91

Protein: 8.2 g

Fat: 5.7 g

Carbs: 1.6 g

99. CREAMY FISH BOWL

Servings: 2

Cook Time: 20 minutes

Ingredients:

- ½ c. onion diced
- 1 carrot diced
- 1 celery diced
- 1 tbsp. oil
- 1 tsp. minced ginger
- 1 tsp. minced garlic
- 1 tsp. light soy sauce
- 1 tbsp. butter
- 1 red chili diced
- 250g white fish fillets cubed
- 100g firm tofu cubes

- ⅓ c. white wine
- Salt and pepper
- 600ml fish stock
- 100ml whipping/heavy cream
- 1 tbsp. rice flour

Directions:

- Season the fish with salt and pepper
- Heat the butter and oil in a wok over med heat and sauté the garlic, ginger, chili, and onion
- Add the carrots, celery, and tofu to cook for a while
- Increase the heat and add the wine and flour, stirring in the stock
- Add the fish and cook for 10 minutes
- Pour in the cream to a boiling point and season well
- Serve

Nutritional Information:

Calories: 74

Protein: 5 g

Fat: 5 g

Carbs: 2.9 g

100.   SPICY FISH STEW

Servings: 4

Cook Time: 30 minutes

Ingredients:

- 15 oz. Chinese yam, peeled and cut into cubes
- 2 lb. any white fish Haddock in cubes
- 3 c. vegetable stock
- 2 tbsp. ginger sliced
- 2 tbsp. vegetable oil
- 1 clove garlic
- 16 oz. Crushed tomatoes
- ½ tsp. brown sugar
- 1 red pepper chopped
- Salt to taste
- ½ tsp. black pepper

Directions:

- Place the peeled yam in a steamer and cook for 5 to 10 minutes until soft but still form
- In a large wok with a lid, heat the oil, sauté ginger, garlic, and chili for 1 minute or two
- Add the tomatoes, stock, sugar, salt, black pepper and bring to a violent boil for 8 to 10 minutes
- Add the potatoes and fish and replace the lid with cooking for 3 minutes or more
- Serve with a sprinkle of cilantro

Nutritional Information:

Calories: 283

Protein: 6.4 g

Fat: 27.15 g

Carbs: 5.66 g

101.   GINGER SCALLION STEAMED FISH FILLETS

Servings: 2

Cook Time: 20 minutes

Ingredients:

- 250g Cod Fillet
- 2 stalks scallion
- 2-inch ginger grated
- 3 tbsp. light soy sauce
- 1 tsp. oyster sauce
- 1 tbsp. Shaoxing rice wine
- 1 tsp. Pepper flakes
- ½ tsp. sesame oil

Directions:

- Marinate the fish in a mix of the ingredients for 10 minutes
- Meanwhile, heat a steamer and place parchment paper over the bamboo base
- After 10 minutes, arrange the fillet and pour a bit of the marinade, and drizzle with sesame oil
- Replace the lid and cook until flaky
- Serve

Nutritional Information:

Calories: 91

Protein: 7.13 g

Fat: 0.59 g

Carbs: 3.88 g

102. FISH AND SUMMER VEGGIES

Servings: 4

Cook Time: 25 minutes

Ingredients:

- 500g white fish fillet
- 1 tsp. garlic
- 2 tbsp. oil
- 300g broccolini
- 1 large carrot into matchsticks
- 120g baby corn halved
- 1 tbsp. soy sauce
- 4 tbsp. oyster sauce
- 1 Chinese chili
- 1 tbsp. water or stock
- Salt and pepper to taste
- Cilantro to garnish

Directions:

- Marinate the fish with garlic and 1 tbsp. of oil for 5 minutes
- In a heated wok, stir fry the fish and set aside
- Add the remaining oil in the wok; stir-fry the veggies with spices until done
- Return the fish to the wok, add the water and cook for 1 minute
- Adjust seasoning and garnish with cilantro when serving

Nutritional Information:

Calories: 77

Protein: 8 g

Fat: 3 g

Carbs: 5 g

103. SIMPLE SPICY FISH BITES

Servings: 4

Cook Time: 20 minutes

Ingredients:

- 900g cod fillet in cubes
- 2 tbsp. garlic minced
- 1 red chili pepper sliced
- 2 tbsp. Chinese wine
- ½ tsp. ginger
- ⅓ c. oil for frying
- Salt and pepper

For the Marinade:

- 1 egg white
- ⅓ c. corn starch or rice flour
- 1 tsp. pepper flakes
- 2 tbsp. water

Directions:

- Marinade the fish in the mix of the marinating ingredients and set aside for 5
- Heat the oil in a wok and fry the battered fish until crisp
- Set aside and reduce the oil in the pan, sauté the garlic, chili and ginger until soft
- Add the fish and toss well
- Pour over the wine and cook for 1 minute more
- Serve

Nutritional Information:

Calories: 119

Protein: 11.4 g

Fat: 5.9 g

Carbs: 4.7 g

104. CHINESE FISH CHEEKS TOMATO STEW

Servings: 4

Cook Time: 90 minutes

Ingredients:

- 1 lb. fish cheeks
- 2 c. diced tomatoes

- 3 c. oyster mushroom cleaned and sliced
- 1 tsp. garlic minced
- 1 med red pepper
- 1 shallot diced
- 2 stalk green onion cut in 2-inch long
- ¼ c. cooking oil, divided
- 1 tbsp. potato flour
- Salt and pepper

Directions:

- Season the fish cheeks with salt, pepper, and potato flour
- Fry in the hot oil until crisp and set aside
- Add the remaining oil, sauté the shallot, garlic, and chili pepper
- Add the tomatoes to cook for 5 minutes, the mushrooms for another 3 minutes
- Throw back the fish and stir
- Serve

Nutritional Information:

Calories: 77

Protein: 5.7 g

Fat: 4.1 g

Carb 5.26 g

105. SWEET & SOUR FRIED FISH ON THE BONE

Servings: 4

Cook Time: 20 minutes

Ingredient:

- 4 – 2-inch-thick fish cut with bone
- 2 tbsp. rice flour to coat the fish
- 1 tbsp. shallot minced
- 1 tsp. pepper flakes
- 1 tsp. garlic
- 1 tsp. ginger minced
- 2 stalks scallion, green and white part separated
- 1 tbsp. Chinese wine
- 2 tbsp. soy sauce
- 1 tsp. dark soy sauce
- 1 tsp. sugar
- 2 tbsp. slurry

- ¼ c. water or vegetable stock
- ⅓ c. oil

Directions:

- Season the fish with salt and pepper and let it sit for a while
- Coat the fish with the rice flour and get ready to fry
- Heat the oil and fry the fish until crisp
- Remove and sauté the shallot, garlic, ginger, and the white part of the scallion to fry
- Pour the sauces and the rest of the ingredients with the stock
- Allow it to simmer down half the initial quantity, then add the fish
- Toss well and serve with the green scallion

Nutritional Information:

Calories: 157

Protein: 10.6 g

Fat: 10.5 g

Carbs: 5.17 g

106. SWEET & SPICY BAKED SALMON STEAK

Servings: 4

Cook Time: 2 hours 30 minutes

Ingredients:

- 4 salmon steaks, skinless
- 1 tbsp. ginger grated
- 1 tsp. Garlic minced
- tbsp. soy sauce light
- 1 tbsp. oyster sauce
- 1 tbsp. Honey
- ½ tbsp. chopped green chili
- 6 white whole pepper corns smashed
- ½ tsp. sesame oil
- Salt to taste

Directions:

- Mix all the ingredients except the fish and sesame oil in a bowl

- This is the base marinade
- Place the salmon in it and allow it to sit for 2 hours in a refrigerator
- After this time, arrange on a lined sheet. Pour some of the marinades over it and bake until flaky
- Just before removing from the oven, drizzle the sesame oil and serve

Nutritional Information:

Calories: 133

Protein: 19.33 g

Fat: 4.7 g

Carbs: 2.33 g

107.   LEMON HONEY-GINGER GLAZED BAKED SALMON

Servings: 4

Cook Time: 30 minutes

Ingredients:

- Salt and pepper
- 4 salmon fillets
- ¼ c. honey
- 2 tbsp. lemon juice
- 1 tbsp. ginger grated
- 1 small red pepper diced
- 2 tbsp. soy sauce

Directions:

- Season the salmon with salt and pepper, be generous
- Mix the rest of the ingredients in a bowl
- Arrange the salmon on a baking tray and use the sauce as a glaze
- Bake in a 400F oven, basting at regular intervals with the sauce
- Serve

Nutritional Information:

Calories: 139

Protein: 18.4 g

Fat: 4.3 g

Carbs: 5.7 g

108.   EXTRA SPICY FISH HEAD

Servings: 2

Cook Time: 20 minutes

Ingredients:

- 4 fish heads, cod preferably
- ½ c. light soy sauce
- 1 c. chili pepper diced
- 1 tsp. sugar
- ½ c. Chinese wine
- 1 tbsp. Ginger
- ½ tsp. garlic
- 1 tsp. sesame sauce
- 2 stalks scallions cut
- ¼ c. water
- 1 tbsp. oil

Directions:

- In the wok, add 1 tbsp. oil and sauté the garlic and ginger
- Next, add the soy, chili, sugar, wine, and water
- Add the fish heads and bring to a boil until it is done
- Serve with a drizzle of sesame oil and scallion

Nutritional Information:

Calories: 85

Protein: 11.5 g

Fat: 3.6 g

Carbs: 2.21 g

109.   SWEET FISH BALLS

Servings: 4

Cook Time: 20 minutes

Ingredients:

- 1 lb. eel fish meat
- 1 egg white
- 1 tsp. garlic powder
- 1 tsp. ginger powder
- 1 tsp. onion
- Salt and pepper
- 1 small chili
- Oil for frying

Directions:

- Add all the ingredients to the blender except the oil
- Whizz until it comes together
- Remove and form into balls and salt boiling water until they start to float
- Next, fry the boiled fish balls until crisp
- Serve with a sauce

Nutritional Information:

Calories: 107

Protein: 9.8 g

Fat: 5.7 g

Carbs: 3.86 g

110. BRAISED FISH HEAD AND BEAN CURD

Servings: 2

Cook Time: 30 minutes

Ingredients:

- 4 med-size cod fish heads cleaned and halved
- ½ tbsp. garlic
- 1 c. bean curd cut into cubes
- 1 tbsp. light soy sauce
- Oil for frying
- Salt to taste

Directions:

- Heat the oil in the wok and fry the fish heads

- Remove and use the same pan to sauté the garlic and add the bean curd with enough water to draw out the flavor
- Add the fish, soy sauce and serve

Nutritional Information:

Calories: 105

Protein: 11.3 g

Fat: 5.6 g

Carbs: 2.22 g

"If you are going to have a roast, a chicken is better than a phoenix" – Chinese proverb

111.   SWEET CHICKEN POPCORN

Cook Time: 40 minutes

Servings: 4

Ingredients:

- 1 lb. chicken breasts, cubes
- 3 egg whites
- ⅓ c. corn flour
- ¼ c. flour
- Oil for frying
- Salt

For the Sauce:

- 1 c. sweet orange juice
- ½ c. sugar
- 2 tbsp. apple cider
- 2 tbsp. Soy sauce
- ½ tsp. ginger-garlic paste
- ½ chili flakes
- 1 tbsp. orange zest
- 1 tbsp. rice flour

Directions:

- To make the sauce, cook all the ingredients for the sauce in a med pan except the rice flour for 3 minutes

- Mix the flour with water to make a slurry and pour it into the pan. Once it starts to thicken, set aside
- For the chicken, in a bowl, mix flour and corn flour with a pinch of salt
- In another beat the egg whites and set aside
- Dip the chicken in the egg white, then the flour mix, and into the oil
- Fry until crisp and repeat until done
- Toss the piece in the orange sauce and enjoy

Nutritional Information:

Calories: 277

Protein: 9.58 g

Fat: 21.37 g

Carb 11.8 g

112.   THE BEST CHINESE CHICKEN BROTH ✓

Cook Time: 3 hours

Ingredients:

- 3-4 lb. by weight whole organic chicken, cleaned
- 2 large onions quartered
- 2 c. cilantro
- 2 inches fresh ginger slices
- 2 stalk scallions
- ½ garlic bulb.
- ½ tbsp. white whole peppercorns
- ½ tsp. black pepper
- Salt

Directions:

- Cover the chicken with water in a large pot and boil for 2 minutes. This will bring all impurities to the surface, strain this liquid and rinse off the chicken
- Return to a clean pot, add water to cover the chicken, and add all the ingredients allowing it to slowly cook and release all its juices for 2 3 hours
- Season, accordingly, strain and serve/store
- It makes the base for many Chinese broth recipes.

Nutritional Information:

Calories: 179

Protein: 14.78 g

Fat: 11.63 g

Carbs: 2.96 g

113. CHICKEN NOODLE BOWL ✓

Servings: 4

Cook Time: 20 minutes

Ingredients:

- 8 c. chicken broth
- 2 dried chili pepper
- 2 c. carrot large dices
- 1 sweet green bell pepper
- 3 c. shredded chicken
- ¼ c. soy sauce
- 2 tbsp. balsamic vinegar
- 350g pasta of choice
- ½ tsp. black pepper
- Salt to taste
- 2 tbsp. cilantro to garnish
- 1 tbsp. sesame seed oil

Directions:

- Pour the chicken broth into a pan and add everything except the chicken, noodles, sesame oil, and cilantro
- Allow it to cook for 5 minutes to bring out the flavor
- Add the noodles, cooking them according to instruction
- Add the chicken just before serving
- When done, serve into a bowl, garnished sesame oil and cilantro
- Enjoy

Nutritional Information:

Calories: 85

Protein: 6.8 g

Fat: 2.4 g

Carbs: 8.6 g

114. CHINESE WHITE CUT CHICKEN

Servings: 6

Cook Time: 60 minutes

Ingredients:

- 2 lb. chicken breast with sk n
- 1 bunch scallions
- 30g ginger
- 3 garlic cloves
- 1 c. dry sherry wine
- 1 tbsp. sesame oil
- 1 tsp. salt or more to taste

Directions:

- Place the chicken breast in a large pan with enough water to cover them
- Add the rest of the ingredients and allow it to cook low and slow until done about 20 minutes
- Bring it to boil for 15 minutes and allow the chicken to sit in the broth for another 15 minutes
- Remove from the broth and slice
- Enjoy

Nutritional Information:

Calories: 209 g

Protein: 18.45 g

Fat: 11.02 g

Carb: 8.05 g

115. CHINESE CHICKEN AND CASHEW DISH

Servings: 6

Cook Time: 40 minutes

Ingredients:

- 2 lb. chicken breasts, skinless & boneless, cut into 1-inch cubes
- 1 tsp. cornstarch
- 1 ½ tbsp. of oil

- 1 tsp. garlic paste
- 1 c. slightly toasted cashew nuts
- 1 c. diced red pepper
- 2 c. broccoli florets
- 1 tsp. ginger minced

For the Sauce:

- ½ c. chicken broth
- ½ c. tamari sauce
- ¼ c. oyster sauce
- 3 tbsp. dry white vinegar
- 1 tbsp. organic honey
- 2 tsp. sesame oil

Directions:

- Bring all the ingredients for the sauce to a boil and set aside
- Coat the chicken with starch and set it aside
- Heat the wok to really hot, add 1 tbsp. oil and pour the chicken and cook until slightly crispy
- Remove from the pan and add the broccoli to the sauté with the remaining ½ tbsp. oil
- Pour the sauce into the pan, add the chicken, toss and warm for 2 to 5 minutes
- Serve

Nutritional Information:

Calories: 165

Protein: 17.34 g

Fat: 8.3 g

Carbs: 5.25 g

116.   BAKED SWEET AND SOUR CHICKEN

Cook Time: 75 minutes

Servings: 6

Ingredients:

- 1 lb. boneless and skinless chicken breasts
- Salt and pepper
- 1 c. corn flour
- Sauce
- ¼ c. soy sauce

- ¾ c. sugar
- ½ c. lemon juice
- 1 tbsp. lemon zest
- 1 tbsp. oyster sauce
- 1 tsp. garlic minced

Directions:

- Coat the chicken with salt and pepper and corn starch
- Place on a baking tray and bake until crisp at 350F
- Cook the sauce ingredients in a saucepan until it coats the back of a spoon
- Toss the chicken in and serve

Nutritional Information:

Calories: 161

Protein: 12.45 g

Fat: 3.05 g

Carbs: 21.04 g

117.   TRADITIONAL SOY SEARED DUCK BREAST

Cook Time: 50 minutes

Servings: 4

Ingredients:

For the Sauce:

- 4 c. Chinese rice wine
- ¾ c. light soy sauce
- ¼ c. sugar
- 1 tbsp. honey
- 1 c. dried seaweed

For the Duck:

- 3 large duck breasts with skin on
- 1 tbsp. vegetable oil
- 1 scallion stalk
- 1 tbsp. toasted sesame seed

Directions:

- Bring the ingredients for the sauce to a boil until syrupy but not thick
- Score the duck breast
- In a hot pan, add the oil and place the duck breasts skin side down to render the excess Fat: and crisp up the skin
- Flip to the rest of the meat and sear thoroughly to seal in the juices and cook the duck
- Repeat the process for the rest and allow it to rest on the counter
- Slice the breast and serve with the sweet sauce

Nutritional Information:

Calories: 176

Protein: 10.5 g

Fat: 9.1 g

Carbs: 3.7 g

118. SPICY SWEET CHICKEN CUBES

Cook Time: 30 minutes

Servings: 4

Ingredients:

- 1 ½ lb. chicken breast
- ½ tsp. salt
- 1 tsp. black pepper
- 1 tbsp. sake
- Oil for frying

For the Sauce:

- ¼ c. dark soy sauce
- 1 red chili chopped
- 1 tsp. chili paste
- 1 tsp. tamarind paste
- 2 tsp. sesame oil
- 1 tbsp. chopped garlic
- 1 tbsp. chopped ginger
- ½ c. cane sugar
- ½ c. water
- ½ c. chicken broth

Directions:

- season the chicken with salt, pepper, and sake, allowing it to sit for 12 minutes
- Meanwhile, bring all the ingredients for the sauce to boil until the sugar dissolves completely
- Fry the chicken bits until crisp
- Pour them into the sauce and serve

Nutritional Information:

Calories: 213

Protein: 11.36 g

Fat: 17.3 g

Carbs: 2.9 g

119. CHICKEN SKIN AND SHRIMP PASTA SOUP

Servings: 2

Cook Time: 45 minutes

Ingredients:

- 300g fresh shrimps cleaned
- 100g chicken skin precooked
- 100g pasta
- 1 tbsp. pork Fat:
- 1 tbsp. chopped cilantro
- Salt to taste
- ½ tsp. white pepper
- 1 tbsp. potato starch
- 4 c. chicken stock
- A dash of black pepper

Directions:

- Cook the pasta in salted water (we are using the same pot for the shrimps, so be mindful about the salt content)
- Meanwhile, blend the shrimps with seasoning, white pepper, and starch and mix well
- Make into small balls and set aside
- Into the boiling water with the pasta, add the shrimp balls to cook, then the chicken skin
- Add the pork Fat: and adjust the seasoning
- Serve with cilantro

Nutritional Information:

Calories: 78

Protein: 7.4 g

Fat: 3.75 g

Carbs: 3.3 g

120. CHICKEN FEET WITH HEALTHY NUTS

Servings: 2

Cook Time: 130 minutes

Ingredients:

- 300g chicken feet, cleaned
- 3 tbsp. cashew paste
- 3 tbsp. chickpea
- 1 stalk scallion
- 1 tsp. Ginger
- ½ tsp. sugar
- Salt to taste
- 1 tsp. chicken seasoning
- 1 red chili
- 1 tbsp. soy sauce
- 2 tbsp. cooking wine or sake
- 100ml water or chicken stock
- Cilantro

Directions:

- Add all the ingredients to a deep pan and allow it to cook until chicken pea is soft and the chicken flesh is almost falling from the bone
- Season accordingly and garnish with cilantro before serving

Nutritional Information:

Calories: 210

Protein: 13.5 g

Fat: 13.2 g

Carbs: 8.8 g

121. COCA-COLA GINGER STICKY CHICKEN WINGS

Servings: 4

Cook Time: 55 minutes

Ingredients:

- 12 chicken wings cleaned
- 1 tsp. salt
- 2 ½ c. Coca-Cola
- 2 tbsp. cooking oil
- 2 tbsp. ginger minced
- 1 tsp. chili pepper
- 1tbsp. soy sauce

Directions:

- Blanch the chicken wings for 10 minutes to remove dirt
- Wash under cold water to clean well
- Fry the wings in the oil until brown
- Remove the oil, return the chicken wings to the wok and add the Coca-Cola, ginger, chili, and soy sauce
- Cook until sticky and serve warm

Nutritional Information:

Calories: 148

Protein: 11.36 g

Fat: 9.97 g

Carbs: 2.9 g

122. ASIAN BBQ CHICKEN DRUMSTICK

Servings: 4

Cook Time: 20 minutes

Ingredients:

- 1.5 lb. chicken drumsticks
- 1 c. BBQ sauce
- 1 tbsp. Soy sauce
- ½ tbsp. oyster sauce
- 1 tbsp. ginger
- 1 tsp. Chili flakes

- ½ tbsp. garlic
- A dash of sake

Directions:

- Marinate the chicken in the ingredients and allow it to stay overnight for better flavor
- The next day, arrange on a grill or bake in the oven until done
- Serve

Nutritional Information:

Calories: 164

Protein: 12.48 g

Fat: 6.64 g

Carbs: 12.42 g

123. SIMPLE CHICKEN AND MUSHROOM SOUP

Servings: 2

Cook Time: 10 minutes

Ingredients:

- 5 shitake mushrooms cut into strips
- 3 Swiss chard leaves in strip
- 1 stalk scallion
- 4 c. shredded chicken
- 50g cook chicken skin
- 4 c. homemade chicken soup

Directions:

- Add everything into the stock and simmer on low for 5 minutes
- Serve piping hot

Nutritional Information:

Calories: 91

Protein: 9.7 g

Fat: 2.69 g

Carbs: 6.84 g

124. CRISP ROAST DUCK

Servings: 8

Cook Time: 90 minutes

Ingredients:

- 4 duck legs with skin on
- ¼ c. honey
- ¼ c. dark soy sauce
- 1 tsp. Chinese 5-spice powder
- ½ c. sake
- 1 tbsp. ginger

Directions:

- Blanch the duck legs. This firms the skin and offers a crisp texture
- Mix the rest of the ingredients in a bowl and add ½ c. warm water
- Simmer this mixture until slightly sticky and pour over the duck in a container
- Allow it to marinate overnight and bake the next day
- Preheat the oven to 375F and arrange the duck legs on a rack, cooking until crisp, golden brown, and delicious

Nutritional Information:

Calories: 196

Protein: 16.5 g

Fat: 6.6 g

Carbs: 12.6 g

125.   DUCK BREAST STIR-FRY

Servings: 4

Cook Time: 40 minutes

Ingredients:

- 2 duck breasts, skinless, boneless cut in strips
- 2 yellow bell pepper strips
- 2 red bell pepper strips
- 2 green bell pepper strips
- 1 tbsp. ginger
- 1 small red chili
- 1 tbsp. sake
- 1 tbsp. Soy sauce
- ½ tbsp. garlic
- 1 tsp. sugar
- 1 tsp. oyster sauce
- Scallions to garnish
- 1 tbsp. rice flour
- Salt and pepper to taste
- 2 tbsp. oil

Directions:

- Marinate the duck breast in salt, rice flour, and sake for 15 minutes
- Heat the oil in a wok and cook the duck breast for 3 to 5 minutes
- Move the meat to the eggs of the pan and cook the rest of the veggies and garlic, ginger, and chili until fragrant
- Add the sauce, sugar, and seasoning, return the duck to the pan, stir-fry for 5 minutes and serve with the scallions

Nutritional Information:

Calories: 63

Protein: 4.4 g

Fat: 2.2 g

Carb 7.2 g

126.   HOMEMADE DUCK SAUCE

Cook Time: 8 minutes   ✓

Ingredients:

- ¾ c. and sticky fruit jam pineapple preferably
- ¼ c. rice vinegar
- 1 tsp. light soy sauce
- 1 tsp. chopped garlic
- 1 tsp. chopped ginger
- 1 tsp. chopped red chili
- 1 tsp. Chinese Five Spice

Directions:

- Whisk all the ingredients together and bring to a gentle boil
- Allow it to cool, then store in a bottle until ready for use

Nutritional Information:

Calories: 60

Protein: 1.1 g

Fat: 0.14 g

Carbs: 14.5 g

127.   EASY CHINESE PAN SEARED DUCK BREAST

Servings: 2

Cook Time: 40 minutes

Ingredients:

- 2 duck breasts about 400g
- ¼ tsp. salt
- 1 tsp. Chinese wine
- ¼ Chinese 5-spice
- 1 tsp. Garlic powder
- ½ tsp. ginger powder
- 1 tbsp. oil
- 2 tbsp. Soy

- ½ tsp. chili flakes

Directions:

- Whisk everything except the oil and duck in a bowl
- Marinate the duck for 30 minutes
- Heat the oil in a pan and sear the duck until the skin is crisp and Fat: rendered
- Cook the rest of the meat in the duck fat. It should take about 6 to 10 minutes
- Allow the duck breasts to rest before slicing and serving

Nutritional Information:

Calories: 390

Protein: 10.9 g

Fat: 37.7 g

Carbs: 1.05 g

128.   CHICKEN AND VEGGIES WRAP

Servings: 4

Cook Time: 5 hours

Ingredients:

- 4-large lettuce for the wrap
- 450g soy-cooked chicken shredded
- 100g carrots in strips
- 100g daikon radish strips
- 1 c. cooked short-grain rice
- ½ c. sweet chili sauce
- 1 tbsp. honey
- 1 red chili chopped
- ¼ c. soy sauce

Directions:

- Mix the sweet chili sauce, honey, chili, and soy in a bowl. This is the dipping sauce
- Take lettuce and assemble with the chicken, rice, carrot, and radish as desired
- Fold and enjoy

Nutritional Information:

Calories: 45

Protein: 4 g

Fat: 0.8 g

Carbs: 5.6 g

129.   DRIED CHILI STIR-FRY CHICKEN

Servings: 4

Cook Time: 40 minutes

Ingredients:

- 500g chicken breast cut in bite-size
- 10 to 15 dried chili pepper cut into bits
- ½ tsp. Salt divided
- ½ tsp. sugar
- 1 egg white
- 1 tbsp. Soy sauce
- ½ tbsp. Chinese cooking wine divided
- 2 tsp. corn starch divided
- ¼ c. oil
- 4 ginger slices
- 1 tsp. garlic minced
- 2 Green stalk onion

Directions:

- Add the cooking wine, salt, egg white, and corn starch to the chicken bits and mix.
- Let this sit for 15 minutes to marinate
- Mix salt, sugar, soy sauce, and corn starch in a bowl and set aside for use
- Heat the oil in a wok and fry the chicken and set aside
- Reduce the oil and add the green onion, pepper and ginger, and garlic to fry well
- Pour the soy mixture and stir again
- Add the chicken, toss and serve

Nutritional Information:

Calories: 114

Protein: 9.1 g

Fat: 6 g

Carbs: 6 g

130. CHICKEN AND WILD SHITAKE MUSHROOM

Servings: 2

Cook Time: 30 minutes

Ingredients:

- 500g chicken breast cut in strips
- 150g dried shitake mushrooms cleaned and cut into strips
- 4 slices of ginger
- 1 shallot diced
- 1 tsp. garlic
- 1 small red chili diced
- 2 c. chicken stock
- 1 tbsp. oil
- 1 tsp. soy sauce
- 2 stalks Scallions

Directions:

- Soak the dried mushroom and flash-dry the chicken for 5 minutes
- Drain and set aside
- In a wok with the oil, sauté the ginger, garlic, red pepper, and scallions, then add the chicken
- Add the soy sauce and chicken stock and allow it to cook until thickened
- Serve as desired

Nutritional Information:

Calories: 103

Protein: 9.3 g

Fat: 2.5 g

Carbs: 12.6 g

131. TERIYAKI MARINATED PAN-SEARED DUCK

Servings: 2

Cook Time: 80 minutes

Ingredients:

- 2-4-oz. duck breast, scored
- ½ c. teriyaki sauce
- ½ c. dark soy sauce
- 1 tsp. garlic
- 1 tsp. ginger
- 1 tsp. chili chopped
- 1 tbsp. sake
- 1 tbsp. honey
- 1 tsp. sesame oil

Directions:

- Mix the ingredients in a Ziploc bag and place the duck for an hour to marinate
- In a hot pan, seared the duck skin side down and set aside
- Pour the leftover marinade into the pan and cook down until sticky
- drizzle over as sauce for the duck with the sesame oil

Nutritional Information:

Calories: 109

Protein: 9 g

Fat: 2 g

Carb 12 g

132. SIMPLE DUCK SALAD

Servings: 2

Preparation Time: 15 minutes

Ingredients:

- 200g Soba Noodles cooked
- 3 c. shredded duck meat
- ½ tsp. grated ginger
- 1 tsp. toasted sesame seeds
- 1 cucumber peeled and cut into cubes
- 1 scallion stalk
- 1 tsp. sesame oil
- 1 tsp. soy sauce
- 1 tbsp. Apricot jam
- ½ tsp. chili flakes

Directions:

- Mix the oil, jam, soy, and chili flakes in a bowl
- Add the rest of the ingredients to a bowl and pour the sauce over
- Sprinkle with sesame seeds
- Serve

Nutritional Information:

Calories: 205

Protein: 15 g

Fat: 12 g

Carbs: 8 g

133. MODERN TAKE ON GINGER DUCK

Servings: 8

Cook Time: 150 minutes

Ingredients:

- 5 lb. whole duck
- 500ml beer
- 350ml ginger ale
- 1 tbsp. chili flakes
- 1 tbsp. ginger powder
- Salt
- 1 tsp. sugar

Directions:

- Mix the ginger ale, chili flakes, ginger powder, salt, and sugar in a bowl
- Apply all over the duck and refrigerate overnight for at least more than 12 hours
- Preheat the oven and sit the duck on the beer can
- Place into the oven and cook until the skin is crisp and juices run clear
- Let it sit for some time before carving
- Serve as desired

Nutritional Information:

Calories: 150

Protein: 9.76 g

Fat: 10.4 g

Carbs: 2.8 g

134. SEARED DUCK BREAST

Servings: 4

Cook Time: 30 minutes

Ingredients:

- 4 (32 oz.) duck breasts
- ¼ c. finely chopped shallots
- 1 tbsp. ginger minced
- 1 tbsp. pineapple syrup
- ¼ c. sake
- 1 tbsp. Tamari sauce
- ½ c. scallions green and white part
- 250ml hot water or chicken broth
- Salt and black pepper to taste

Directions:

- Score the skin, but do not get to the flesh
- Season with salt and pepper and let it sit for 5 minutes
- In a hot wok, place the breast skin side down to cook on low for 8 minutes to render the Fat:
- Drain the Fat: before flipping to cook the flesh, about 4 minutes, then set aside
- In the same wok, sauté the shallots and ginger, then add the sake and pineapple syrup with the hot broth
- Cook for 2 minutes, then add the Tamari sauce
- Slice the duck and pour the sauce over it

Nutritional Information:

Calories: 358

Protein: 10.7 g

Fat: 31.3 g

Carb 10.1 g

135. LEMON & GINGER DUCK

Servings: 2

Cook Time: 30 minutes

Ingredients:

- 2 duck breasts
- 1 lime juiced
- 1 small red chili chopped
- 1 tsp. ginger
- 2 tsp. garlic
- 1 tbsp. lemongrass paste
- 2 tbsp. scallions
- A bunch of coriander
- Salt and pepper

Directions:

- Blend everything except the coriander and duck breasts to form a paste, add some water to loosen it
- Score the duck breast and season with salt and pepper
- On a hot pan, cook skin side down for 10 minutes until Fat: is done
- Flip to the flesh and add your marinade, reducing the heat to low for 3 to 5 minutes according to the desired doneness
- Allow the duck to rest, slice, and garnish with coriander

Nutritional Information:

Calories: 91

Protein: 13 g

Fat: 2.8 g

Carbs: 3.1 g

"The way you cut your meat reflects the way you live." – Confucius

Seeing this quote for the first time, one would wonder the correlation between meat cutting and life, but looking at it from a deeper understanding, you'd see that in the real sense of life how a person handles and prepares his meat (beef in this case) shows a lot.

If a person prepares his beef hastily, they lack finesse. But if prepared decently and sweetly, it shows that they are a person of great character!

136.   BRAISED BEEF

Preparation Time: 5 Minutes

Cooking Time: 25 Minutes

Servings: 2

Ingredients:

- 10g minced ginger
- 1 tbsp. canola oil
- 3 c. chunked beef
- 1 minced garlic clove
- 1 chopped small onion
- 1 tbsp. Chinese five-spice powder
- 1 handful chopped coriander stalk
- 30g dark brown muscovado sugar
- 2-star anise
- 30ml soy sauce
- 1 tbsp. tomato puree
- 1 tsp. black peppercorn
- 1 c. beef stock

Directions:

- Preheat the oven to 320F.
- Brown the beef chunks in a pan of oil. Cook-stir till done. Transfer to a lined plate.
- In that same pan, sauté the onion, coriander, garlic, and ginger for 3 minutes.
- Transfer this mixture to your food processor and blitz till you get a smooth paste.
- Transfer to a clean pan, add 2 tbsp. Of water, and everything else.
- Cook for 2 minutes before adding the browned beef and any accumulated juices.
- Cover the pan and transfer to the heated oven.
- Cook till the sauce is thick.
- Serve with rice.

Nutritional Information:

Calories: 163

Protein: 3.28 g

Fat: 7.25 g

Carbs: 22.01 g

137.   CRISPY CHILI BEEF

Preparation Time: 5 Minutes

Cooking Time: 15 Minutes

Servings: 1

Ingredients:

- 1 tsp. Chinese five-spice powder
- 150g thin-sliced steak
- 30ml sunflower oil
- 1 tbsp. cornflour
- 1 sliced red chili
- 1 sliced, separated spring onion (separate white and green)
- 1 tbsp. sweet chili sauce
- 1 minced garlic clove
- 1 sliced red pepper
- 1 tbsp. ketchup
- 1 tbsp. water
- 2 tbsp. white wine vinegar

Directions:

- Combine the five-spice powder, steak, and corn flour in a bowl. Toss well.
- Then combine the vinegar, ketchup, sauce, and water in a bowl. Keep aside.
- Fry the coated steak in a pan of oil.
- Transfer to a lined plate.
- Sauté the chili, red pepper, garlic, and white spring onion in the pan.
- Stir-fry for 2 minutes and add the vinegar mixture.
- Cook for 2 more minutes.
- Return the beef to the mixture.
- Serve with rice. Garnish with the remaining green scallions.

Nutritional Information:

Calories: 526

Protein: 26.79 g

Fat: 40.84 g

Carbs: 14.69 g

138. BEEF, SCALLION, AND GINGER STIR-FRY

Preparation Time: 08 Minutes

Cooking Time: 16 Minutes

Servings: 2

Ingredients:

- 2 oz. sliced beef tenderloin
- 1 cut scallion stalk
- 1 pinch cornstarch
- 1 shredded peeled ginger
- 1 tbsp. rapeseed oil
- 1 c. sweet Shaoxing sauce

Directions:

- Coat the beef in cornstarch.
- Sauté the ginger in a pan of oil. Cook-stir for 3 minutes.
- Add the beef. Cook for 4 minutes before adding the Shaoxing sauce.

- Cook till beef is tender.
- Toss in the scallion.
- Serve with rice.

Nutritional Information:

Protein: 10.79g

Fat: 9.76g

Carbs: 9.29g

Calories: 162

139. BEEF, PINEAPPLE, AND GINGER STIR-FRY

Preparation Time: 20 Minutes

Cooking Time: 22 Minutes

Servings: 1

Ingredients:

- 1 tsp. white wine vinegar
- 250g sliced rump beef
- 1 tbsp. rapeseed oil
- 1 cut ginger (into matchstick sizes)
- 1 minced garlic clove
- 2 tbsp. soy sauce
- 1 tsp. sweet chili sauce
- 2 cut spring onions
- 1 tbsp. brown sugar
- 150g chunked pineapple

Directions:

- Combine the sugar, sauces, and vinegar in a large bowl.
- Mix well before tossing in the beef.
- Marinate for 10 minutes.
- While that is marinating, sauté the spring onion, garlic, and ginger in a pan of oil. Cook-stir for 3 minutes. Transfer to a lined plate.
- Proceed to fry the coated beef in the oil. (Add extra oil if needed). When the beef is fried, add the pineapples and sautéed ginger mixture.
- Add the marinade mixture too.
- Cook for 3 minutes till the marinade is thick.
- Serve.

Nutritional Information:

Protein: 58.13 g

Carbs: 35.85 g

Fat: 35.1 g

Calories: 680

140. BEEF AND BROCCOLI NOODLES

Preparation Time: 07 Minutes

Cooking Time: 10 Minutes

Servings: 2

Ingredients:

- 1 minced garlic clove
- 200g sliced beef fillet
- 200g egg noodles
- 1 handful sliced onion
- 1 tbsp. peanut oil
- 2 c. chopped broccoli florets
- 1 handful sesame seed
- 1 c. Sweet Shaoxing sauce

Directions:

- Marinate the beef fillet in half of the sauce. Set aside.
- Cook the noodles and broccoli al dente.
- When ready, drain, rinse, and set aside.
- Sauté the onion, beef, and garlic in a pan of oil.
- Cook-stir till beef is browned.
- Toss in the other half of the sauce, the remaining marinade, and broccoli/noodles.
- Mix well. Cook for 2 minutes.
- Serve. Garnish with sesame seeds.

Nutritional Information:

Protein: 6.06 g

Fat: 13.09 g

Carbs: 41.66 g

Calories: 424

141. STICKY GREEN STIR-FRY AND BEEF

Preparation Time: 07 Minutes

Cooking Time: 14 Minutes

Servings: 4

Ingredients:

- 35g minced ginger
- 1 large deseeded chopped green pepper
- 50ml soy sauce
- 50ml Chinese rice wine
- 450ml minced Beef
- 70g hoisin sauce
- 8g toasted sesame seeds
- 2 chopped brown onions
- 5 minced garlic cloves
- 2 sliced red chili
- 25ml toasted sesame oil

Directions:

- Sauté the onion, green pepper, beef, garlic, and ginger in a pan of oil.
- Cook-stir for 3 minutes.
- Add everything else asides from the red pepper.
- Cook-stir till you get a thick sticky sauce.
- Serve with rice.
- Garnish with the red chili.
- Enjoy

Nutritional Information:

Calories: 115

Protein: 2.64 g

Fat: 1.77 g

Carbs: 23.52 g

142. SUGAR SNAP NOODLES AND BEEF

Preparation Time: 08 Minutes

Cooking Time: 14 Minutes

Servings: 6

Ingredients:

- 1 tsp. chili powder
- 450g minced beef
- 1 tbsp. peanut oil
- 4 grated garlic cloves
- 3 large egg noodles nests
- 500g sugar snap peas
- 2 tbsp. five-spice powder
- 5 tbsp. hoisin sauce
- 1 minced ginger
- 600ml beef broth

Directions:

- Cook your noodles al dente and drain after. Set aside.
- Sauté the beef, ginger, chili powder, five-spice powder, snap peas, and garlic in a pan of oil.
- Cook-stir for 6 minutes till beef is browned.
- Add the Hoisin sauce, noodles, and broth.
- Serve.

Nutritional Information:

Calories: 224

Protein: 17.13 g

Fat: 107.03 g

Carbs: 49.65 g

143.   BEEF NOODLES CAKE

Preparation Time: 10 Minutes

Cooking Time: 20 Minutes

Servings: 8

Ingredients:

- 1 handful chopped mint leaves
- 600g sirloin steak
- 300g Stir-fry mixed veggies
- 400g cooked egg noodles
- 6 beaten eggs
- 5 tbsp. soy sauce
- 4 tbsp. peanut oil

- 2 tbsp. chili sauce

Directions:

- Combine the eggs, veggies, sauces, and noodles in a bowl.
- Mix well.
- Heat your oil in a pan.
- When it's heated, pour the noodles mixture into it.
- Cook both sides till brown.
- Turn off the heat.
- Marinate the beef in a bowl of sauce and pepper. After 10 Minutes, heat another pan of oil. Cook the beef in the pan till done.
- Serve the noodle cake and beef. Garnish with mint.

Nutritional Information:

Calories: 452

Protein: 31:69 g

Fat: 27.47 g

Carbs: 18.18 g

144.   CHILI BEEF, BROCCOLI, AND OYSTER SAUCE

Preparation Time: 08 Minutes

Cooking Time: 11 Minutes

Servings: 2

Ingredients:

- 1 tbsp. dry sherry
- 300g sliced steak
- 1 tbsp. five-spice powder
- 2 tbsp. rapeseed oil
- 1 tbsp. hoisin sauce
- 1 tbsp. oyster sauce
- 1 seeded chunked pepper
- 1 tbsp. cornflour
- 100g sliced broccoli
- 1 small sliced red chili
- 150ml beef broth

Directions:

- Combine the beef, Hoisin sauce, five-spice powder, red chili, corn flour, and dry sherry in a bowl.
- Toss to be well combined. Keep aside to marinate for a while.
- Heat the oil in a pan. Proceed to cook the marinated beef in the pan till done.
- Add the broccoli and chunked pepper.
- Cook-stir for 4 minutes before adding the oyster sauce
- After 3 minutes, add the beef broth.
- Cook till your mixture becomes thick. Serve.

Nutritional Information:

Calories: 489

Protein: 44.55 g

Fat: 29.84 g

Carbs: 12.57 g

145.   HONEY BEEF NOODLES

Preparation Time: 08 Minutes

Cooking Time: 17 Minutes

Servings: 4

Ingredients:

- 250g egg noodles
- 300g cut broccoli
- 7 chunked spring onions
- 4 tbsp. peanut oil
- 2 handfuls sesame seeds
- 4 tbsp. soy sauce
- 4 tbsp. honey
- 400g sliced beef

- 180g cut sugar snap peas

Directions:

- Boil your noodles al dente.
- Sauté the beef, half of the sauce, and sesame seeds first in a pan of oil. Cook till done. Transfer to a bowl.
- Then add the peas, honey, spring onion, and broccoli to the oil pan. Stir-fry till veggies are tender.
- Add the noodles and sauce.
- Serve the noodles, veggies, and beef.

Nutritional Information:

Calories: 493

Carbs: 44.45 g

Protein: 28.67 g

Fat: 23.89 g

146.   CHILI AND LIME STEAK SALAD

Preparation Time: 08 Minutes

Cooking Time: Nil

Servings: 1

Ingredients:

- 1 tbsp. toasted halved hazelnuts
- 50g herb salad
- 1 chopped chili
- 1 handful chopped coriander
- 2 sliced radishes
- 1small garlic clove minced
- 1 tbsp. lemon juice
- 1 tsp. plum sauce
- 1 small, chopped cucumber
- 60g cooked sliced steak
- 1 tsp. sugar

Directions:

- Combine the coriander, cucumber, radishes, herb salad in a bowl.
- Toss everything else in another bowl.
- Mix the content of both bowls.

- Serve.

Nutritional Information:

Calories: 510

Carbs: 10.05 g

Protein: 18.43 g

Fat: 43.88 g

147. BEEF AND BOK CHOY

Preparation Time: 07 Minutes

Cooking Time: 09 Minutes

Servings: 4

Ingredients:

- 1 handful peanut oil
- 1 tbsp. pepper
- 18oz. Sliced steak fillet.
- 4 tbsp. five-spice powder
- 1 c. plum sauce
- 3 c. cooked crunchy chopped Bok choy

Directions:

- Combine the five-spice powder, pepper, and salt in a bowl. Add the steak. Toss well.
- Proceed to cook the steak in a pan of oil till done.
- Serve the Bok choy, sauce, and steak.

Nutritional Information:

Calories: 523

Fat: 23.66 g

Carbs: 41.44 g

Protein: 35.59 g

148. SPICY BEEF, SHIITAKE, AND AUBERGINE STIR-FRY

Preparation Time: 07 Minutes

Cooking Time: 13 Minutes

Servings: 2

Ingredients:

- 1 tsp. sugar
- 1 tbsp. canola oil
- 2 cut spring onions
- 1 tbsp. minced red chili
- 300g cooked minced beef
- 2 tbsp. plum sauce
- 3 minced garlic cloves
- 1 sliced medium Aubergine
- 100g sliced mushroom

Directions:

- Cook the Aubergine in a pan of oil till soft. Toss in the mushrooms, garlic, minced beef, and chili. Cook well.
- Add the sugar, spring onions, and sauce. Cook till done
- Serve

Nutritional Information:

Calories: 520

Fat: 24.89 g

Protein: 59.9 g

Carbs: 15.5 g

149. BEEF CURRY

Preparation Time: 08 Minutes

Cooking Time: 15 Minutes

Servings: 1

Ingredients:

- 2 c. cubed beef
- 30ml almond milk
- 1 handful diced carrot
- 30g curry paste
- 1 handful sliced red onion
- 1 tbsp. sunflower oil
- 2 c. chunked potato

Directions:

- Cook the beef in a pan of oil till browned.
- Then add everything else.
- Cook till sauce is thick and well cooked.
- Serve.

Nutritional Information:

Calories: 471

Protein: 10.8 g

Fat: 18.56 g

Carbs: 73.78 g

150. BEEF AND AUBERGINE SAUCE

Preparation Time: 10 Minutes

Cooking Time: 20 Minutes

Servings: 2

Ingredients:

- 1 tbsp. toasted ground cinnamon
- 3 c. beef broth
- 2 toasted star anise
- 2 c. Aubergine wedges
- 1 tsp. brown sugar
- 2 tbsp. peanut oil
- 30g sliced ginger
- 3 c. cooked chunked braising steak
- 1 deseeded sliced red chili
- 50ml plum sauce
- 2 kaffir lime leaves

Directions:

- Preheat your oven to 301F.
- Combine the meat, star anise, cinnamon, sugar, lime leaves, sauce, ginger, oil, and broth in a casserole dish.
- Cook in the oven till boiled.
- When it's boiled, toss in the Aubergine.
- Continue cooking till Aubergine is soft.
- Serve and garnish with red chili.

Nutritional Information:

Calories: 623

Fat: 24.79 g

Protein: 60.98 g

Carbs: 42.88 g

151. BEEF, MANGETOUT, AND PEANUTS

Preparation Time: 07 Minutes

Cooking Time: 17 Minutes

Servings: 1

Ingredients:

- 1 minced ginger
- 15g toasted peanuts
- 50g sliced mangetout
- 90g sliced rump chin
- 1 tsp. rice vinegar
- 1 sprinkle cornflour
- 1 tbsp. oyster sauce
- 1 tsp. plum sauce
- 1 tsp. brown sugar
- 1 minced garlic clove

Directions:

- Combine the sauces, sugar, corn flour, and vinegar in a bowl. Mix well.
- Cook the beef in a pan of oil until it burns slightly.
- Then toss in the sauce and everything else except for the peanuts.
- Stir and allow cooking till done.
- Serve and garnish with peanuts.
- Enjoy.

Nutritional Information:

Calories: 309

Carbs: 15.85 g

Fat: 14.65 g

Protein: 30.22 g

152. MONGOLIAN BEEF

Preparation Time: 05 Minutes

Cooking Time: 14 Minutes

Servings: 16

Ingredients:

- 3 minced gingers
- 7 c. chunked steak
- 1 c. honey
- 1 c. Hoisin sauce
- 1 c. cornstarch
- 2 minced garlic cloves
- 1 c. soy oil
- 7 cut green onions

Directions:

- Combine the beef and cornstarch in a large bowl. Toss well so that the beef is well coated.
- When it's well coated, cook the beef in a pan of oil.
- Cook till all sides are done.
- Then toss the garlic, ginger, water, honey, and sauce into the pan.
- Cook till the sauce gets thick.
- Throw in the scallions.
- Serve.

Nutritional Information:

Calories: 416

Carbs: 42.87g

Fat: 20.23g

Protein: 18.11g

153. BEEF AND BROCCOLI √

Preparation Time: 04 Minutes

Cooking Time: 16 Minutes

Servings: 2

Ingredients:

- 2 tbsp. Chinese Black Bean Sauce

- 2 tbsp. beef broth
- 2 tbsp. honey
- 1 tsp. toasted sunflower oil
- 1 tsp. red wine
- 1 tsp. cornstarch
- 1 pinch ground black pepper
- 2 tbsp. oyster sauce
- 2 handfuls of bean sprouts
- 3 c. strip lean beef
- 1 tsp. dry white wine
- 1 minced ginger
- 2 c. chunked broccoli florets
- 1 tsp. plum sauce
- 1 sliced yellow onion
- 1 tbsp. canola oil
- 1 minced garlic clove

Directions:

- Combine the bean sauce, broth, oyster sauce, oil, honey, wine, pepper, and cornstarch in a bowl. Mix well.
- Proceed to combine the beef, plum sauce, and dry white wine. Toss well
- Sauté the onion, ginger, and garlic in a pan of oil. Cook-stir for 3 minutes.
- Add the beef. Cook till browned.
- Then toss in the broccoli. Cook for 2 minutes.
- Toss in the oyster sauce, bean sprouts, and first sauce mixture.
- Cook for 3 minutes.
- Serve.

Nutritional Information:

Calories: 192

Carbs: 26.94g

Fat: 9.59g

Protein: 2.24g

154. BEEF IN OYSTER SAUCE √

Preparation Time: 08 Minutes

Cooking Time: 13 Minutes

Servings: 1

Ingredients:

- 110g sliced ribeye steak
- 1 tsp. honey
- 1 tsp. plum sauce
- 1 tsp. baking soda ✓
- 80g Pak Choi
- 1 tbsp. coconut oil
- 1 minced garlic
- 1 small, grated ginger
- 1 handful sliced red onion
- 1 tbsp. honey
- 1 pinch cornstarch
- 2 tbsp. Hoisin sauce
- 1 tbsp. water
- 1 tbsp. dark soy sauce
- 1 tbsp. sesame oil

Directions:

- Combine the steak, sauce, honey, and baking soda in a bowl. Toss well.
- Combine the last 6 ingredients in another bowl. Set aside.
- Cook the beef slices in a pan of oil.
- Cook till all sides are done.
- Toss in everything else.
- Cook-stir for 6 minutes till the sauce is glossy and thick.
- Serve.

Nutritional Information:

Calories: 633

Fat: 41.1g

Carbs: 45.3g

Protein: 25.19g

155.   CHINESE PEPPER STEAK ✓

Preparation Time: 04 Minutes

Cooking Time: 13 Minutes

Servings: 2

Ingredients:

- 1 tbsp. baking soda

- 3 c. chunked chuck roast
- 1 pinch ground ginger
- 1 tbsp. honey
- 1 chopped tomato
- 1 sliced red onion
- 2 tbsp. canola oil
- 2 tbsp. dark soy sauce
- 1 chopped green bell pepper
- 1 chopped red bell pepper

Directions:

- Combine the roast, ginger, baking soda, honey, and sauce in a bowl. Toss well to marinate the beef.
- Cook the marinated beef in a pan of oil till browned.
- Toss in the onion, tomato, and peppers.
- Cook till pepper and tomato are well cooked.
- Serve.

Nutritional Information:

Calories: 1861

Fat: 91.52g

Carbs: 15.89g

Protein: 246.36g

156.   BEEF STEW AND POTATOES

Preparation Time: 10 Minutes

Cooking Time: 33 Minutes

Servings: 2

Ingredients:

- 1 sliced red onion
- 1-star anise
- 2 small, chunked potatoes
- 1lb. cooked chunked sirloin steak
- 1 bay leaf
- 1 c. chunked carrots
- 1 minced ginger
- 1 c. beef sauce broth
- 1 tbsp. canola oil
- 1 tbsp. ground cinnamon
- 1 clove
- 1 tsp. white wine vinegar
- 1 c. hot water

Directions:

- Sauté the onion, ginger, and other spices in a pan oil.
- Cook-stir for 3 minutes till fragrant.
- Toss in the beef, sauce, broth, bay leaf, vinegar, and water. Cook for 20 minutes before adding the carrot and potatoes.
- Cook till veggies are tender and the sauce thickened.
- Serve.

Nutritional Information:

Calories: 862

Fat: 29.45g

Carbs: 73.32g

Protein: 74 69g

157. SWEET AND STICKY CRISPY BEEF

Preparation Time: 20 Minutes

Cooking Time: 25 Minutes

Servings: 3

Ingredients:

- 3 c. sliced steak
- 3 c. canola oil for frying
- 12 tbsp. cornstarch
- 1 grated red onion

- 2 tbsp. baking soda
- 1 c. sweet and sticky sauce
- 1 tbsp. grated garlic
- 1 tbsp. grated ginger
- 2 tbsp. plum sauce

Directions:

- Combine the onion, baking soda, sliced steak, garlic, plum sauce, and ginger in a bowl.
- Mix well. Marinate for 10 minutes.
- Proceed to coat the marinated beef in part of the cornstarch. Set aside for 5 Minutes.
- Then deep fry the coated beef in a pan of oil till crispy.
- Pour the sweet and sticky sauce into a pot. When it's boiling, toss in the drained fried beef.
- Add the remaining cornstarch.
- Cook till sauce is thick.
- Serve.

Nutritional Information:

Calories: 2124

Fats: 218.2g

Carbs: 38.46g

Protein: 1.82g

158. PANDA EXPRESS BEIJING BEEF

Preparation Time: 25 Minutes

Cooking Time: 20 Minutes

Servings: 2

Ingredients:

- 3 c. sliced chuck roast
- 3 tbsp. potato starch (divided)
- 2 minced garlic cloves
- 8 tbsp. sunflower oil
- 4 tbsp. water
- 1 chopped red bell pepper
- 1 sliced yellow onion
- 1 tbsp. rice vinegar
- 1 tsp. plum sauce
- 3 tbsp. hoisin sauce
- 1 tbsp. sweet chili sauce

- 2 tbsp. honey
- 1 pinch salt
- 2 tbsp. ketchup
- 2 beaten egg whites
- 1 pinch crushed red pepper

Directions:

- Combine the sauces, water, honey, red pepper, ketchup, and vinegar in a bowl. Keep aside. Cook this mixture till it thickens.
- Marinate the beef in a bowl of salt, egg whites, and 1 pinch of potato starch.
- Set aside for 20 minutes.
- Coat the marinated beef in the remaining potato starch.
- Proceed to fry the beef till browned.
- In another pan, sauté the bell pepper, garlic, and onion in oil till caramelized.
- Serve the caramelized veggies with the fried beef and vinegar mixture.
- Enjoy

Nutritional Information:

Calories: 1204

Fats: 107.03g

Protein: 17.13g

Carbs: 49.65g

159. BIG BATCH CHINESE BEEF

Preparation Time: 08 Minutes

Cooking Time: 24 Minutes

Servings: 4

Ingredients:

- 1 c. canola oil
- 1 small chopped yellow onion
- 1 lb. chunked sirloin steak
- 1 pinch Chinese five spice
- 1 dash salt

- 1 tbsp. flour
- 1 dash pepper
- 10 chopped mushrooms
- 2 minced garlic cloves
- 2 c. beef broth
- 1 minced ginger
- 1 tsp. honey
- 1 handful sliced scallions
- 45ml soy sauce

Directions:

- Combine the beef, pepper, salt, and flour in a bowl. Toss well.
- Heat the oil in a pan. Fry the coated beef till brown. Reduce the oil when you're done frying.
- Toss in five-spice ginger, onion, and garlic into the pan.
- Sauté till fried.
- Return the beef to the pan. Stir well.
- Toss in the remaining ingredients asides from the scallion
- Cook till beef is tender.
- Serve with rice and garnish with the scallions

Nutritional Information:

Carbs: 31.53g

Protein: 34.46g

Calories: 1088

Fat: 92.98g

160. BEEF TERIYAKI SKILLET

Preparation Time: 06 Minutes

Cooking Time: 14 Minutes

Servings: 2

Ingredients:

- 6 tbsp. Teriyaki sauce
- 3 c. ground beef
- 1 minced garlic clove
- 2 tbsp. canola oil
- 1 dash ground ginger
- 2 handfuls chopped red onion

Directions:

- Sauté the garlic clove, ginger, and red onion in a pan of oil. Cook-stir till onion is soft.
- Add the beef. Continue to cook-stir till beef is done.
- Toss in the last ingredient, which is the sauce.
- Cook for 4 minutes more.
- Serve.

Nutritional Information:

Protein: 4.51g

Calories: 215

Fats: 14.13g

Carbs: 19.18g

161.   LOW SYN SWEET CHILI BEEF

Preparation Time: 05 Minutes

Cooking Time: 16 Minutes

Servings: 1

Ingredients:

- 1 chopped spring onion
- 1 tsp. sunflower oil
- 1 tsp. tapioca
- 1 tbsp. hoisin sauce
- 1 dash salt
- 1 tsp. tomato paste
- 200g sliced beef
- 50ml water
- 1 tbsp. sweet chili sauce

Directions:

- Combine the sauces, water, and tomato paste in a bowl.
- Toss well. In another bowl, combine the beef, salt, and tapioca. Mix well to coat the beef.
- Fry the beef in a pan of oil till golden.
- Toss in the first mixture.
- Cook till the sauce thickens.
- Toss in the spring onion. Cook for 2 minutes.
- Serve.

Nutritional Information:

Calories: 378

Fat: 16.57g

Protein: 42.52g

Carbs: 15.42

162.   HUNAN BEEF

Preparation Time: 09 Minutes

Cooking Time: 17 Minutes

Servings: 2

Ingredients:

- 2 handfuls drained baby corn (cut into halves)
- 2 c. sliced flank steak
- 1 tsp. canola oil
- 4 tbsp. beef stock
- 1 tbsp. pepper
- 1 tsp. salt
- 1 tbsp. Hoisin sauce
- 1 tbsp. rice vinegar
- 1 minced garlic clove
- 1 diced red bell pepper
- 1 tsp. chili paste
- 1 handful chopped yellow onion
- 1 tbsp. plum sauce
- 1 handful sliced celery
- 2 handfuls cut broccoli florets
- 1 tbsp. tapioca
- 1 pinch brown sugar

Directions:

- Fry the beef slices in a pan of oil till browned.
- Transfer to a lined plate.
- Sauté the onion, garlic, broccoli, bell pepper, baby corn, and celery in the pan.
- Add pepper and salt.
- Cook-stir till veggies are done.
- Toss in the sauces, beef, stock, vinegar, paste, sugar, and tapioca into the pan.
- Cook till sauce is thick.
- Serve.

Nutritional Information:

Fats: 16.17g

Carbs: 31.88g

Protein: 59.33g

Calories: 516

163. BEEF AND TOMATO

Preparation Time: 07 Minutes

Cooking Time: 18 Minutes

Servings: 2

Ingredients:

- 2 tbsp. soy sauce
- 1 tsp. rice vinegar
- 1 tbsp. baking powder
- 1 tbsp. plum sauce
- 1 tbsp. pepper
- 1 tsp. salt
- 2 c. sliced sirloin steak
- 2 chopped large tomatoes
- 2 tbsp. canola oil
- 2 c. sliced green onions

Directions:

- Combine the pepper, salt, sauces, vinegar, and baking powder in a bowl. Mix well.
- Cook the beef in a pan oil till browned.
- Transfer to a lined plate.
- Throw the tomatoes, garlic, and green onions into the same pan.
- Cook stir till fragrant.
- Throw in the sauce.
- Cook for 3 minutes before adding the beef.
- Cook for 3 minutes more.
- Serve.

Nutritional Information:

Calories: 1376

Protein: 126.81g

Carbs: 24.86g

Fats: 83.87g

"If I had to narrow my choice of meats down to one for the rest of my life, I am quite certain that meat would be pork." – James Beard culled from GoodRead

It is no gainsaying that pork is one of the most favored meats eaten by the Chinese, and they show this by preparing this meat in different ways. Either stewed, roasted, stir-fried, it glazed, you'd always find a Chinese man doing one thing or the other with pork meat!

Listed below are 28 ways that the Chinese enjoy pork meat.

164.   SWEET AND SOUR PORK

Preparation Time: 15 Minutes

Cooking Time: 25 Minutes

Servings: 1

Ingredients:

- 100g chopped pork
- 70g corn flour
- 300ml canola oil
- 1 tbsp. ketchup
- 1 handful chopped red bell pepper
- 2 tbsp. brown sugar
- 1 minced garlic clove
- 2 tbsp. soy sauce
- 80g pineapple
- 1 pinch tapioca
- 1 handful toasted sesame seeds
- 1 beaten egg
- 1 pinch salt
- 1 handful chopped green bell pepper

Directions:

- Combine the pork, egg, salt, and tapioca in a bowl. Toss well. Keep aside to marinate.
- When the pork is marinated, coat it in cornflour. Keep aside.
- Take 2 tbsp. from the oil and pour into a pan.
- Sauté the peppers and garlic till fragrant.
- Toss in the ketchup, pineapple, sauce, and sugar. Cook till the mixture boils.
- While boiling, fry the coated pork in a pan of oil till browned.
- Then toss the fried pork into the pan of sauce.
- Serve and garnish with sesame seeds.

Nutritional Information:

Calories: 538

Fats: 26.74g

Carbs: 35.67g

Protein: 39.35g

165.   CHAR SIU BBQ PORK

Preparation Time: 14 Minutes

Cooking Time: 30 Minutes

Servings: 4

Ingredients:

- 1 pinch five-spice powder
- 2 tbsp. honey
- 1 tsp. soy sauce
- 1 dash pepper
- 1 tbsp. brown sugar
- 1 dash canola oil
- 1 tsp. salt
- 1 tsp. Shaoxing rice wine
- 1 minced garlic clove
- 1 tsp. plum sauce
- 2 lb. sliced pork meat

Directions:

- Preheat your oven to 382F.

- Combine the oil, pepper, salt, sugar, rice wine, five-spice, honey, sauces, and garlic in a bowl. Toss well.
- Drizzle this sauce over the pork slices. (Don't finish the sauce).
- Use your hand to toss the pork and sauce well till well combined.
- Place foil over a sheet pan, and arrange the pork slices on the foiled pan.
- Roast till all sides of the pork are almost done.
- Brush the sauce over the pork again. And roast some more.
- Turn the pork after a while and brush sauce over the other side too.
- Continue roasting till the pork is done.
- Bring out the pork.
- Serve.
- Enjoy.

Nutritional Information:

Calories: 343

Carbs: 15.95g

Fats: 8.99g

Protein: 51.66g

166. GARLIC GINGER PORK

Preparation Time: 13 Minutes

Cooking Time: 20 Minutes

Servings: 2

Ingredients:

- 1 c. pork broth
- 1 dash minced red pepper flakes
- 1 tbsp. brown sugar
- 3 tsp. soy sauce
- 1 tbsp. plum sauce
- 1 tbsp. potato starch
- 1 tsp. grated ginger
- 1 dash chili paste
- 2 handfuls of snow peas
- 2 c. sliced pork chops
- 1 minced ginger
- 2 handfuls sliced mushrooms
- 2 minced garlic cloves

- 1 tbsp. toasted sunflower oil

Directions:

- Combine the broth, pepper flakes, sauces, potato starch, sugar, ginger, and chili paste in a bowl. Mix well. Keep aside.
- Then sauté the pork dryly in a pan till brown.
- Transfer to a lined plate.
- Sauté the ginger and garlic in a pan of oil for 3 minutes.
- Add the broth, mushrooms, and snow peas.
- Cook for 5 minutes before adding the pork.
- Cook till pork is tender and well cooked.
- Serve.

Nutritional Information:

Calories: 590

Fats: 26.17g

Carbs: 42.03g

Protein: 45.53g

167. MONGOLIAN PORK

Preparation Time: 07 Minutes

Cooking Time: 20 Minutes

Servings: 2

Ingredients:

- 1 tsp. toasted sesame seeds
- 2 c. pork tenderloin slices
- 1 grated ginger
- 2 tbsp. baking soda
- 4 tbsp. soy sauce
- 4 tbsp. honey
- 1 tbsp. sunflower oil
- 1 handful chopped green onions
- 1 tsp. minced garlic
- 2 tbsp. water

Directions

- Combine the honey, water, and sauce in a bowl. Toss well.

- Combine the baking soda and pork slices in a bowl. Toss well to coat your pork.
- Cook the pork in a pan of oil till browned.
- Transfer to a plate.
- Sauté the ginger and garlic in the pan for 1 minute.
- Toss in the pork and sauce mixture.
- Cook till boiled.
- Serve and garnish with green onions and sesame seeds.

Nutritional Information:

Calories: 546

Fats: 19.36g

Protein: 40.09g

Carbs: 55.84

168. BRAISED PORK BELLY

Preparation Time: 04 Minutes

Cooking Time: 15 Minutes

Servings: 8

Ingredients:

- 4 c. water
- 2 tbsp. granulated brown sugar
- 4 tbsp. almond oil
- 2 tbsp. hoisin sauce
- 1 tbsp. soy sauce
- 5 tbsp. Shaoxing rice wine
- 700g pork belly chunks

Directions:

- Combine the pork, sugar, oil, rice wine, water, and sauces into a pan.
- Cook till pork is soft and the sauce is glossy.
- Serve. Easy peasy, right?

Nutritional Information:

Calories: 322

Protein: 22.83g

Carbs: 4.55g

Fats: 23.74g

169. PORK AND PEPPER STIR-FRY

Preparation Time: 07 Minutes

Cooking Time: 20 Minutes

Servings: 2

Ingredients:

- 3 c. sliced pork loin
- 1 dash Shaoxing rice wine
- 1 pinch potato starch
- 1 dash soy sauce
- 1 dash hoisin sauce
- 1 dash water
- 1 dash sesame oil
- 1 dash Plum sauce
- 1 minced ginger
- 1 tbsp. honey
- 150g chopped hot green peppers
- 1 tsp. Shaoxing rice wine
- 1 handful chopped red onion
- 2 minced garlic cloves
- 1 tbsp. canola oil

Directions:

- Combine the pork, rice wine, sauces, potato starch, oil, and water in a bowl. Toss well to coat the pork.
- Sauté the pork in a pan of oil till browned.
- Transfer to a lined plate.
- Sauté the onion, peppers, garlic, and ginger in a pan of oil.
- Cook-stir for a minute.
- Toss in the pork, honey, plum sauce, and rice wine.
- Cook till pork is tender.
- Serve.

Nutritional Information:

Calories: 1628

Protein: 72.22g

Fats: 14.25g

Carbs: 366.91g

170. CHINESE STIR-FRY PORK ✓

Preparation Time: 09 Minutes

Cooking Time: 22 Minutes

Servings: 2

Ingredients:

- 1 sliced yellow onion
- 3 c. sliced pork loin
- 1 tsp. Chinese five-spice powder
- 1 tbsp. canola oil
- 1 tbsp. honey
- 1 minced ginger
- 1 tbsp. soy sauce
- 1 minced garlic clove
- 1 handful chopped Pak Choy
- 1 sliced red capsicum
- 1 handful scallions
- 2 tbsp. plum sauce
- 1 sliced carrot
- 150g trimmed snap peas
- 2 tbsp. pork broth
- 1 handful of toasted cashews
- 1 sliced red pepper

Directions:

- Combine the sauces, pork, five-spice powder, and honey in a bowl. Toss well.
- Cook the pork in a pan of oil till brown.
- Transfer to a lined plate
- Sauté the capsicum, pepper, onion, carrot, garlic, and ginger in a pan of oil.
- Cook-stir for 4 minutes before tossing the broth, snow peas, pork, and Pak Choy.
- Cook-stir till pork is done.
- Serve and garnish with scallions and cashews.

Nutritional Information:

Protein: 23.71g

Carbs: 27.76g

Calories: 362

Fats: 17.61g

171. PORK FRIED RICE ✓

Preparation Time: 06 Minutes

Cooking Time: 21 Minutes

Servings: 2

Ingredients:

- 1 dash brown sugar
- 2 c. chunked pork
- 1 dash dry sherry
- 1 tbsp. canola oil
- 2 tbsp. soy sauce
- 1 diced yellow onion
- 1 tbsp. pepper
- 1 tsp. salt
- 2 c. cooked Chinese rice
- 1 scrambled egg
- 1 minced garlic clove
- 1 handful diced carrots
- 1 handful chopped green onions

Directions:

- Sauté the pork, onion, carrot, and garlic in a pan of oil for 6 minutes.
- Toss in the rice, sugar, pepper, sherry, sauce, salt, carrots, and green onions.
- Cook till everything is well combined.
- Serve and garnish with scrambled egg.

Nutritional Information:

Calories: 659

Protein: 46.11g

Carbs: 66.78g

Fats: 22.61g

172. HUNAN PORK STIR-FRY

Preparation Time: 05 Minutes

Cooking Time: 16 Minutes

Servings: 3

Ingredients:

- 1 minced ginger
- 1 tbsp. canola oil
- 1 tsp. plum sauce
- 2 c. sliced pork loin
- 1 minced garlic clove
- 2 chopped hot green chili peppers
- 1 tbsp. salt
- 1 handful sliced white onion

Directions:

- Sauté the onion, ginger, peppers, and garlic in a pan of oil.
- Cook till fragrant.
- Toss in the salt and pork.
- Cook for 6 minutes.
- Add sauce.
- Cook for 4 minutes more.
- Serve.

Nutritional Information:

Protein: 1.07g

Carbs: 6.54g

Calories: 90

Fats: 7.14g

173.　　STICKY CHINESE PORK

Preparation Time: 08 Minutes

Cooking Time: 20 Minutes

Servings: 3

Ingredients:

- 1 sliced toasted medium red pepper
- 2 tbsp. granulated brown sugar
- 1 handful chopped white onion
- 300g chopped pork chop
- 2 tbsp. peanut oil (divided)
- 40g sliced Mangetout
- 1 minced garlic clove
- 2 tbsp. soy sauce
- 1 tbsp. five-spice powder
- 1 chopped Pak Choy
- 1 minced ginger
- 1 c. bean sprouts

Directions:

- Combine the ginger, pork, garlic, onion, sauce, sugar, spice powder, and 1 tbsp. Oil in a bowl.
- Toss well.
- Fry the marinated pork in a pan of oil till browned.
- Toss in the bean sprouts, Pak Choy, Mangetout, and pepper.
- Cook till done.
- Serve.

Nutritional Information:

Protein: 46.24g

Fats: 28.92

Carbs: 17.35g

Calories: 515

174.　　PORK AND MUSHROOM STIR-FRY

Preparation Time: 50 Minutes

Cooking Time: 25 Minutes

Servings: 8

Ingredients:

- 8 tbsp. hoisin sauce
- 5 c. bean sprouts
- 8 chopped green onions
- 2 lb. chopped pork
- 3 c. chopped broccoli

- 4 tbsp. rice wine
- 3 tbsp. sunflower oil (divided)
- 1 minced garlic clove
- 3 c. chopped long red pepper
- 3 c. chopped broccoli florets
- 1 handful chopped coriander
- 2 c. mushrooms

Directions:

- Combine the pork chunks, sauce, rice wine, pepper, garlic, and 1 tbsp. Oil in a bowl. Toss well.
- After 40 minutes, pour the bowl's content (plus the marinade) into a pan of oil. Cook till pork is browned.
- Then toss in everything else asides from the coriander.
- Cook for 6 minutes.
- Serve and garnish with coriander.

Nutritional Information:

Calories: 403

Protein: 37.64g

Carbs: 21.03g

Fats: 20.28g

175.   PEKING PORK CHOPS

Preparation Time: 07 Minutes

Cooking Time: 27 Minutes

Servings: 3

Ingredients:

- 1 tbsp. Worcestershire sauce
- 1 tsp. Plum sauce
- 2 tbsp. soy sauce
- 2 tbsp. honey
- 1 tbsp. ketchup
- 1 tbsp. rice vinegar
- 1 tsp. chili sauce
- 1 dash Shaoxing wine
- 1 lb. chopped pork chops
- 1 tbsp. pepper
- 1 tsp. salt
- 1 minced garlic

- 1 minced ginger

Directions:

- Combine the sauces, wine, vinegar, ketchup, and honey in a bowl. Toss well.
- Add the pork chops to this mixture. Toss well.
- Sauté the ginger and garlic in a pan of oil.
- Cook till fragrant.
- Add the marinade and pork.
- Continue cooking till pork is tender.
- Add pepper and salt.
- Cook till done.
- Serve.

Nutritional Information:

Calories: 412

Protein: 39.95g

Fats: 18.71 g

Carbs: 19.59g

176.   BARBEQUED ROAST PORK ✓

Preparation Time: 10 Minutes

Cooking Time: 25 Minutes

Servings: 2

Ingredients:

- 1 tbsp. sunflower oil
- 1 tbsp. sweet paprika
- 1 tsp. ground garlic
- 1 tbsp. white pepper
- 1 tsp. honey
- 1 tsp. salt
- 2 lb. chopped pork
- 1 c. BBQ sauce

Directions:

- Toss the pork and the other ingredients in a bowl.
- Ensure that the pork is well coated.
- Preheat your oven to 330F.
- Arrange the pork and marinade in a roast pan.
- Roast till pork is tender.
- Serve.

Nutritional Information:

Calories: 1081

Protein: 119.12g

Carbs: 16.4g

Fats: 57.91g

177. ASIAN NOODLES BOWL WITH PORK

Preparation Time: 15 Minutes

Cooking Time: 35 Minutes

Servings: 2

Ingredients:

- 4 oz. spaghetti
- 1 tbsp. Shaoxing rice wine
- 3 tbsp. sunflower oil (divided)
- 1 minced garlic clove
- 3 c. sliced into strips pork loin
- 1 handful sliced white onion
- 1 tsp. brown sugar
- 2 tbsp. Hoisin sauce
- 2 tbsp. plum sauce
- 1 minced ginger
- 1 tbsp. water
- 1 minced red chili

Directions:

- Cook the spaghetti al dente.
- Sauté the onion, ginger, and garlic in a pan of oil. Cook-stir for 3 minutes.
- Add the pork. Cook till browned.
- Toss in the sauces, rice wine, spaghetti, water, sugar, and chili.
- Toss well.
- Cook till the sauce gets thick.
- Serve.

Nutritional Information:

Calories: 359

Protein: 4.36g

Fats: 22.83g

Carbs: 35.35g

178. GRILLED CHINESE PORK

Preparation Time: 10 Minutes

Cooking Time: 28 Minutes

Servings: 4

Ingredients:

- 16 oz. Sliced pork shoulder
- 1 crushed ginger
- 1 crushed garlic clove
- 2 tbsp. Shaoxing rice wine
- 2 tbsp. soy sauce
- 1 tbsp. lime juice

Directions:

- Preheat your grill to 356F.
- Combine everything in a big bowl.
- Marinated the pork for 7 minutes.
- Grill the marinated pork till all sides are browned.
- Serve.

Nutritional Information:

Calories: 369

Protein: 29.55g

Fats: 22.28g

Carbs: 4.39g

179. SWEET GLAZED PORK

Preparation Time: 15 Minutes

Cooking Time: 25 Minutes

Servings: 6

Ingredients:

- 3 tbsp. five-spice powder
- 3 c. halved cabbage
- 7 chopped pork bellies

- 1 tbsp. orange juice
- 1 tbsp. plum sauce
- 7 tbsp. honey

Directions:

- Preheat your grill to 358F.
- Combine the pork, juice, sauce, spice powder, and honey in a bowl.
- Toss well.
- Grill the pork belly till done.
- Serve and garnish with cabbage.

Nutritional Information:

Carbs: 27.85g

Fats: 0.14g

Protein: 1.11g

Calories: 107

180.   STICKY HONEY GINGER PORK

Preparation Time: 20 Minutes

Cooking Time: 25 Minutes

Servings: 3

Ingredients:

- 350g diced pork
- 3 minced garlic cloves
- 10 tbsp. honey
- 2 tbsp. peanut oil
- 2 tbsp. plum sauce
- 2 tbsp. potato starch
- 2 tbsp. rice wine vinegar
- 2 tbsp. Chinese cooking wine
- 7 tbsp. Sriracha sauce
- 2 tbsp. Worcestershire sauce
- 2 minced gingers

Directions:

- Combine the pork, cooking wine, and plum sauce in a bowl. Toss well.
- In another bowl, combine the rest of the ingredients minus the oil and potato starch. Toss well.

- Coat the marinated pork in potato starch. Proceed to Stir-fry the garlic and ginger in a pan.
- Toss in the pork and fry till crispy brown.
- Pour in the vinegar mixture.
- Cook for 12 minutes till thick.

Nutritional Information:

Calories: 650

Carbs: 113.45g

Fats: 13.43g

Protein: 25.89g

181.   CHINESE PORK RIBS

Preparation Time: 05 Minutes

Cooking Time: 25 Minutes

Servings: 6

Ingredients:

- 2 tbsp. Chinese five-spice powder
- 250ml plum sauce
- 2 tbsp. honey
- 2 tbsp. rice wine
- 3 tbsp. soy sauce
- 16 cooked pork ribs

Directions:

- Preheat the grill to 346F.
- Combine the pork, rice wine, sauces, spice powder, and honey in a bowl.
- Toss well.
- Grill for 25 minutes till all sides are done.
- Serve.

Nutritional Information:

Calories: 581

Protein: 60.23g

Carbs: 9.29g

Fats: 32.41g

182.   CHINESE PORK CHOPS STEAK

Preparation Time: 06 Minutes

Cooking Time: 20 Minutes

Servings: 1

Ingredients:

- 2 c. cut pork chop steaks
- 1 tsp. canola oil
- 1 tsp. honey
- 2 handfuls green onions
- 1 pinch salt
- 1 dash ground white pepper
- 3 tbsp. plum sauce

Directions:

- Preheat your grill to 344F.
- Marinate the plum in a mixture of oil, sauce, salt, pepper, and honey. Toss well.
- Grill the pork chops till done.
- Serve.
- Garnish with onions.

Nutritional Information:

Calories: 395

Protein: 6.72g

Carbs: 84.49g

Fats: 5.71g

183.   CHINESE PORK CURRY

Preparation Time: 09 Minutes

Cooking Time: 27 Minutes

Servings: 2

Ingredients:

- 1 tbsp. salt
- 1 tbsp. ground cinnamon
- 3 c. chopped blanched pork loin
- 1 sliced yellow onion
- 2 tbsp. ground curry
- 150ml almond milk
- 2 c. water
- 1 chopped tomato
- 2 c. chopped potatoes
- 1 c. spicy Gāoliáng jiāng and lemongrass paste

Directions:

- Sauté the cinnamon, onion, and curry in a pan of oil.
- Cook-stir for 4 minutes.
- Add the lemongrass paste.
- Cook-stir for 2 minutes.
- Add the water, salt, almond milk, and pork.
- Cook till pork is almost tender.
- Cook for 4 minutes before adding the potatoes and tomatoes.
- Cook till the veggies are soft and the sauce is thick.
- Serve.

Nutritional Information:

Calories: 755

Protein: 70.74g

Carbs: 59.59g

Fats: 27.84g

184.   FRUITY PORK STEAK

Preparation Time: 15 Minutes

Cooking Time: 27 Minutes

Servings: 3

Ingredients:

- 150ml pork broth
- 3 pork loin steaks
- 3 chopped red apples
- 1 tbsp. ground ginger
- 1 tbsp. ground cinnamon
- 1 medium chopped yellow onion
- 1 tsp. cider vinegar
- 1 tsp. canola oil
- 1 tbsp. red currant jelly
- 1 tbsp. five-spice powder

Directions:

- Combine the five-spice, half of the ginger, and half of the cinnamon in a bowl.
- Then toss the pork in it.
- Cook the coated pork in a pan of oil.
- Transfer to a lined plate.
- Sauté the remaining cinnamon, remaining ginger, and onion in the pan. Add oil if the remaining oil in the pan is not enough.
- Toss in the jelly and apples. Cook for 4 minutes before adding the broth and vinegar.
- Cook till apples are soft.

Nutritional Information:

Calories: 198

Protein: 1.38g

Carbs: 37.58g

Fats: 5.19g

185.   SPICED PINEAPPLE PORK

Preparation Time: 10 Minutes

Cooking Time: 25 Minutes

Servings: 6

Ingredients:

- 3 tbsp. sunflower oil
- 1 tbsp. Chinese Chili powder
- 3 tbsp. honey
- 2 tbsp. Chinese five-spice powder
- 1 minced garlic
- 1 minced ginger
- 6 chopped pork steaks

- 2 tbsp. soy sauce
- 700g sliced pineapple with juices
- 2 tbsp. tomato paste

Directions:

- Combine the soy sauce, tomato paste, honey, and pineapple juice in a bowl. Toss well.
- Sauté the garlic and ginger in a pan of oil.
- Add the pork into the pan. Fry till golden.
- Toss in the pineapples, five-spice, and Chili. Continue cooking for 6 minutes
- Add the tomato paste mixture. Cook for 4 minutes more.
- Serve.

Nutritional Information:

Protein: 47.75g

Fats: 41.07g

Carbs: 26.97g

Calories: 674

186.   PORK AND NOODLE STIR-FRY

Preparation Time: 05 Minutes

Cooking Time: 13 Minutes

Servings: 8

Ingredients:

- 5 c. Stir-fry mixed veggies of your choice
- 6 tbsp. sunflower oil
- 3 tbsp. garlic puree
- 10 c. minced pork
- 2 minced small gingers
- 750g egg noodles
- 7 tbsp. plum sauce
- 7 tbsp. sweet chili sauce
- 4 tbsp. potato starch

Directions:

- Cook the noodles al dente. Drain after cooking. Keep aside.
- Sauté the ginger and garlic in a pan of oil. Cook till fragrant.

- Toss in the minced pork and vegetables. Cook till the vegetables are tender.
- Then add in the sauces, potato starch, and noodles.
- Cook-stir for 3 minutes.
- Serve.

Nutritional Information:

Calories: 692

Protein: 53.39g

Fats: 20.44g

Carbs: 72.63g

187.   SPICED HONEY SOY PORK

Preparation Time: 07 Minutes

Cooking Time: 20 Minutes

Servings: 3

Ingredients:

- 300ml pork broth
- 2 tbsp. canola oil
- 1 tbsp. pepper
- 1 tsp. salt
- 4 minced garlic
- 1 chopped red chili
- 6 c. sliced pork loin
- 2 tbsp. honey
- 1 tbsp. Sriracha sauce
- 6 tbsp. orange marmalade
- 2 tbsp. plum sauce
- 1 tsp. five-spice powder
- 1 small sliced onion
- 2 c. chopped scallions
- 200ml Chinese cooking wine

Directions:

- Combine the sauces, honey, spice powder, orange marmalade, and cooking wine in a bowl. Toss well.
- Sauté the garlic and onion in a pan of oil.
- Cook-stir for 3 minutes.
- Add the pork. Cook till done.

- Add the honey mixture, red chili, pepper, salt, and broth.
- Cook till sauce is thick.
- Serve and garnish with scallions.

Nutritional Information:

Carbs: 53.01g

Protein: 2.23g

Fats: 9.66g

Calories: 288

188.   TWICE COOKED PORK

Preparation Time: 12 Minutes

Cooking Time: 25 Minutes

Servings: 2

Ingredients:

- 3 c. sliced pork belly
- 1 minced ginger
- 1 minced garlic
- 2 dashes honey
- 1 chopped leek
- 3 tbsp. sesame oil
- 1 chopped deseeded hot green pepper
- 1 tsp. Sriracha sauce
- 1 tbsp. spicy bean paste
- 1 tsp. Chinese cooking wine

Directions:

- Cook the pork in a pan of oil. Cook till done.
- Transfer to a lined plate.
- Sauté the garlic and ginger in the pan (add more oil if necessary).
- Add the bean paste. Cook for 1 minute.
- Then add the pepper, wine, pork, honey, sauce, and leek into the pan.
- Cook till veggies are tender.
- Serve

Nutritional Information:

Calories: 218

Protein: 1.17g

Carbs: 8.64g

Fats: 20.59g

189. PORK AND TOMATOES

Preparation Time: 08 Minutes

Cooking Time: 23 Minutes

Servings: 1

Ingredients:

- 10g honey
- 2 c. sliced pork loin
- 1 handful chopped green pepper
- 2 chopped red bell pepper
- 1 handful green onions
- 1 medium chopped white onion
- 1 medium egg white
- 1 minced garlic clove
- 10g potato starch
- 10g tomato ketchup
- 20g tomato puree
- 10g Shaoxing wine
- 2 tbsp. canola oil

Directions:

- Cook the pork in a pan of oil till browned.
- Transfer to a lined plate.
- Sauté the onions, garlic, and peppers in the pan.
- When the veggies are soft and fragrant, toss in the wine, tomato puree, ketchup, starch, egg white, honey, and pork.
- Cook till pork is well done.
- Serve. Garnish with the scallions.

Nutritional Information:

Calories: 458

Protein: 8.96g

Carbs: 46.95g

Fats: 28.59g

190. FISH FLAVORED SHREDDED PORK

Preparation Time: 13 Minutes

Cooking Time: 24 Minutes

Servings: 2

Ingredients:

- 1 tbsp. potato starch
- 1 tbsp. spicy bean paste
- 1 tbsp. honey
- 1 tbsp. hoisin sauce
- 3 tbsp. fish sauce
- 2 tbsp. rice vinegar
- 350g shredded pork shoulder
- 1 sliced carrot
- 2 chopped spring onion
- 1 tbsp. Chinese cooking wine
- 1 minced ginger
- 1 tbsp. canola oil
- 3 minced garlic cloves
- 1 tsp. salt

Directions:

- Combine the cooking wine, pork slices, potato starch, salt, and oil in a bowl. Toss well. Set aside for 7 minutes.
- Cook-stir the marinated pork in a pan of oil till done.
- Transfer pork to a lined plate.
- Then sauté the spring onions, ginger, and garlic for 3 minutes.
- Toss in the carrots, bean paste, honey, sauces, and vinegar.
- Cook-stir till pork is well cooked and sauce thickens.
- Serve.

Nutritional Information:

Calories: 884

Protein: 53.59g

Carbs: 80.6g

Fats: 38.65g

191.   PORK MEDALLIONS

Preparation Time: 10 Minutes

Cooking Time: 24 Minutes

Servings: 2

Ingredients:

- 230g pork medallions
- 1 sliced spring onion
- 1 tbsp. brown sugar
- 1 minced garlic
- 1 minced ginger
- 1 tsp. salt
- 1 tbsp. pepper
- 1 tsp. five-spice powder
- 1 tbsp. Worcestershire sauce
- 1 tbsp. Plum sauce
- 1 handful chopped carrots
- 1 tsp. potato starch

Directions:

- Combine the spice, sauces, pepper, and salt in a bowl.
- Toss well.
- Sauté the garlic and ginger in a pan of oil till fragrant. Add the pork. Fry till all sides are cooked.
- Add sugar, marinade, potato starch, and carrots.
- Cook well till carrots and pork are well cooked.
- Serve and garnish with spring onions.

Nutritional Information:

Calories: 495

Protein: 33.53g

Carbs: 43.47

Fats: 20.72g

"If you throw a lamb chop in the oven, what's to keep it from getting done?" – Joan Crawford

Talking about lamb meat in China is a dicey and complicated affair. The Northern Chinese love lamb meat as much as any other meat, but the Southern Chinese wouldn't touch lamb meat with a long pole.

Regardless, lamb meat is still one of the meats enjoyed by the Chinese, and this can be proven by these 28 lamb recipes that the Chinese don't joke with!

192.   CUMIN LAMB STIR-FRY

Preparation Time: 06 Minutes

Cooking Time: 15 Minutes

Servings: 2

Ingredients:

- 1 pinch salt
- 2 c. sliced lamb shoulder
- 1 tsp. toasted Sichuan peppercorns
- 1 handful chopped coriander
- 1 tsp. toasted cumin seeds
- 1 minced garlic clove
- 1 small sliced white onion
- 1 tbsp. crushed red pepper
- 1 handful chopped green onions (separate white and green)
- 1 pinch cumin powder
- 1 tbsp. Chinese cooking wine
- 1 tbsp. plum sauce
- 1 tbsp. sesame oil

Directions:

- Combine the lamb, salt, red pepper, peppercorn, cumin powder, and cumin seeds in a bowl. Toss well.
- Sauté the onion and white part of green onions in a pan of oil.
- Cook for 3 minutes before adding the marinated lamb, garlic, cooking wine, sauce, and marinade.
- Cook till lamb is well cooked.
- Serve and garnish with the green part of scallion and coriander.
- Enjoy.

Nutritional Information:

Protein: 20.78g

Carbs: 5.76g

Fats: 16.5g

Calories: 257

193.   SHREDDED LAMB

Preparation Time: 3 Hours 10 Minutes

Cooking Time: 25 Minutes

Servings: 2

Ingredients:

- 4 c. shredded lamb breast
- 1 tsp. Chinese five-spice
- 2 minced garlic cloves
- 1 tsp. peppercorns
- 2 tbsp. dry sherry
- 1 tsp. salt
- 1 crushed red pepper
- 1 minced ginger
- 1 c. chopped spring onion

Directions:

- Preheat your grill to 356F.
- Combine the honey, pepper, spice, peppercorn, salt, ginger, garlic, sherry, and lamb in a bowl. Marinate for 3 hours.
- Toss well.
- Roast till lamb is crispy tender.

- Serve with spring onion.

Nutritional Information:

Calories: 56

Carbs: 10.43g

Protein: 1.67g

Fats: 1.56g

194.   LAMB AND SESAME FRIED RICE ✓

Preparation Time: 10 Minutes

Cooking Time: 30 Minutes

Servings: 5

Ingredients:

- 2 tbsp. plum sauce
- 5 c. sliced lamb fillets
- 1 minced garlic clove
- 1 medium chopped yellow onion
- 1 tsp. Chinese five-spice powder
- 70g cooked Chinese rice
- 1 tsp. minced ginger
- 1 tbsp. Sesame oil
- 1 sliced spring onion
- 1 handful chopped blanched Chinese broccoli

Directions:

- Combine the garlic, sauce, five-spice, lamb, and ginger in a bowl. Toss well.
- Cook the marinated lamb in a pan of oil.
- Cook till done.
- Transfer to a lined plate.
- Wipe the pan and pour in the oil.
- Sauté the ginger, garlic, and onion in the pan.
- Cook-stir for 3 minutes.
- Add the rice, broccoli, and marinade.
- Cook till done.
- Serve rice with lamb and spring onion.

Nutritional Information:

Calories: 92

Protein: 1.24g

Carbs: 10.42g

Fats: 5.28g

195.   CHINESE SPICED LAMB

Servings: 4

Cook Time: 30 minutes

Ingredients:

- 1 tbsp. olive oil
- 150g lamb leg meat cut in cubes
- ½ tbsp. dark soy
- 1 tsp. Chinese cooking wine
- 1 tsp. rice or potato flour
- 1 tsp. Toasted cumin ground
- ½ c. shallots diced
- ½ tsp. chili flakes
- 1 tsp. minced ginger
- 1 tsp. garlic minced
- 2 sprig cilantro roughly chopped
- 1 tbsp. water

Directions:

- Combine the wine, soy sauce, potato flour, and lamb in a bowl
- Set it aside for 15 minutes
- In a non-stick pan, add ½ the oil and cook the lamb for 3 minutes or until brown on all sides
- Add the remaining oil and sauté the ginger, garlic, onion, chili, and cumin until fragrant
- Return the lamb to the pan, add a tbsp. water, and cook for 2 minutes
- Serve with cilantro

Nutritional Information:

Calories: 176

Fat: 14g

Protein: 9g

Carbs: 3.3g

196.   BRAISED LAMB

Preparation Time: 05 Minutes

Cooking Time: 27 Minutes

Servings: 6

Ingredients:

- 2lb. diced blanched lamb shoulder
- 5-star anise
- 5 minced gingers
- 3 sliced yellow onions
- 4 sliced spring onions
- 2 tbsp. peanut oil
- 5 tbsp. Chinese cooking wine
- 4 oz. brown sugar
- 2 points lamb broth
- 4 tbsp. plum sauce
- 2 tbsp. ground cinnamon
- 4 tbsp. peanut butter

Directions:

- Sauté the onions, ginger, star anise, and spring onion in a pan of oil.
- Cook-stir till fragrant.
- Toss in the lamb, wine, sugar, broth, cinnamon, plum sauce, and peanut butter.
- Braise till lamb is tender.
- Serve the lamb and sauce.

Nutritional Information:

Calories: 409

Protein: 31.05g

Carbs: 29.61g

Fats: 19.19g

197.   MONGOLIAN LAMB ✓

Preparation Time: 25 Minutes

Cooking Time: 16 Minutes

Servings: 2

Ingredients:

- 1 tbsp. Hoisin sauce
- 300g sliced lamb back strap
- 1 minced garlic
- 2 tbsp. Chinese cooking wine
- 1 tbsp. sesame oil
- 1 tsp. potato starch
- 1 tsp. brown sugar
- 1 minced ginger
- 1 tbsp. oyster sauce
- 1 tbsp. Worcestershire sauce
- 1 chopped capsicum
- 1 sliced red onion

Directions:

- Mix the cooking wine and potato starch in a bowl.
- Add the lamb slices.
- Marinate for 20 minutes.
- Cook the lamb in a pan of oil till browned.
- In another pan, sauté the onion, capsicum, ginger, and garlic.
- Cook-stir for 3 minutes.
- Throw in the meat, sauces, and sugar.
- Cook for 3 minutes.
- Serve.

Nutritional Information:

Protein: 55.31g

Fats: 25.11g

Carbs: 41.28g

Calories: 621

198.   LAMB CUTLETS ✓

Preparation Time: 28 Minutes

Cooking Time: 23 Minutes

Servings: 2

Ingredients:

- 350g cut lamb loin chop
- 1 tsp. black bean sauce
- 1 tsp. chili sauce
- 1 tsp. tapioca
- 3 tbsp. peanut oil
- 1 tbsp. potato starch

For the Sauce:

- 1 tbsp. plum sauce
- 1 dash peanut oil
- 1 tbsp. honey
- 1 tbsp. dry sherry

Directions:

- Combine the sauce ingredients in a bowl. Toss well. Set aside
- Combine the potato starch, sauces, lamb, and tapioca in another bowl.
- Toss well. Marinate for 20 Minutes.
- Go ahead to fry the lamb till golden.
- Transfer the sauce mixture into the pan.
- You can add the marinade if you choose.
- Cook till sauce is thick.
- Serve.

Nutritional Information:

Calories: 633

Protein: 38.91g

Fats: 32.57g

Carbs: 48.71g

199. HOISIN LAMB CHOPS

Preparation Time: 07 Minutes

Cooking Time: 25 Minutes

Servings: 3

Ingredients:

- 2 c. black bean sauce
- 1 tsp. crumbled red pepper flakes
- 1 tbsp. peanut oil
- 2lb. chopped lamb loin
- 3 minced garlic cloves
- 1 tsp. salt
- 1 tbsp. black pepper

Directions:

- Preheat your grill to 348F.

- Mix the peppers, salt, pepper flakes, chopped lamb, sauce, oil, and garlic in a bowl.
- Toss well.
- Place the marinated pork loin chops on the grill.
- Cook till done
- Serve.

Nutritional Information:

Calories: 652

Protein: 68.12g

Carbs: 23.66g

Fats: 30.56g

200. HUNAN LAMB ✓

Preparation Time: 05 Minutes

Cooking Time: 17 Minutes

Servings: 2

Ingredients:

- 3 tbsp. black bean sauce
- 1 tbsp. plum sauce
- 1 tbsp. sesame oil
- 1 tbsp. chili pepper
- 1 tsp. salt
- 1 diced white onion
- 1 tsp. white rice vinegar
- 1 tbsp. Chinese cooking wine
- 2 minced garlic cloves
- 3 chopped lamb shank

Directions:

- Sauté the onion, garlic, and pepper in a pan of oil.
- Cook till fragrant.
- Add everything else.
- Cook till done.
- Serve.

Tried - has flavour. I added vegetable stock (1 cup) and used lamb chops

Nutritional Information:

Protein: 0.76g

Carbs: 7.32g

Fats: 6.78g

Calories: 92

201. LAMB STEW ✓

Preparation Time: 50 Minutes

Cooking Time: 35 Minutes

Servings: 3

Ingredients:

- 400g chopped lamb breast
- 2 handfuls chopped mushrooms
- 30g chopped carrot
- 1 minced garlic clove
- 1 tbsp. dry sherry
- 1 handful chopped broccoli
- 1 minced ginger
- 2 tbsp. peanut oil
- 1 tbsp. ground cinnamon
- 1 tsp. minced soybean paste
- 1 tbsp. ground cumin
- 1 tsp. dry thyme

~~1½ cups vegetable stock~~ *(2½ cups vegetable stock instead)*

For the Marinade:

- 1 tbsp. hoisin sauce
- 1 tsp. potato starch
- 2 tbsp. plum sauce
- 1 tbsp. honey

Directions: *Recipe Tried*
Nice recipe

- Combine the lamb and the marinade ingredients in a bowl. Toss well.
- Keep aside for 40 minutes.
- Sauté the ginger, garlic, cumin, cinnamon, thyme, and bean paste in a pan of oil.
- Cook stirring for 6 minutes.
- Add the broccoli, lamb, and mushrooms.
- Fry till veggies are tender.
- Add the sherry, carrot, and marinade.
- Cook for 15 minutes.
- Serve.

Dumplings - Page 25

Nutritional Information:

Calories: 318   *Dumplings - Page 26*

Protein: 25.85g

Fats: 20.27g

Carbs: 10.2g

202. LAMB CURRY ✓

Preparation Time: 05 Minutes

Cooking Time: 30 Minutes

Servings: 3

Ingredients:

- 2 tbsp. soy sauce
- 2 tbsp. plum sauce ✓
- 1 tbsp. peanut oil
- 8 tbsp. water
- 1lb. blanched chopped lamb tenderloin
- 1 tsp. honey
- 1 chopped small ginger
- 3 tbsp. ground curry
- 200g chopped potatoes
- 1 minced garlic clove
- 100g chopped carrots

½ chopped onion
meat marinade - page 16

Directions:

- Sauté the ginger and garlic in a pan of oil.
- Cook-stir for 3 minutes.
- Add sauces, honey, curry, 8 tbsp. of water.
- Cook till the mixture is well boiled.
- Then add your lamb, carrots, and potatoes.
- Cook till the veggies are tender.
- Serve.

Nutritional Information:

Calories: 514   *(this recipe has been tried and has a lot of flavour).*

Carbs: 42.37g

Fats: 19.98g

Protein: 51.72g

marinade for lamb
page 16
soy sauce, rice wine,
cornflour, ginger, garlic,
salt, pepper.

113

203.   STICKY LAMB

Preparation Time: 12 Minutes

Cooking Time: 25 Minutes

Servings: 2

Ingredients:

- 1 tbsp. gochujang
- 3 lamb cutlets
- 1 tbsp. Chinese sweet rice wine vinegar
- 3 minced garlic cloves
- 2 tbsp. dry thyme
- 1 tsp. Five-spice
- 3 tbsp. maltose
- 2 tbsp. Thai sauce
- 1 tbsp. granulated sugar

Directions:

- Preheat your oven to 361F.
- Combine everything else in a bowl. Set aside for 9 minutes.
- Place the marinated lamb cutlets in a lined baking tray.
- Bake till caramelized.
- Serve with juices.

Nutritional Information:

Carbs: 9g

Fats: 0.36g

Protein: 0.86g

Calories: 38

204.   SALT AND PEPPER LAMB

Preparation Time: 25 Minutes

Cooking Time: 30 Minutes

Servings: 2

Ingredients:

- 4 c. diced lamb meat
- 2 minced garlic cloves
- 1 pinch crushed peppercorn
- 1 c. groundnut oil
- 1 small, crushed ginger
- 1 tsp. brown sugar
- 1 tbsp. Thai sauce
- 2 chopped red chilies
- 1 tbsp. potato starch
- 1 bunch chopped scallions
- 1 handful chopped mixed capsicum
- 1 bunch chopped celery stalk
- 1 tsp. salt

Directions:

- Combine the ginger, garlic, potato starch, peppercorns, sauce, 1 tbsp. Oil and salt in a bowl.
- Add the lamb meat.
- Marinate for 25 minutes.
- Deep fry the meat till crispy golden.
- Sauté the red chili, ginger, garlic, pepper, salt, and celery in a pan of 2 tbsp. oil.
- Cook for 4 minutes.
- Add the sugar and capsicum. Cook for 2 minutes.
- Then add the marinade. Cook till glossy.
- Add the scallions.
- Serve.

Nutritional Information:

Calories: 1287

Protein: 20.51g

Fats: 117.73g

Carbs: 7.76g

205.   ROAST LAMB

Preparation Time: 10 Minutes

Cooking Time: 25 Minutes

Servings: 3

Ingredients:

- 2 tbsp. canola oil
- 1 tbsp. ground black pepper
- 1 tbsp. black bean sauce
- 1 tbsp. lemon juice
- 6 lamb leg cutlets
- 1 minced garlic
- 1 crushed ginger
- 1 tsp. chopped Thai basil

Directions:

- Combine the ingredients except for the lamb in a bowl.
- Mix well.
- Preheat your grill to 361F.
- Dip the lamb into this marinade.
- Hold still till lamb is well coated.
- Place the lamb on the grill.
- Roast till well cooked.
- Serve.

Nutritional Information:

Calories: 90

Fats: 9.39g

Carbs: 1.88g

Protein: 0.37g

206.   SPICED ORANGE LAMB

Preparation Time: 35 Minutes

Cooking Time: 33 Minutes

Servings: 2

Ingredients:

- 1 tbsp. sunflower oil
- 1 crushed ginger
- 350g sliced lamb fillets
- 4 tbsp. plum sauce
- 4 tbsp. orange juice
- 1 tbsp. orange zest
- 1 chopped white onion
- 2 minced garlic cloves
- 1 tsp. chili sauce
- 2 tbsp. lamb broth
- 1 tsp. honey

Directions:

- Combine the ginger, honey, sauces, orange juice, orange zest, and garlic in a bowl. Add the lamb. Set aside for 35 minutes.
- Stir-fry the onions in a pan of oil for 3 minutes.
- Toss in the lamb. Cook till browned.
- Add marinade and broth.
- Cook for 5 minutes more.
- Serve.

Nutritional Information:

Protein: 37.01g

Carbs: 25.24g

Fats: 18.11g

Calories: 101

207. PAK CHOY BBQ LAMB

Preparation Time: 06 Minutes

Cooking Time: 25 Minutes

Servings: 3

Ingredients:

- 6 lamb breast chops
- 3 c. steamed chopped Bok choy
- 5 tbsp. Thai sauce
- 1 tbsp. groundnut oil
- 1 tbsp. honey

Directions:

- Preheat your chargrill pan to 398F.
- Combine oil, honey, and sauce in a bowl. Mix well.
- Dunk your lamb chops into this marinade.
- Place the lamb on the grill.
- Cook till all sides are well roasted.
- Serve with Bok choy.

Nutritional Information:

Fats: 45.47g

Protein: 45.96g

Carbs: 9.31g

Calories: 636

208. 5-SPICE LAMB

Preparation Time: 10 Minutes

Cooking Time: 30 Minutes

Servings: 2

Ingredients:

- 6 tbsp. dry sherry
- 2 minced garlic cloves
- 2 tbsp. maltose
- 1 sliced lamb ribs
- 3 tbsp. ketchup
- 1 tbsp. peanut oil
- 2 tbsp. hoisin sauce
- 1 crushed ginger
- 1 tbsp. Sriracha
- 2 tbsp. Chinese five-spice powder

Directions:

- Combine the sauce, maltose, ketchup, sherry, and Sriracha in a bowl. Toss well.
- Sauté the ginger and garlic in a pan of oil.
- Cook-stir till fragrant. Toss the lamb ribs with the five-spice powder. Make sure that it is well coated.
- Then add the lamb ribs to the pan.
- Cook till browned.
- Then add the ketchup mixture.
- Cook till done.
- Serve.

Nutritional Information:

Carbs: 26.61g

Calories: 170

Protein: 1.53g

Fats: 7.47g

209. PEPPER LAMB STIR-FRY

Preparation Time: 07 Minutes

Cooking Time: 25 Minutes

Servings: 3

Ingredients:

- 1 sliced small green chili pepper
- 1 minced garlic clove
- 300g diced lamb
- 1 handful chopped white onion
- 1 small chopped red bell pepper
- 1 chopped small ginger
- 1 medium chopped red chili
- 1 tbsp. peanut oil
- 1 tbsp. soy sauce
- 1 small chopped green bell pepper

Directions:

- Combine the diced lamb and soy sauce in a bowl. Toss well.
- Sauté the garlic and ginger in a pan of oil.
- Add the peppers, red chili, and onion. Cook-stir till it caramelized.
- Lastly, add the lamb.
- Cook till the meat is down.
- Serve.

Nutritional Information:

Calories: 367

Protein: 26.74g

Carbs: 14.24g

Fats: 22.46g

210.   SESAME LAMB, GINGER, AND GARLIC

Preparation Time: 15 Minutes

Cooking Time: 23 Minutes

Servings: 6

Ingredients:

- 2 tbsp. dry sherry
- 1 chopped ginger
- 3 minced garlic cloves
- 3 tsp. potato starch mixed in water
- 7 c. sliced lamb
- 3 tsp. sunflower oil
- 8 sliced spring onions
- 3 tsp. Chee Hou Sauce

Directions:

- Marinate the lamb in a bowl of sherry and sauces.
- While you're at it, pour oil into your pan and wait till it's heated.
- When heated, sauté the ginger, garlic, and spring onion. Cook-stir for 3 minutes.
- Then throw in the lamb and fry till golden.
- Add the potato starch/water mixture and marinade.
- Cook for 2 minutes.
- Serve.

Nutritional Information:

Calories: 367

Protein: 26 74g

Carbs: 14.24g

Fats: 22.46g

211.   CHINESE LAMB NODDLE SOUP ✓

Preparation Time: 10 Minutes

Cooking Time: 30 Minutes

Servings: 2

Ingredients:

- 50g dried Mai fun noodles
- 1 tbsp. pepper
- 4g chopped mushrooms
- 3 c. lamb stock
- 1 pinch salt
- 2 c. shredded cabbage
- 3 c. chopped lamb ribs
- 1 dash rice wine
- 2 tbsp. cumin
- 1 dash fennel seeds
- 1-star anise
- 1 minced garlic clove
- 1 minced white onion
- 1 dash peppercorns

Directions:

- Combine the cabbage, stock, and mushrooms in a pot.
- While that is boiling, combine the lamb ribs, rice wine, fennel seeds, cumin, star anise, onion, peppercorns, and garlic in a bowl.
- Toss well so that the lamb absorbs the spices.
- Then add the lamb, salt, pepper, and noodles to the pot.
- Cook till the lamb is done.
- Serve.

Nutritional Information:

Calories: 163

Protein: 6.62g

Fats: 2.66g

Carbs: 31.16g

212.   CHINESE LAMB RIBS

Preparation Time: 08 Minutes

Cooking Time: 25 Minutes

Servings: 4

Ingredients:

- 1 pinch chili flakes
- 1 tbsp. sunflower oil
- 1kg cut lamb ribs
- 1 tbsp. pepper
- 1 grated garlic clove
- 30g maltose
- 1 tbsp. cumin
- 25ml hoisin sauce
- 50ml dry sherry
- 2 minced gingers

Directions:

- Preheat your oven to 282F.
- Combine the chili flakes, cumin, sherry, sauce, pepper, maltose, lamb ribs cuts, garlic, oil, and ginger in a bowl.
- Toss well.
- Arrange the coated meat in a lined baking sheet.
- Roast well till done.
- Serve.

Nutritional Information:

Calories: 938

Protein: 55.37g

Carbs: 1.73g

Fats: 77.21g

213.   LAMB AND VEGGIES

Preparation Time: 10 Minutes

Cooking Time: 25 Minutes

Servings: 2

Ingredients:

- 500g Stir-fry mixed veggies
- 350g lamb tenderloin cut in strips
- 1 c. sliced scallions
- 3 tbsp. plum sauce
- 2 tbsp. peanut oil

Directions:

- Toss the sauce and lamb in a bowl.
- Pour the oil into a pan. When it's heated, cook the lamb.
- Stir-fry till done.
- Add the veggies.
- Add the scallions and marinade.
- Cook till veggies and Lamb is tender.
- Serve.

Nutritional Information:

Calories: 703

Protein: 53.03g

Carbs: 25.67g

Fats: 44.15g

214.   GRILLED LAMB CHOPS

Preparation Time: 1 Hour 10 Minutes

Cooking Time: 25 Minutes

Servings: 3

Ingredients:

- 1 tbsp. brown sugar
- 2 tbsp. shrimp sauce
- 1 dash salt
- 1 tbsp. hoisin sauce
- 2 lb. lamb meat cut into 12 chops
- 1 tbsp. dry sherry
- 1 pinch five-spice powder

Directions:

- Preheat the barbequed grill to 347F.
- Combine the lamb, salt, sugar, sauces, sherry, and spice powder in a bowl.
- Toss well.
- Marinate for 1 hour.
- Grill the chops till done.
- Serve.

Nutritional Information:

Calories: 513

Protein: 62.55g

Carbs: 3.54g

Fats: 27.64g

215.   LAMB CHUANR

Preparation Time: 05 Minutes

Cooking Time: 25 Minutes

Servings: 15

Ingredients:

- 1 lb. chunked lamb loin
- 1 tsp. salt
- 1 minced garlic clove
- 1 tbsp. chili powder
- 1 tsp. five-spice powder
- 1 tbsp. fennel seeds
- 1 tsp. ground coriander

Directions:

- Preheat your grill to 398F.
- Combine the salt, coriander, spice powder, garlic, fennel seeds, and chili powder in a bowl. Then thread the lamb chunks into wooden skewers.
- Douse spice mix all over the skewered lamb meat.
- Grill till the meat is done.
- Serve the meat with the skewers. It is fun eating from the skewers!

Nutritional Information:

Protein: 6.2g

Carbs: 0.66g

Fats: 2.22g

Calories: 49

216.   SCALLION LAMB

Preparation Time: 25 Minutes

Cooking Time: 30 Minutes

Servings: 2

Ingredients:

- 7ml rice wine
- 6 oz. sliced lamb fillets
- 1 tsp. soy sauce
- 1 tsp. honey
- 5 chopped spring onions
- 1 minced garlic clove
- 1 sliced ginger
- 1 tsp. potato starch paste
- 200ml sunflower oil
- 1 handful chopped broccoli
- 1 tbsp. Xo Sauce

Directions:

- Combine the soy sauce, potato starch paste, lamb fillets, honey, and wine in a bowl. Toss well.
- Marinate for 25 minutes.
- Pour oil into a pan. Cook-stir the meat till done. Transfer to a lined plate. Then proceed to sauté the spring onion, ginger, and garlic in the pan.
- Add the broccoli.
- Cook-stir for 6 minutes.
- Add the meat and Xo sauce.
- Cook for 4 minutes more.
- Serve.

Nutritional Information:

Fats: 6.02g

Protein: 23.06g

Carbs: 40.44g

Calories: 304

217. SPICY, SWEET, AND SOUR LAMB CHOPS

Preparation Time: 05 Minutes

Cooking Time: 25 Minutes

Servings: 3

Ingredients:

- 1 chopped white onion
- 1 minced garlic clove
- 5 c. chunked lamb chops
- 2 tbsp. honey
- 3 tbsp. sweet and sour sauce
- 1 chopped ginger
- 3 tbsp. peanut oil
- 2 tbsp. ketchup
- 1 tbsp. Thai sauce
- 2 tbsp. chili sauce
- 3 tbsp. Chinese five-spice powder
- 1 tbsp. dry sherry

Directions:

- Sauté the onion, garlic, and ginger in a pan. Cook-stir till fragrant.
- Add the lamb. Cook till browned.
- Then throw in everything else.
- Toss the lamb with the mixture.
- Cook-stir till lamb is well cooked.
- Serve.

Nutritional Information:

Calories: 224

Fats: 13.66g

Carbs: 26.44g

Protein: 1.06g

218. HERBAL LAMB SOUP

Preparation Time: 05 Minutes

Cooking Time: 20 Minutes

Servings: 2

Ingredients:

- 10g ginseng
- 300g sliced blanched lamb
- 10g Dang Quai
- 1 c. chopped carrot
- 10g Huang-qi
- 7g cranberries
- 2 tbsp. ground Chinese orange peel
- 8g jujube fruits

Directions:

- Throw in all in a pot of water.
- Cook till lamb is tender and everything is well combined.
- Serve.

Nutritional Information:

Calories: 418

Protein: 37.43g

Fats: 25.39g

Carbs: 8.05g

219. CHILIES AND CUMIN LAMB

Preparation Time: 10 Minutes

Cooking Time: 20 Minutes

Servings: 3

Ingredients:

- 1 tbsp. canola oil
- 1 tbsp. cumin
- 1 chopped green bell pepper
- 1 chopped red bell pepper
- 1 minced garlic
- 1 chopped yellow bell pepper
- 1 tsp. chili flakes
- 1 sliced yellow onion
- 1 tsp. fennel seeds
- 1 tbsp. Thai sauce

Directions

- Combine the fennel seeds, sauce, cumin, and lamb in a bowl. Toss well.
- Sauté the onion and garlic in a pan of oil.
- Cook-stir for 4 minutes.
- Add the chili flakes, bell peppers, and lamb.
- Cook till browned.
- Toss in the marinade.
- Cook for 3 minutes.
- Serve.

Nutritional Information:

Calories: 73

Fats: 5.44g

Carbs: 6.34g

Protein: 1.58g

Nutritional Information:

Calories: 312

Carbs: 8.09g

Fats: 24.37g

Protein: 17.94g

220. TOOTHPICK LAMB

Preparation Time: 20 Minutes

Cooking Time: 10 Minutes

Servings: 2

Ingredients:

- 150g cut lamb shank (cut into bite able sizes)
- 1 tbsp. cumin
- 2 tbsp. Thai sauce
- 1 dash salt
- 1 tsp. ground coriander
- 1 tbsp. chili powder
- 3 tbsp. peanut oil
- 2 tbsp. dry sherry

Directions:

- Marinate the lamb in a bowl of sauce. Keep aside.
- After 20 minutes, thread the lamb meat through prepared toothpicks.
- Pour oil into a pan.
- When heated, sauté the coriander, cumin, salt, and chili powder in the pan.
- Cook-stir for 6 minutes.
- Add the toothpick skewered lamb and sherry.
- Cook-stir for 7 minutes.
- Serve.

"All the dreamers in all the world are dizzy in the noodle!"

221. PAN-FRIED NOODLES

Preparation Time: 25 minutes

Servings: 4-6

Ingredients:

- 1½ tbsp. corn oil
- 750g of fresh noodles
- 1 tsp. of toasted sesame oil
- 3 c. of water

Directions:

- Boil the three cups of water in a large pot.
- Add the noodles and stir for about 5 minutes until half-done. Then drain the noodles into a sieve, add sesame oil, and toss.
- Then transfer noodles into a greased cake pan and cool for 2 minutes.
- Place your stainless Wok over high heat till it's very hot for 30 seconds.
- Then add the 1 ½ tbsp. of corn oil, let it heat for 5 seconds (make sure it becomes hot).
- Next, reduce the heat to medium and upturn the noodles into the Wok. Twirl infrequently to avoid sticking until it becomes deep golden brown on the bottom for 5 minutes.
- Use a pancake-turner and flip the noodle cake over to brown for another 5 minutes. Then, turn off the heat and transfer it into a plate ready to serve.

Nutritional Information:

Calories: 287

Fat: 11g

Protein: 7.1g

Carbs: 40g

222. CHINESE NOODLES SALAD

Preparation Time: 10 min,

Serving: 4

Ingredients:

- 1 c. of Oriental sesame oil
- 3 ½ Tbs. soy sauce
- 1 ¼ Tbs. balsamic vinegar
- 1 lb. of Chinese noodles
- 3 chopped scallions

- 9 oz. of broccoli (divide into florets)

Directions:

- In boiling salted water, put your noodles and allow them to simmer for 5 minutes. Then mix the first three ingredients in a neat bowl and set aside.

- Next, drain the noodles in a colander. Make sure to do this thoroughly. Then stir in the chopped scallions and set them aside.

- Now put your broccoli in a steamer basket over boiling water, cover it and let it steam for 5 minutes. When it becomes tender, drain and mix with the noodles and sauce (first three ingredients) until it blends well before serving.

Nutritional Information:

Calories: 247

Fat: 14g

Protein: 250g

Carbs: 29g

223.   NOODLES WITH FRIED BEAN-PASTE SAUCE

Preparation Time: 15 minutes

Servings: 5

Ingredients:

- 500g flour noodles

- 250g of minced lean meat

- 4 tsp. of sweet bean sauce

- 4 peppercorns

- 3 ¼tblsp vegetable oil

- One sliced scallion

- 1tsp. ground ginger

- 5tblsp soy sauce

- 1 ½ tsp. salt,

- 1 c. of clear stock

- 1 ½tblsp corn starch (dissolved in 1 tbsp. water)

Directions:

- Put the sweet bean sauce in a bowl and add ½ c. of water to make a thin paste.

- Put your noodle in boiling water and simmer for 5 minutes. Remove and drain thoroughly and put it aside in a bowl.

- Next, heat your vegetable oil in a wok over medium heat until it becomes hot.

- Add the peppercorns and make sure to deep-fry for two minutes until scented.

- Then remove and get rid of the peppercorns. Put the sliced scallions, the lean meat, ground ginger, soy sauce, salt, paste into the oil and stir-fry for two minutes, add the stock and corn-starch and a c. of water, then stir for 30 seconds until it is thickened.

- Transfer it to a serving bowl and enjoy with your noodles.

Nutritional Information:

Calories: 640

Fat: 16g

Carbs: 117g

Protein: 40g

224.   HOT AND SPICY MEAT SAUCE NOODLES

Preparation Time: 15 minutes

Servings: 4 to 6

Ingredients:

- 1 c. of vegetable oil
- 4 lb. ground pork (not too lean)
- 2 c. of brown bean sauce
- 2 tbsp. bottled red chili paste with garlic
- 3 tbsp. sugar
- 5 tbs dry Sherry
- 2 lb. fresh Chinese egg noodles
- 1 ½ c. of minced scallions

Directions:

- Heat a wok over high heat and the vegetable oil. Add the ground pork and cook quickly, stirring and chopping down to avoid lumps.
- Keep stirring until the pork loses its raw look.
- Add two cups of brown bean sauce and the red chili paste with garlic. Stir quickly for two minutes.
- Then add the sugar and the Sherry and cook one minute longer over high heat.

- Add the scallions to the simmering sauce and stir. Remove from the heat and turn it into an oven dish.
- Next, boil water in a pot. Add the noodles and cook for four minutes.
- Drain the noodles and cut them into bits of convenient length.
- Pour the noodles into a heatproof serving dish.
- Now Pour the sauce over the hot noodles and toss gently to blend perfectly. Your guests can help themselves to a dish.

Nutritional Information:

Calories: 220

Fat: 6g

Carbs: 20g

Protein: 20g

225.   COLD NOODLES WITH SESAME SAUCE

Preparation Time: 10 minutes

Servings: 4

Ingredients:

- 500g Chinese egg noodles
- 1 tsp. of toasted sesame oil
- 5 tbsp. of sesame paste
- 2 c. of water
- 1tsp. of white vinegar
- 3 tbsp. soy sauce

- 1 tsp. sugar

- 3 cloves of garlic (minced)

- 1 sliced scallion both white and green parts

- 1 inch of fresh chopped ginger

- Chinese chili

Directions:

- In boiling water, add the noodles, cook until barely tender for 5 minutes.

- Drain well in a sieve and mix them with the sesame oil to coat. Then cover and refrigerate.

- In the meantime, get a bowl, put the sesame paste, and stir enough water into the paste to make it thick. Continue stirring for two minutes.

- Swiftly beat the vinegar, soy sauce, and sugar together in a bowl. Then add the mixture to the sesame paste.

- Next, stir two-quarters of the scallion, the ginger, and minced garlic in the paste. Do this for about three minutes and set aside.

- Then bring out your noodles from the refrigerator, which should be chilled.

- Mix the chilled noodles with the sauce.

- Then garnish with the remaining scallion and drizzle with the chili oil for a better taste.

Nutritional Information:

Calories: 300

Fat: 12g

Carb 50g

Protein: 15g

226.   SPICY PORK NOODLES

Preparation Time: 15 minutes

Servings: 4

Ingredients:

- 1 c. of vegetable oil

- 1¼ tsp. of red chili pepper

- Minced ginger

- 2 pieces of garlic

- Sliced white onions

- 1 bowl of pound Pork

- 500g of steamed noodles

- 1tlb. of sesame oil

- ½tlb. of Soy sauce

- Ground white pepper

add shrimps/spring onions

Directions:

- Under medium heat, pour your 1 c. of vegetable oil into your stainless Wok, add the minced ginger, chopped garlic, and sliced white onions, and make sure to stir-fry for 30 seconds.

- Then add the red chili pepper to the pound of pork, raise the heat high and allow to fry for 2 two minutes.

- Next, turn the heat to a low level and put your steamed noodles. Add 1 tbsp. to taste sesame oil, ½ of soy sauce, and ground pepper. Mix quickly for three minutes to make a perfect blend of flavor.

- Turn off the heat, transfer into a bowl, and cover for three minutes. Uncover the bowl, stir again and get ready to serve.

Nutritional Information:

Calories: 150

Carb: 97g

Protein: 9g

Fat: 14g

227. STIR-FRY HOKKIEN NOODLES WITH CHICKEN

Preparation Time: 10 minutes

Servings: 3

Ingredients:

- 600g stir-fry Hokkien noodles

- 1 c. Hoisin sauce

- 300g rainbow vegetables

- 500g chicken

- 2 tbsp. of vegetable oil

Directions:

- In a heatproof bowl of boiled water, put your noodles and cover for 3 minutes and drain. Then separate noodles with a fork to avoid sticking.

- Slice your rainbow veggie, place it in a bowl and set it aside.

- After that, heat a wok over high heat. Then add 1 tbsp. of oil, and twirl to cover round.

- Put the chicken, half of it, and stir fry for 4 minutes until it is cooked well. Then transfer it into a bowl.

- Pour the remaining oil into the wok, let it be hot for 2 minutes, put your rainbow veggie, and stir fry for 1 minute until it's tender.

- Add the remaining chicken and stir fry until it is cooked through. Then add the Hokkien sauce, noodles, and other chicken, mix until it is heated through. Turn off the heat, divide among bowls and serve.

Nutritional Information:

Calories: 450

Carbs: 45g

Fat: 30g

Protein: 15g

228. CHICKEN CHOW MEIN NOODLES

Preparation Time: 15 minutes

Servings: 3

Ingredients:

- 2 pack of continental noodles

- 1 carrot

- ½ c. of cabbage

- 100g snow peas
- 1 tbsp. of Soy Sauce
- 1 ½ tbsp. of salt
- 500g of chicken mince
- 1 tbsp. canola oil
- 1 tbsp. canola oil
- 440g Singapore style noodles

Directions:

- Prepare the noodles according to the packet direction and drain thoroughly over medium-high heat. Heat oil in a wok. Stir-fry until it is brown.

- Add carrot, stir fry for 3 minutes. Add cabbage, stir-fry for another 3 minutes.

- Then add snow peas and stir fry. Add your prepared noodles and stir together.

- Add 150ml of water and soy sauce. Stir-fry until sauce thickens and noodles are heated through.

Nutritional Information:

Calories: 250

Fat: 20g

Protein: 19g

Carbs: 25g

229.   SZECHUAN SPICY COLD NOODLES

Preparation Time: 15 minutes

Servings: 4-6

Ingredients:

- 3 quarts of chicken broth
- 2 lb. of dry Asian noodles
- 2 ½ tbsp. of spicy chili oil
- 1 oz. dried chili
- 1 ½ tsp. soy sauce
- 2 tsp. of salt
- 2 tsp. chicken bouillon granules
- 1c. Chopped green onions
- ½ tsp. garlic powder

Directions:

- In a Wok over medium-high heat, bring 3 quarts of chicken broth to a boil.

- Turn off heat, add the dry noodles, and for 5 minutes. Drain the noodles, reserving 2 tbsp of broth.

- Put the noodles back in the wok, and while it's still hot, add the chili oil and dried chili. Let cool for 4 minutes.

- Add salt, chicken-bouillon granules, soy sauce, green onions, garlic powder, and the reserved chicken broth when the noodles are cool. Put it in the refrigerator. And serve chilled.

Nutritional Information:

Calories: 478

Fat: 10g

Protein: 15g

Carb 87g

230. SPICY BEEF NOODLE SOUP

Preparation Time: 10 minutes

Servings: 2

Ingredients:

- 5 sliced gingers
- 2 scallions
- 1.3 kg beef chuck
- ½ c. of Shaoxing wine
- 2 tbsp. of oil
- 2 tbsp. of Sichuan peppercorns
- Chopped garlic
- 1 onion
- 3 bay leaves
- ½ c. spicy bean paste
- 5-star anise
- 2 large tomatoes (sliced)
- ½ c. light soy sauce
- 1 tbsp. sugar
- 1 large piece of dried tangerine peel
- Chopped scallion and cilantro to garnish

Directions:

- In a pot filled with 10 c. of cold water. Add the ginger, scallions, Shaoxing wine, and beef chunks.

- Allow boiling for 5 minutes. Then turn down the heat and simmer for 5 minutes. Turn off the heat after that and set it aside.

- Get a large wok and heat oil over medium-low heat. Add the Sichuan peppercorns, garlic cloves, onion, star anise, and bay leaves. Cook for 5 minutes.

- Add the spicy bean paste and stir. Then add the tomatoes. Stir in the light soy sauce and sugar to cook for two minutes. Turn off the heat.

- Next, get your cooked beef, ginger, and scallions, transfer them into the wok. Then, pour in the stock through a fine-mesh strainer. Turn on the heat again and add in the tangerine peel.

- Cover and allow it to boil for a while, then reduce the heat and let it simmer for 10 minutes.

- Turn off the heat but keep the lid on for another 10 minutes so that the flavours meld together.

- Cook your noodles in a separate pot according to the package instructions, and divide among your serving bowls

Nutritional Information:

Calories: 570

Fat: 18g

Carbs: 36.4g

Protein: 60g

231. STIR-FRIED NOODLES WITH STEAMED DRIED SCALLOPS

Preparation Time: 15 minutes

Servings: 3

Ingredients:

- 5 dried scallops
- 4 c. water
- 1 tsp. salt
- 12 oz. fresh egg noodles
- 2 tbsp. Onion Oil
- 1 tbsp. of peeled ginger
- 1 tbsp. oyster sauce
- 1 ½ tsp. light soy sauce
- 1 tsp. Sugar
- ½ c.
- 2 scallions (white portion)
- 2 oz. of mung bean sprouts, with the ends, removed

Directions:

- Steam the dried scallops. Remove and let it cool. Then Shred into strands, removing any hard ends, and reserve.
- Put the water and salt in a pot and boil over high heat. Add the noodles, stir well with chopsticks, and cook for 10 seconds.
- Turn off the heat, run cold water into the pot, then drain the noodles with a mesh strainer and allow to dry thoroughly. Then cut the noodles into 1-inch lengths.
- Heat a wok over high heat for 40 seconds. Add 2 tbsp. of the onion oil and, using a spatula, cover the wok with the oil.
- Then add the noodles and stir-fry for 2 minutes. Reduce the heat to medium and cook for 2 minutes more, or until very hot.
- Add the scallops, add the ginger, mix well, and stir for 3 minutes.
- Add the oyster sauce, soy sauce, sugar, and stir-fry for 2 minutes.
- Add the scallions, the bean sprouts, and stir-fry for 2 minutes. Turn off the heat, transfer to a heated dish, and serve.

Nutritional Information:

Calories: 275

Carbs: 34g

Protein: 18g

Fat: 10g

232. ONE-WOK FRIED VEGGIE NOODLES ✓

Servings: 4

Cook Time: 45 minutes

Ingredients:

- 1 c. carrot grated packed
- 1 c. mung bean sprouts
- ½ c. green onion chopped
- 1 tsp. garlic
- 1 tbsp. olive oil
- 2 tbsp. sesame oil
- 6 tbsp. light soy sauce
- 1 tbsp. Hoisin
- 1 tsp. chili chopped
- 150 pre-boiled noodles

Add sliced onion and shrimps

Directions:

- Heat the oil in the wok and cook the carrots until soft, then set it aside.
- In the same wok, add the sesame oil and fry the noodles until crisp, throwback the carrots, green onion, and the rest of the ingredients except the bean sprouts.
- Cook for 2 minutes, then toss in the bean sprouts.
- Combine and adjust for seasoning.
- Serve.

Nutritional Information:

Calories: 119

Protein: 4.14g

Fat: 5.8g

Carbs: 14.4g

233. SPINACH, SHRIMP, AND BEAN THREAD NOODLE SOUP ✓

Preparation Time: 15 minutes

Servings: 6

Ingredients:

- 1-oz. package bean thread noodles
- 7 oz. large shrimp
- 2 c. of water
- 1 tbsp. salt
- ½ tsp. baking soda
- ½ -lb. spinach leaves
- 5 c. Chicken Stock
- 1 sliced ginger
- 2 garlic cloves,
- 1½ tsp. salt
- 1 c. of Garlic Oil

Directions:

- Soak the bean threads in hot water to cover for 15 minutes. Drain well, cut into 4-inch lengths, and reserve.

- Boil water in a pot over high heat. Add the salt and baking soda. Add the spinach and cook when water boils until leaves turn bright green. Turn off the heat instantly and then drain off the water.

- Get a wok, put the stock, ginger, garlic, and salt and allow to boil over high heat.

- Add the reserved spinach, stir well, and let it boil for 10 minutes.

- Then add the garlic oil, cleaned shrimp, stir, and boil for 5 minutes.

- Next, Add the bean threads, stir well and boil again for 3 minutes. At this point, the shrimp will have curled and turned pink, indicating they are cooked. Turn off the heat, and transfer to a serving bowl.

Nutritional Information:

Calories: 150

Fat: 4g

Carb 29g

Protein: 1g

234.   NOODLE SOUP WITH CHICKEN AND MUSHROOMS

Preparation Time: 15 minutes

Servings: 2- 4

Ingredients:

- 4 lb. noodles

- 2 tsp. Chinese sauce

- 1 ½ tsp. oil

- 2 drops of sesame seed oil

- 1 ½ c. of chicken

- 1 c. of mushrooms

- 2 c. of water chestnuts

Directions:

- Put the noodles into boiling water, and boil for 3 minutes. Then put it into a clean bowl containing the oil, sesame seed oil, Chinese sauce, and a little pepper. Allow boiling for 5 minutes.

- Next, Cut the chicken, mushrooms, and water chestnuts into pieces 1 ½ inch long, add and mix well, then add Chinese gravy.

- Reduce the heat and allow to simmer for 5 seconds. Turn off the heat and serve.

Nutritional Information:

Calories: 420

Fat: 9g

Carbs: 47.6g

Protein: 36.5g

235.   SWEET AND SPICY CHICKEN NOODLES

Preparation Time: 10 minutes

Servings: 4

Ingredients:

- 450g thin egg noodles

- 350g stir fry traditional vegetables

- 1 ½ tbsp. soy sauce

- 2 tbsp. olive oil

- 35g of Smokey Texan style seasoning

- 600g chicken thigh fillets

Directions:

- First, combine chicken with Texan-style seasoning in a bowl. Cover and set aside for 20 minutes. Then Prepare noodles as per packet directions. Drain thoroughly and set aside.

- Heat 1 tbsp. of the oil in a large frying pan over high heat. Add the chicken and cook, stirring from time to time, do this for about 3 minutes. Then put it in a bowl and cover.

- Heat the remaining oil in a frying pan. Then add vegetables and stir-fry for 4 minutes. Add noodles and soy sauce, mix well.

- Then add the reserved chicken and cook for 2 minutes until heated through. Turn off heat and serve.

Nutritional Information:

Calories: 390

Fat: 18g

Protein: 7g

Carb 60g

236.   SPICY COLD SKIN NOODLES

Preparation Time: 15 Minutes

Servings: 2-3

Ingredients:

For the Sauce:

- ½ c. of chili oil

- 2 tsp. of Chinese black vinegar

- 1 ½ tsp. of light soy sauce

- 1 tbsp. toasted sesame seeds

- 1 tsp. sesame oil

- ½ tsp. sugar

- ¼ tsp. salt

- 1 ½ tsp. of Sichuan peppercorn powder

- 3 cloves garlic

For the Noodles:

- 250 fresh Liang pi noodles

- 2 c. bean sprouts

- 150 g wheat gluten

- ¼ c. cilantro leaves

- 1 small cucumber

Directions:

- Combine all sauce ingredients in a pot under medium heat and cook for 10 minutes. Then turn off the heat.

- Then cook the noodles in another pot for 5 minutes. Drain and put it in a bowl.

- Steam or blanch the beansprouts and wheat gluten. Steam for about 4 minutes over high heat. Turn off the heat and then pour them into the bowl with the noodles, cilantro, and cucumber.

- Add the sauce as well and mix everything. Taste to see if there is a need to adjust seasonings.

- Mix again and until all flavours are perfectly blended. Pour into a serving dish and enjoy.

Nutritional Information:

Calories: 500

Carbohydrates: 39g

Protein: 17g

Fat: 32g

237.   SESAME PEANUT BUTTER NOODLES RECIPE

Preparation Time: 10 minutes

Servings: 4

Ingredients:

- 5 oz. of noodles

- 1 ½ tbsp. pure sesame oil

- 1 tbsp. peanut butter

- 1 ½ tbsp. honey

- 2 ½ tbsp. soy sauce

- 1 tbsp. rice vinegar

- 2 garlic cloves

- 1 tsp. of grated ginger root

- 3 sliced green onions

- 1 tbsp. of salt

Directions:

- Cook noodles in boiling water for 5 minutes. Drain and put in a bowl aside.

- Get a medium bowl, and add the sesame oil, peanut butter, honey, soy sauce, rice vinegar, garlic, ginger, salt, and green onion.

- Mix thoroughly until it is well blended. Make sure the peanut butter breaks down totally to create a smooth sauce.

- Get your Wok, pour the sauce and the prepared noodles. Stir well and heat for 3 minutes under low heat. Turn off the heat and serve.

Nutritional Information:

Calories: 391

Carbohydrates: 56.7g

Protein: 11.5g

 Fat: 14.4g

Saturated Fat: 2.2g

Fibre: 2.5g

238.   NOODLES WITH GRAVY ✓

Preparation Time: 15 minutes

Servings: 2-4

Ingredients:

- 200 g flat rice noodles

- 1 ½ tsp. vegetable oil

- 2 crushed garlic cloves

- 3 sliced carrots

- 450g chopped mushrooms
- 100g of chopped broccoli
- 100g Pak choi
- 1 ½ tbsp. yellow bean paste
- 800 ml vegetable stock
- 3 tbsp. of cornflour
- ½ tsp. white pepper
- 2 tbsp. light soy sauce
- Sliced red chili

Directions:

- Soak the noodles in hot water for ten minutes and drain. Then heat the oil in a wok, add the garlic, mushrooms, carrots, and broccoli, then stir fry for 5 minutes.

- Pour in the veggie stock and yellow bean paste as soon as the mushrooms start to release liquid.

- Next, put in your cornflour and watch as the sauce thickens. Add the soy sauce and white pepper and stir very well. Allow cooking for 4 minutes.

- Now add the Pak choi and for one minute. Reduce the heat, turn in the noodles and mix well the sauce. Turn off the heat and serve with chopped chili.

Nutritional Information:

Calories: 309

Carbohydrates: 64g

Protein: 9g

Fat: 2g

239.   SIMPLE CRISPY NOODLES

Preparation Time: 15 minutes

Servings: 3

Ingredients:

- 3 oz.' fresh egg noodles
- 2 c. vegetable oil
- 1 tbsp. of Salt
- 2 tbsp. of Cornflour
- 1 ½ c. of Canola Oil

Directions:

- In a wok, heat the oil to 400°F. Then carefully drop the noodles into the oil. Use a pair of wooden chopsticks to break apart to prevent sticking together as they fry. Let it fry for 20 seconds.

- Use a spatula, carefully flip the noodles, and keep frying until equally golden brown.

- Drain the fried noodles of excess oil, and transfer them to a plate to cool.

- Sprinkle salt over the noodles to taste. Repeat until you've fried all of your noodles.

Nutritional Information:

Calories: 109

Carbohydrates: 9g

Protein: 1g

Fat: 8g

240. FRIED EGGS WITH CHINESE NOODLES

Preparation Time: 15 minutes

Servings: 4

Ingredients:

- 2 lb. of noodles
- 1 ½ tbsp. of vegetable oil
- 3 cloves of garlic (sliced)
- 1 tbsp. of grated ginger
- 2 green onions
- 10 oz package of fresh stir fry vegetables
- 2 tbsp. dry sherry
- 2 tbsp. light soy sauce
- 1 ½ tbsp. of low sodium dark soy sauce
- 1 ½ tbsp. oyster sauce
- 1 tbsp. of ground black pepper
- 4 eggs

Directions:

- Cook the noodles a little less than stated on the package instructions, drain, rinse with cold water and set aside.
- Heat the oil in the wok over high heat. Once hot, add the garlic, ginger, and green onions and stir-fry for 30 secs before adding the stir fry vegetables. Stir fry for 2-3 minutes.

- Add the sherry and allow it to evaporate before adding any meat you are using and cooked noodles almost. Toss so that all of the ingredients are combined.
- Turn the heat down to medium and add soy sauces, oyster sauce, and pepper.
- Stir-fry for a further 2 mins before adding the green onions, then toss to combine.
- Fry the eggs to your liking and serve on top of the noodles.

Nutritional Information:

Calories: 561

Carbohydrates: 97g

Protein: 11g

Fat: 11g

241. STIR-FRIED RICE NOODLES WITH EGGS AND GREENS

Preparation Time: 15 minutes

Servings: 3

Ingredients:

- 5 oz. dry rice noodles
- 4 tbsp. vegetable oil
- 4 eggs
- 1 tbsp. of salt
- 3 small heads Bok choy
- 2 tsp. of garlic
- 2 tiny, sliced scallions

- 1 ½ tsp. chili flakes
- 3 tsp. of light soy sauce

Directions:

- Prepare your noodles according to the package instruction. Rinse cooked noodles with water running water, drain thoroughly, and set aside.

- Next, break eggs in a bowl and beat with 1 tbsp. of salt. Pour 2 tbsp. of oil in a wok and heat over high heat for 2 minutes.

- Add the eggs, scrambling, and stir-frying with a spatula for 20 seconds. Then transfer it to a plate and set it aside.

- Wipe out wok and add 1 tbsp. of oil. Place under high heat and let it heat for 25 seconds. Add the greens and stir fry for 1 minute, then transfer to a plate and set aside.

- After that, take the remaining tbsp. of oil to wok and heat over high heat until it's hot.

- Add the scallions, garlic, chili pepper flakes, and stir-fry for 30 seconds until the oil smells fragrant.

- Then add the drained noodles, round with a spatula, add the soy sauce and mix well.

- Keep frying until noodles are dry and evenly seasoned, do this for 5 minutes.

- Add the eggs and vegetables and stir well until well blended. Turn off the heat and serve in a bowl.

Nutritional Information:

Calories: 419.6

Fat: 13.8 g

Carbohydrate 33.9 g

Protein: 38.8 g

242.   CRISPY PAN-FRIED NOODLES WITH GRAVY

Preparation Time: 20 minutes

Servings: 2-5

Ingredients:

- 6 oz. cooked egg noodles
- 5 large shrimp
- 4 pieces of tender cut chicken
- 1 c. of broccoli florets
- 5 oz. Bok choy stems cut off
- 4 tbsp. vegetable oil

For the Gravy:

- 1 ½ c. of chicken stock
- 2 ½ cloves garlic minced
- 2 tsp. of oyster sauce
- 1 ½ tsp. of soy sauce
- 2 tsp. corn starch
- 1 tbsp. water

Directions:

- Form your noodles into a noodles disk first, then add 2 tbsp. Of oil into a large wok under medium-high heat.

- Place noodle disc in once heated and let it cook slowly until noodles turn brown and crispy at the bottom. Take out the noodles in one piece, using two spatulas, and place them in a bowl.

- Next, add another 1 tbsp. of oil into the pan. Place noodles back into the pan and let the non-crispy side face down. Do this for 3 minutes until the bottom is crispy. Take it out and place it in a pan.

- Now add the remaining tbsp. of oil into the pan, add chicken and shrimp, and stir-fry for 5 minutes. Then put in the vegetables and cook until everything is fully cooked. Remove from heat and put aside.

- Get a small pot and add gravy ingredients except for corn starch and water. And allow boiling for about 5 minutes.

- Add your dissolved corn starch and allow it to cook until it thickens, stirring continuously.

- Add the gravy into the pan of vegetables and Protein. Cook for about 2-3 minutes, coating and flavouring stir fry with the gravy.

- Add the stir fry on top of crispy noodles.

- Add remaining gravy over noodles. Serve immediately.

Nutritional Information:

Calories: 441

Carbohydrates: 40g

Protein: 16g

Fat: 24g

243.   SPICY SICHUAN NOODLES WITH EGGPLANT

Servings: 4

Preparation Time: 20 mins

Ingredients:

- 1 tbsp. of ground Sichuan peppercorn

- 2 lb. frozen noodles

- 4 tbsp. of vegetable oil

- 1 ½ lb. Japanese eggplant,

- 9oz fried tofu, or half-block of extra firm tofu

- 1 bunch green onions, sliced, light and dark parts separate

- 3 cloves of garlic

- 5 Thai minced chilies,

- 2 ½ tbsp. Light soy sauce

- ½ tbsp. dark soy sauce

- 1 ½ tbsp. Chinese cooking wine

Directions:

- Cook the noodles according to package direction, then drain and rinse in cold water to arrest cooking. Set aside.

- Heat a wok over medium-high heat and add some oil and the eggplant. Cook the eggplant until very tender, about 8 minutes. Remove from wok.

- Add a drizzle of oil and the tofu and cook until golden in spots, 2 minutes. Take it out and keep it in a bowl. Add more oil and the light part of the green onions, garlic, and chili. Allow cooking for 2 minutes. Add the 1 tsp. of Sichuan peppercorn and stir to coat well

- Put the eggplant and tofu to the wok along with the noodles. Then add the soy sauces and cooking wine and stir to coat. Turn off heat and garnish with the dark part of the green onions to serve.

Nutritional Information:

Calories: 242.6

Fat: 19.0 g

Carbohydrate 17.4 g

Protein: 1.9 g

244.   SHRIMP NOODLE SOUP

Preparation Time: 15 minutes

Servings: 4

Ingredients:

- 7 oz. Chinese noodle

- 3 c. of chicken stock

- 1 ½ tsp. fish sauce

- 2 tsp. low sodium dark soy sauce

- 3 tbsp. light soy sauce

- lime juice

- 2-star anise

- ½ Tsp. brown sugar

- 2 green onions (chopped)

- 25 cleaned raw shrimps

- Red chili flakes
- Bok choy

Directions:

- Cook the noodles according to the package instructions and then drain.

- Add the chicken stock, fish sauce, soy sauces, lime juice, star anise, brown sugar, green onions, and Bok choy.

- Bring to the boil and add the shrimp until they turn pink and add the noodles.

- Warm through, pour into a bowl, and serve topped with chili flakes.

Nutritional Information:

Calories: 312

Carbohydrates: 50g

Protein: 18g

Fat: 4g

245.   PARMESAN CHICKEN NOODLES

Servings: 3

Preparation Time: 30 minutes

Ingredients:

- 300g of egg noodles
- 2 tbsp. of corn oil
- Parmesan cheese
- 170g of scallops
- 2 tbsp. of soy sauce
- 500g of tender chicken
- 2tbsp. of paprika

Directions:

- Boil the noodles for 5 minutes and drain.
- Add the oil into a wok and add the scallop, paprika, soy sauce. Allow cooking for 4 minutes.
- Cook the chicken for 15minutes in another pot.
- Drain the chicken and add to the sauce mix.
- Add the noodles into the mix and stir.
- Allow to cool for 4 minutes.

Nutritional Information:

Calories: 270kal

Fat: 11g

Carb 28g

Protein: 18.7g

246. LEMON CHOW CHEDDAR NOODLE

Servings: 3

Preparation Time: 40 minutes

Ingredients:

- 450g of flour noodles
- 3 tbsp. of lemon juice
- 400g of shrimps
- 3 tbsp. of paprika
- 2½ tbsp. of vegetable oil
- 1tsp. of sea salt
- 200g of cheddar

Directions:

- Boil the noodles and shrimp in a pot for 3 minutes and drain.
- Make a sauce with the remaining ingredients apart from the cheddar.
- Add the noodles into the mix and stir fry for 5 minutes.
- Add the cheddar and allow to cook for 6 minutes.
- Serve hot.

Nutritional Information:

Calories: 430kal

Carbs: 80g

Protein: 11g

Fat: 9.2g

247. MUTTON FRY NOODLES

Servings: 2-3

Preparation Time: 30 mins

Ingredients:

- 450g of steamed noodles
- 3tbso of canola oil
- Chopped onions
- 240g of thinly sliced mutton
- 1tsp. of sesame seed
- 2 tsp. of sesame oil
- 1 tsp. of blended ginger
- 3 tsp. of dark soy sauce
- 2 tsp. of ground pepper

Directions:

- Cook the noodles based on the manufacturer's instructions and drain the water.
- Cook the mutton and soy sauce in a pot with medium heat for 13 mins.
- Make a sauce with the remaining ingredients and cook for 6 mins.
- Add the noodles into the mix and stir until the mutton gets a pinkish colour.

Nutritional Information:

Calories: 369

Carbs: 75g

Fat: 6.2g

Protein: 16g

248.   WHITE SCALLOP NOODLES

Servings: 3

Preparation Time: 15 minutes

Ingredients:

- 17oz of egg noodles
- 2 tsp. of oyster sauce
- 2½ tbsp. of onion oil
- 2tsp. of garlic
- 1 tbsp. of black pepper
- 60g of finely cut Spinach
- 6 dried scallops

Directions:

- Heat your oil for 3 mins in a wok.
- Add the scallop, oyster sauce, pepper, and allow to cook for 4 minutes.
- Boil grilled your noodles in another braid pot and add into the sauce.
- Stir fry for another 3 minutes, and then add your spinach.
- Serve while hot.

Nutritional Information:

Calories: 290

Carb: 80g

Fat: 6.4g

Protein: 19g

249.   MUSHROOM-PEANUT BUTTER NOODLE

Servings: 3

Preparation Time: 15 minutes

Ingredients:

- 600g of ramen

- 2 tbsp. of canola oil

- 2 tbsp. of peanut butter

- 240g of mushroom

- 30g of scallops

- 1 garlic clove.

- 2tbsp. of paprika

- 2 medium-sized onions

Directions:

- Boil the ramen and mushroom until tender.

- In a pan, heat some oil and add the onions, paprika, garlic, and scallops. Stir fry for 4 minutes.

- Drain the ramen and mushroom, mix with the sauce, add the peanut butter, and stir.

- Allow to cook for 3 more minutes, and then it is ready.

Nutritional Information:

Calories: 450

Carbs: 78g

Fat: 11g

Protein: 12.2g

"Even though you have ten thousand fields, you can eat but one measure of rice a day."

250. CHINESE CHICKEN FRIED RICE

Preparation Time: 15 minutes

Servings: 4

Ingredients:

- 1 egg
- 1 tbsp. water
- 1 tbsp. butter
- 1 onion (chopped)
- 2 c. of rice (cooked but cold white rice)
- 2 tbsp. soy sauce
- 1 tsp. ground pepper (black pepper)
- 1 c. cooked chicken meat (chopped)

Directions:

- Get a small bowl, whisk the egg with water.

- Melt butter in a large saucepan over low to medium heat.

- Add the whisked egg and leave flat for about 2 minutes. Remove from the saucepan and cut into shreds.

- Heat oil in the same saucepan, add chopped onion, and sauté until it softens.

- Then add rice, pepper, chicken, and soy sauce. Stir fry together for about 5 minutes, then stir in the egg. Serve while hot.

Nutritional Information:

Calories: 255

Protein: 14.1g

Carbohydrates: 25.9g

Fat: 10.2g

Cholesterol: 83.2mg

Sodium: 515.6mg

251. CHINESE FRIED RICE √

Preparation Time: 28 minutes

Servings: 4

Ingredients:

- 1 c. of onion (finely chopped)
- 2½ tbsp. oil
- 1 egg (lightly whisked) or more eggs to taste
- 3 drops of soy sauce
- 3drops of sesame oil

- 8 oz. of chicken (chopped)

- 1 c. of frozen peas

- 2c. of rice (cooked but cold white rice)

- 4 green onions (chopped)

- 2 tbsp. light soy sauce (you can add more)

- 1 c. of Small finely chopped carrot

Directions:

- Heat 1 tbsp. Oil in pan; add chopped onions and stir-fry until onions turn a nice brown colour, about 8-10 minutes; remove from pan.

- Allow the wok to cool slightly. Mix egg with 3 drops of soy and 3 drops of sesame oil; set aside.

- Add ½ tbsp. Oil to a pan, swirling to coat surfaces; add egg mixture; working quickly, swirl egg until egg sets against pan; when egg puffs, flip the egg and cook another side briefly; remove from pan, and chop into small pieces.

- Heat 1 tbsp. Oil in pan; add selected meat to the pan, along with carrots, peas, and cooked onion; stir-fry for 2 minutes.

- Add rice, green onions, and bean sprouts, mix well; stir-fry for 3 minutes.

- Add 2 tbsp. of light soy sauce and chopped egg to rice mixture and fold in; stir-fry for 1 minute more; serve.

- Set out additional soy sauce on the table, if desired.

Nutritional Information:

Calories: 497.8

Cholesterol: 80 mg

Sodium: 606.8 mg

Carbohydrate: 64.6 g

Protein: 22.3 g

252.   CHINESE PINEAPPLE RICE

Preparation Time: 30 minutes

Servings: 2

Ingredients:

- 1 medium Pineapple

- Cooking oil

- Dried prawns (optional)

- 3 tbsp. Chopped garlic

- 800g Cooked Jasmine rice

- 3 tbsp. Fish sauce

- 1 tbsp. Sugar

- Chilli powder (optional)

For the Garnishing:

- Crisp-fried shallots

- Roasted cashews

- Coriander leaves (cilantro)

- Sliced red chilies

- Pork or chicken floss (optional)

Directions:

- Peel, core, remove pineapple eyes, then chop into small cubes. Alternatively, halve unpeeled pineapple lengthways and run a sharp knife about 2-cm (1-in) from the edge all around, then scoop out pineapple flesh. Reserve pineapple shells for serving later.

- Heat oil in a wok or large pan. Fry dried prawns, if using, until fragrant, then dish out and set aside.

- In the same oil, fry garlic until lightly brown and fragrant. Add rice and stir-fry, breaking up lumps. Season with fish sauce, sugar, and chili powder if used.

- Add pineapple cubes and fried prawns if using. Stir until ingredients are well mixed and rice is dry after absorbing juices from pineapple cubes. Adjust seasoning to taste.

- Dish out to a serving platter, individual serving plates, or pineapple shells. Garnish as desired and serve hot.

Nutritional Information:

Calories: 285

Protein: 24.1g

Carbohydrates 25.9g

Fat: 10.2g

Cholesterol: 87.2mg

Sodium: 435.6mg

253.   CHINESE MUSHROOM SOUP WITH BROWN RICE

Preparation Time: 25 minutes

Servings: 4

Ingredients:

- 4 c. of Dashi

- 1 tsp. Salt

- 3 tbsp. Chinese light soy sauce

- 100g Fresh shiitake mushrooms

- 1 sprig of Chinese chives

- 2 medium-sized eggs

- 500g Cooked brown rice

Directions:

- Combine dashi stock, salt, and soy sauce in a pot. Bring to the boil.

- Reduce heat, add mushrooms and simmer for 5 minutes or until mushrooms are cooked.

- Add chives and adjust seasoning to taste. Add eggs in a slow, steady stream to form egg ribbons. Remove from heat.

- Divide brown rice among individual serving bowls. Shape rice in each bowl into a mound, if desired.

- Ladle soup over and serve. If serving rice in a mound, add soup slowly around it to keep its shape.

Nutritional Information:

Calories: 255

Protein: 34.1g

Carbohydrates 25.9g

Fat: 10.2g

Cholesterol: 83.2mg

Sodium: 515.6mg

254.   CHINESE LENTIL RICE

Preparation Time: 20 minutes

Servings: 4

Ingredients:

- 240g of Long-grain rice (washed and drained)

- 120g of Moong dal or yellow lentils

- 5 tbsp. of Butter

- 1 c. of Onion (peeled and finely chopped)

- 1 c. of Ginger (peeled and finely chopped)

- 1 clove Garlic (peeled and chopped)

- 6 medium-sized Black peppercorns

- 1 Bay leaf

- 1 tsp. of Salt

- ½ tsp. of Ground turmeric

- 1 pint of Boiling water

Directions:

- Combine rice and dal or lentils in a large bowl. Add enough water to cover and leave to soak for 1 hour. Drain before use.

- Melt 3 Tbsp. Butter in a large saucepan over moderate heat. When foam subsides, add onion and fry for 4 minutes, stirring occasionally.

- Add ginger, garlic, peppercorns, and bay leaf. Fry for another 4 minutes or until the onion is golden brown.

- Add rice, dhal, salt, and turmeric. Stir and toss the mixture gently. Reduce heat to moderate–low and cook for 5 minutes, stirring gently.

- Add hot water and stir once, then cover the pan and reduce heat to low. Cook for 15–20 minutes or until rice and dhal are cooked, and all the water has been absorbed.

- Stir in remaining butter with a fork and remove from heat. Transfer to a serving dish, garnish as desired, and serve.

Nutritional Information:

Calories: 205

Protein: 41g

Carbohydrates: 25.9g

Fat: 10.2g

Cholesterol: 83.2mg

Sodium: 515.6mg

255.   CHINESE AUBERGINE RICE DISH AND POTATOES

Preparation Time: 25 minutes

Servings: 4

Ingredients:

- 300g Long-grain rice (soaked in cold water and drained)

- 1 pint of Water

- 1 tsp. of Salt

- Ghee (clarified butter)

- 360g of Potatoes (peeled and cut into cubes)

- 1 large-sized Aubergine/Eggplant (cubed and disgorged)

- 60g of Butter

- Spice paste

- 1 tsp. of Ground turmeric

- 1 tsp. of ground cumin seeds

- 1 tbsp. Ground coriander seeds

- ½ tsp. Cayenne pepper

- ½ tsp. Sugar

- ½ tsp. Salt

- 2 tsp. Chickpea flour

- 1 tsp. Lemon juice

Directions:

- Combine rice, water, and salt in a large saucepan. Bring to the boil over high heat.

- Cover saucepan, reduce heat to very low, and simmer for 15–20 minutes or until rice is tender and all the water has been absorbed. Remove from heat, set aside, and keep warm.

- Meanwhile, combine all spice paste ingredients in a small bowl. Mix until pasty, adding extra lemon juice, if necessary. Set aside.

- Melt ghee in a large frying pan (skillet) over moderate heat. When foam subsides, add potatoes and aubergine. Fry for 5 minutes, stirring frequently.

- Add the spice paste and fry for 10 minutes, stirring constantly. Add 1–2 Tbsp. Water if the mixture is too dry.

Nutritional Information:

Calories: 255

Protein: 14.1g

Carbohydrates 25.9g

Fat: 10.2g

Cholesterol 83.2mg

Sodium 515.6mg

256. PILAF WITH PINEAPPLE AND CASHEW NUTS

Preparation Time: 20 minutes

Servings: 3

Ingredients:

- 90g (3 oz) of Butter

- 1 medium-sized Pineapple (peeled)

- 1 tbsp. Raisins

- 12 Spring onions (scallions) - (chopped)

- 75g of Cashew nuts

- 1 tbsp. Coriander seeds (lightly crushed)

- ¼ tsp. Cayenne pepper

- 360 Long-grain rice.

- Salt to taste

- 2½ c. of Vegetable or chicken stock

Directions:

- Melt half the butter in a medium frying pan (skillet) over moderate heat. When foam subsides, add pineapple and raisins. Fry for 2–3 minutes, turning frequently.

- When the pineapple is lightly coloured, remove the pan from heat and set it aside.

- Melt the remaining butter in a large saucepan over moderate heat. When foam subsides, add spring onions. Fry, occasionally stirring, for 4–5 minutes or until golden brown.

- Add cashew nuts, coriander seeds, and cayenne pepper. Fry for about 4 minutes, stirring occasionally.

- Add rice and salt. Fry mixture, constantly stirring, for 5 minutes. Stir in pineapple and raisins, then add stock and bring to the boil.

- Cover the pan, reduce heat to low, and cook for 20–25 minutes or until rice is tender and all the liquid has been absorbed.

- Adjust seasoning to taste, then remove the pan from heat. Spoon pilaf onto a serving platter.

- Garnish as desired and serve immediately.

Nutritional Information:

Calories: 255

Protein: 14.1g

Carbohydrates 25.9g

Fat: 10.2g

Cholesterol 83.2mg

Sodium 515.6mg

257.   ASIAN TOMATO RICE

Preparation Time: 20 minutes

Servings: 2

Ingredients:

- 3 tbsp. Butter

- 2 bulbs of Onions (chopped)

- 1clove of Garlic (peeled and crushed)

- ¼ c. of Ginger (peeled, finely chopped)

- 1 large-sized red bell pepper (seeded, disgorged, and nicely sliced)

- 2 c. of Long-grain rice (soaked in water for 30 minutes and drained)

- 420g Canned peeled tomatoes

- Salt to taste

- ¼ tsp. Freshly ground black pepper

- 2 spring onions

Directions:

- Melt butter in a large skillet over moderate heat. When foam subsides, add onions, garlic, and ginger. Fry, occasionally stirring, for 5–7 minutes or until onions are soft and translucent but not brown.

- Add capsicum and fry for 3 minutes, stirring occasionally.

- Add rice and fry for 3 minutes, stirring constantly.

- Add tomatoes and can juice, then top with water until liquid covers rice by 1-cm (1/2-in). Season to taste and bring to a boil.

- When liquid is boiling vigorously, cover the pan and reduce heat to very low. Simmer for 15–20 minutes or until rice is tender and all the liquid has been absorbed.

- Remove from heat and dish out, then garnish with spring onions and serve immediately.

Nutritional Information:

Calories: 255

Protein: 14.1g

Carbohydrates 25.9g

Fat: 10.2g

Cholesterol 83.2mg

Sodium 515.6mg

258. CHINESE RICE IN GREEN TEA WITH SALMON

Preparation Time: 25 minutes

Servings: 2

Ingredients:

- 180g Salmon fillet.

- 1 tsp. Salt

- 250g Cooked Chinese rice

- 3¼ c. of Hot water

- 1 tbsp. green tea leaves

- 1 tbsp. Chinese light soy sauce

- Chinese seaweed (nori) strips (to taste)

Directions:

- Pan-fry salmon until lightly browned and cooked, seasoning to taste with salt. Remove and set aside.

- Divide rice equally among individual bowls and top with a few salmon slices.

- Prepare green tea. Pour hot water over tea leaves, infuse for about 1 minute, then strain and pour over rice.

- Drizzle with soy sauce and sprinkle seaweed strips over. Serve immediately.

Nutritional Information:

Calories: 265

Protein: 24.1g

Carbohydrates 25.9g

Fat: 10.2g

Cholesterol: 83.2mg

Sodium: 515.6mg

259. CHINESE SEAFOOD FRIED RICE

Preparation Time: 25 minutes

Servings: 2

Ingredients:

- 240g Long-grain rice. (Soaked in cold water for 30 minutes and drained)

- 500ml of Water

- 1½ tbsp. Salt

- 3 tbsp. cooking oil

- 2 medium-sized Onions (finely chopped)

- 120g Cooked ham (nicely chopped)

- 2 tbsp. Baby peas

- 2 medium-sized Tomatoes (peeled and cut into quarters)

- 240g of Prawns (parboiled and shelled)

- 180g of Squid tubes (parboiled and cut into circles)

- 1 tbsp. Light soy sauce

- Ground white pepper (to taste)

- 1 large-sized Egg (lightly whisked)

Directions:

- Put rice in a medium, heavy saucepan. Add water and add 1 tsp. Salt. Bring to the boil over high heat.

- Reduce heat to low, cover, and simmer for 15 minutes or until all the water has been absorbed. Remove from heat. Alternatively, use a rice cooker.

- Heat oil in a large saucepan over moderate heat. Fry onions for 2 minutes, stirring constantly.

- Add ham, peas, tomatoes, prawns, squid, and remaining salt. Cook for 1 minute, stirring constantly.

- Stir in cooked rice and cook for 2 minutes, still stirring constantly. Add soy sauce and pepper, adjusting to taste.

- Make a well in the ingredients and add the egg. Briskly fold ingredients in towards liquid egg and stir continuously for 2 minutes.

- Remove from heat and serve immediately.

Nutritional Information:

Calories: 295

Protein: 27.1g

Carbohydrates 25.9g

Fat: 12.2g

Cholesterol 85.2mg

Sodium 515.6mg

260. CHINESE FISH SOUP WITH RICE

Preparation Time: 25 minutes

Servings: 4

Ingredients:

- 500g Fish fillet

- 2 tsp. Light soy sauce

- 1 tbsp. cooking oil

- 1 clove of Garlic (peeled, crushed)

- 3 c. of Water

- 1 finger of Ginger (peeled and shredded)

- 2 tbsp. Corn flour and 3 tbsp. of water (corn starch)

- 1 large Egg (lightly beaten)

- 2 Fresh Tomatoes (cut in wedges)

- 1 sprig of Coriander leaves (chopped)

- 500g Cooked long-grain rice

- 3 Red chilies (seeded and sliced)

- Red chili strips (optional) for garnishing

Directions:

- Season fish slices with soy sauce to taste. Leave for 10 minutes.

- Heat oil in a pot and stir-fry garlic until fragrant.

- Add water, bring to a boil, and then add ginger and fish slices.

- Stir in cornflour solution to thicken the soup slightly.

- Lower heat until soup is just simmering. Pour in the egg while stirring, so that egg ribbons are formed.

- Add tomatoes and coriander. Turn off heat when tomatoes are tender but not mushy.

- Spoon rice onto deep plates, ladle soup, and ingredients over.

- Serve hot with a side dip of chilies in soy sauce, garnished with chili strips, if you want.

Nutritional Information:

Calories: 255

Protein: 14.1g

Carbohydrates 25.9g

Fat: 10.2g

Cholesterol: 83.2mg

Sodium: 515.6mg

261.   CHINESE STEAMED GLUTINOUS RICE

Preparation Time: 30 minutes

Servings: 4

Ingredients:

- 500g of Chicken meat (sliced)

- 2 tbsp. cooking oil.

- 80g Dried Chinese mushrooms (soaked to soften and cut into strips)

- 1kg Glutinous rice

- 1½ tsp. of Salt

- 1 tsp. Dark soy sauce

- 1 tsp. Light soy sauce

- 1 tsp. Five-spice powder

- 1 tsp. of ground white pepper

- 1 litre of Water

- 1 sprig of Coriander leaves (cilantro)

- Chilli sauce of choice

Seasonings:

- 3 tbsp. Oyster sauce
- 2 tbsp. dark soy sauce
- 2 Light soy sauce
- 2 tsp. Ground white pepper

Directions:

- Combine seasoning ingredients and mix in chicken. Leave for 1 hour, refrigerated.
- Heat cooking oil in a wok or large pan. Stir-fry mushrooms for 2–3 minutes. Drain and set aside.
- Reheat wok or pan and add rice. Stir-fry and season with salt, soy sauces, five-spice powder, and pepper. Add water and simmer for 10 minutes until rice is partially cooked. Remove from heat.
- Grease some heatproof (flameproof) bowls. Line each one with chicken and mushrooms, then fill three-quarters way with glutinous rice, packing in tightly.
- Steam bowls rapidly, boiling water for 45 minutes or until rice is well done. Turn out onto serving plates to serve. Alternatively, scoop out from steaming bowls.
- Garnish with coriander and serve with chili sauce.

Nutritional Information:

Calories: 255

Protein: 14.1g

Carbohydrates: 25.9g

Fat: 10.2g

Cholesterol: 83.2mg

Sodium: 515.6mg

262.   CHICKEN CONGEE

Preparation Time: 20 minutes

Servings: 4

Ingredients:

- 2 medium-sized chicken breasts
- 1 tsp. Salt
- 1 tsp. Ground white pepper
- 1.5 litre/ 6 c. Water
- 200g Long-grain rice (washed and drained)

Garnishing:

- Crisp-fried shallots
- Shredded ginger
- Chopped spring onions (scallions)
- Sliced red chilies
- Ground white pepper
- Light soy sauce
- Sesame oil

Directions:

- Season chicken with salt and pepper and set aside for 20 minutes, refrigerated.

- Combine seasoned chicken and water in a pot. Bring to the boil and simmer for 15 minutes or until chicken is cooked. Remove from heat.

- If time permits, leave the chicken to cool in the stock. Otherwise, drain and set aside to cool, reserving stock.

- Add rice to stock and bring to a boil. Reduce heat and simmer, partially covered, for 45–60 minutes or until rice is soft and broken up. Stir occasionally to prevent sticking.

- Meanwhile, remove and discard chicken skin if still attached. Shred chicken meat and discard bones, if any.

- Ladle congee into individual serving bowls. Top with chicken and desired amounts of each garnishing ingredient. Alternatively, serve garnishing ingredients on the side for diners to adjust to their taste.

Nutritional Information:

Calories: 255

Protein: 14.1g

Carbohydrates 25.9g

Fat: 10.2g

Cholesterol: 83.2mg

Sodium: 515.6mg

263. CHINESE RICE WITH EGG AND CHICKEN

Preparation Time: 15 minutes

Servings: 2

Ingredients:

- 1 c. of Dashi

- 1 tbsp. Sugar

- 4 tbsp. Mirin

- 4 tbsp. Chinese light soy sauce

- 1 Large onion (peeled and nicely sliced into rings)

- 350gChicken fillet (cubed)

- 4 Large Eggs (lightly whisked)

- 300g Cooked Chinese rice

- Nanami togarashi (to taste)

Directions:

- Combine dashi, sugar, mirin, and soy sauce in a bowl. Pour into a medium frying pan (skillet) with a lid and bring to a boil.

- Add onion rings and chicken cubes and turn the heat up to high. Cook for 2–3 minutes, shaking pan frequently to ensure chicken is evenly cooked.

- Pour in eggs to cover chicken and onion rings. Cover the pan and leave for about 30 seconds. Remove from heat and leave to stand for about 1 minute; this allows eggs to cook lightly but remain soft.

- Divide rice evenly among 4 serving bowls. Pour warm egg mixture over each bowl and serve, sprinkled with Nanami togarashi, or Chinese seven-spice seasoning, to taste.

Nutritional Information:

Calories: 255

Protein: 14.1g

Carbohydrates 25.9g

Fat: 10.2g

Cholesterol: 83.2mg

Sodium: 515.6mg

264.   YEUNG CHOW FRIED RICE

Preparation Time: 20 minutes

Servings: 2

Ingredients:

- 4 tbsp. cooking oil

- 120g Cooked pork (diced)

- 120g Cooked chicken (diced)

- 120g Prawns (shelled, deveined)

- 4 Large Dried Chinese mushrooms (soaked to soften, stems removed, sliced)

- 1 Ginger (peeled and cut in shreds)

- 120g Cooked long-grain rice

- 4 tbsp. Light soy sauce

- ½ tsp. Ground white pepper

- 60g Bean sprouts

- 3 Spring onions (scallions - trimmed and finely chopped)

- 2 eggs (scrambled and kept warm)

- 6 Fresh Chinese lettuce leaves (washed, dried, and shredded)

Directions:

- Heat oil in a wok or large pan over moderate heat. Add pork, chicken, prawns, mushrooms, and ginger. Stir-fry continuously for 2 minutes.

- Add rice, soy sauce, pepper, bean sprouts, and spring onions. Stir-fry until ingredients are well mixed. Adjust seasoning to taste, then remove from heat.

- Stir in eggs, then spoon onto a serving platter or individual serving plates. Garnish with shredded lettuce and serve immediately.

Nutritional Information:

Calories: 255

Protein: 14.1g

Carbohydrates 25.9g

Fat: 10.2g

Cholesterol: 83.2mg

Sodium: 515.6mg

265.   CHINESE DICED PORK ON CRACKLING RICE

Preparation Time: 30 minutes

Servings: 4

Ingredients:

- 450g Lean pork fillets

- 1 tsp. Salt

- ½ tsp. Freshly ground black pepper

- 1 ½ tbsp. Corn flour (corn-starch)

- 450g Cooked rice

- Cooking oil for deep-frying

For the Sauce:

- 150ml Chicken stock

- 3 tbsp. Light soy sauce

- 1 tbsp. Sugar

- 1 tbsp. of Chinese cooking wine (Hua Tiao)

- 1 tbsp. Corn oil

- 1 large onion (small, thinly sliced)

- 1 clove of Garlic (peeled and crushed)

- 1 ½ tbsp. Contour mixed with 4 tbsp. of water

Directions:

- Season pork with salt and pepper, then sprinkle with cornflour and rub into meat with fingers. Set aside.

- Put rice in an ovenproof (flameproof) baking dish and place in a preheated oven at 140°C (275°F) for 15–20 minutes to dry out; rice should be slightly crisp.

- Meanwhile, heat sufficient oil for deep-frying in a deep pan over moderate heat. If using a deep fryer, preheat to 180°C (350°F) and dip the basket in hot oil before using.

- Deep-fry pork cubes, a few at a time, for 3–4 minutes or until golden brown. Drain pork on absorbent paper towels and maintain oil at 180°C (350°F).

- Prepare sauce. Combine stock, soy sauce, sugar, and wine in a small bowl, beating with a fork until well blended. Set aside.

- Heat corn oil in a large frying pan (skillet) over moderate heat. Stir-fry onion and garlic for 1 minute, then add stock mixture and bring to the boil.

- Add pork and reduce heat to low. Baste well and simmer for 2 minutes or until sauce is hot, then add cornflour solution to thicken. Remove from heat and keep warm.

- Remove rice from the oven and transfer to a narrow-mesh basket for deep-frying. Carefully lower the basket into hot oil, cook for 11/2 minutes, and drain on absorbent paper.

- Arrange rice on a serving dish and spoon sauce over. Serve immediately.

Nutritional Information:

Calories: 255

Protein: 19.1g

Carbohydrates 25.9g

Fat: 10.2g

Cholesterol: 83.2mg

Sodium: 515.6mg

266. LAMB AND APRICOT PILAF

Preparation Time: 20 minutes

Servings: 2

Ingredients:

- 120g Butter

- 1 medium-sized onion (peeled and thinly sliced)

- 675g Boned leg of lamb

- 90g Dried apricots (soaked overnight, drained, and halved)

- 3 tbsp. Raisins

- 2 tbsp. Salt

- ½ tsp. ground Cinnamon

- ½ tsp. Freshly ground black pepper

- 1 litre of Water

- 240g Long-grain rice (washed soaked in water for 30 minutes and drained)

Directions:

- Melt butter in a large frying pan (skillet) over moderate heat. When foam subsides, add onion, and cook, occasionally stirring, for 5 minutes or until soft and translucent but not brown.

- Add lamb and cook, stirring and occasionally turning, for 5–8 minutes or until lightly browned all over.

- Add apricots, raisins, 1 tsp. Salt, cinnamon, pepper, and half the water. Bring to the boil, stirring occasionally.

- Reduce heat to low, cover the pan and simmer for 1–1¼ hours or until meat is tender.

- Meanwhile, combine rice and remaining water and salt in a medium saucepan over high heat. Bring to the boil.

- Reduce heat to very low, cover, and simmer for 15 minutes. If all the liquid has not been absorbed, continue to cook, uncovered, until rice is dry. Remove from heat.

- Spread one-third of rice over a medium ovenproof (flameproof) casserole base, then top with half the meat mixture.

- Spread another third of rice on top and top with the remaining meat mixture. Finish by covering meat with the last third of the rice.

- Cover the casserole and bake in a preheated oven at 180°C (350°F) for 50 minutes or until rice is cooked through.

- Remove from the oven, dish out, and serve.

Nutritional Information:

Calories: 255

Protein: 34.1g

Carbohydrates 25.9g

Fat: 15.2g

Cholesterol: 83.2mg

Sodium: 505.6mg

267.   ASIAN MANGO AND STICKY RICE

Preparation Time: 25 minutes

Servings: 2

Ingredients:

- 360g Glutinous rice

- 2 c. Water

- 1 c. Coconut milk

- 3 large Ripe mangoes (peeled)

- Coconut sauce

- 1 c. Coconut cream

- 2 Screw pine (pandan leaves)

- 1 tbsp. Sugar

- 1 tbsp. Salt

Directions:

- Drain rice and place in a rice cooker with water, coconut milk, and salt. Cook until rice is tender. Cool thoroughly before using.

- Prepare sauce. Combine all ingredients in a saucepan and simmer, stirring until sugar is dissolved and sauce is slightly thickened.

- Spoon rice onto dessert plates and add mango slices. Spoon sauce over and serve

Nutritional Information:

Calories: 255

Protein: 28.1g

Carbohydrates: 25.9g

Fat: 10.2g

Cholesterol: 83.2mg

Sodium: 515.6mg

Preparation Time: 15 minutes

Servings: 2

Ingredients:

- 400g Black glutinous rice

- 6 c. of Water

- 2 Screw pine (pandan leaves)

- ¼ Salt

- 250ml Coconut milk

Syrup:

- 50g Palm sugar (gula Melaka)

- ½ c. of Water

Directions:

- Rinse rice thoroughly and remove impurities. Soak in plenty of water for about 4 hours or preferably overnight.

- Drain rice and transfer to a large saucepan. Add 1.5 litres of water and screwpine leaves. Simmer over medium heat for about 45 minutes or until tender but not mushy.

- Meanwhile, combine syrup ingredients in a small saucepan. Place over moderate–low heat and stir sugar is dissolved. Strain to remove impurities.

- When rice is tender, stir in syrup and salt. Adjust to taste with granulated sugar, if necessary.

- Remove from heat. Serve hot or at room temperature, topped with the desired amount of coconut milk.

Nutritional Information:

Calories: 235

Protein: 25.9g

Carbohydrates: 25.9g

Fat: 10.2g

Cholesterol 83.2mg

Sodium 515.6mg

269. DATE AND RICE PUDDING

Preparation Time: 15 minutes

Servings: 2

Ingredients:

- 5 c. Milk
- 4 tbsp. Rice
- 5 tbsp. Sugar
- 60g Almond slivers
- 180g Dates (pitted and chopped)
- 2 tbsp. Butter
- 2 Egg yolks
- 2 tsp. Rosewater
- Crystallized (candied)
- Rose petals (optional)

Directions:

- Combine milk and rice in a heavy, medium saucepan. Bring to the boil over moderate heat.

- Reduce heat to very low and simmer for 1–1½ hours, frequently stirring with a wooden spoon, or until the consistency is that of thick cream.

- Add sugar, almonds, and dates. Still stirring, bring to the simmer and cook the mixture until it regains the consistency of thick cream.

- Stir in butter and when it is well blended, remove from heat.

- Beat in egg yolks, one at a time. Stir in rose water. Pour pudding into a shallow dish or ramekins for individual servings. Leave to cool.

- Cover dish or ramekins with aluminium foil or cling film (plastic wrap) and refrigerate until chilled.

- Decorate with crystallized rose petals, if using, and serve

Nutritional Information:

Calories: 288

Protein: 18.6g

Carbohydrates 25.9g

Fat: 10.2g

Cholesterol 83.2mg

Sodium 515.6mg

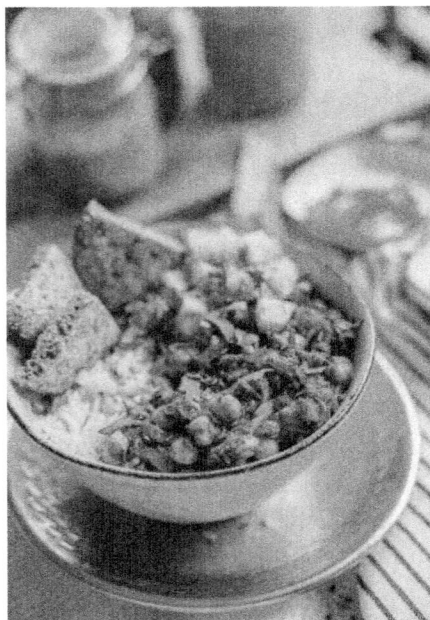

Preparation Time: 30 minutes

Servings: 4

Ingredients:

- 120g Butter

- 12 Pickling (pearl) onions

- 900 Stewing steak (cubed)

- 120g Chickpeas (soaked overnight and drained)

- 1 c. Beef stock

- ½ tsp. Salt

- ½ tsp. Freshly ground black pepper

- 1 tsp. ground cumin

- ½ tsp. Ground turmeric

- 450g Long-grain rice (washed, soaked for 30 minutes, and drained)

Directions:

- Melt butter in a large, heavy saucepan over moderate heat. When foam subsides, add onions and meat. Cook, stirring and turning, for 8–10 minutes or until onions are golden brown and meat is evenly browned.

- Add chickpeas and stock, then top up with enough water to completely cover solid ingredients.

- Add seasoning to taste, cumin and turmeric. Stir to blend, cover saucepan, and cook for 2 hours or until meat and chickpeas are tender.

- Increase heat to moderate–high and bring to the boil. Stir in rice, cover, and reduce heat to low. Simmer for 15–20 minutes or until rice is tender and all the liquid has been absorbed.

- Remove from heat and serve immediately.

Nutritional Information:

Calories: 295

Protein: 24.1g

Carbohydrates: 25.9g

Fat: 10.2g

Cholesterol: 83.2mg

Sodium: 515.6mg

271.   CHINESE BRAISED SAFFRON RICE

Preparation Time: 30 minutes

Servings: 4

Ingredients:

- 4 tbsp. Butter
- 2 Beef marrow (chopped)
- 1 large onion (peeled and thinly sliced)
- 450g Italian rice
- 90 ml Dry white wine
- 5 c. of hot Beef stock
- ½ tsp. Saffron threads soaked in 1 tbsp. hot water
- 60g Parmesan cheese (grated + extra for garnishing)

Directions:

- Melt 3 Tbsp. Butter in a large, heavy saucepan over moderate heat.
- When foam subsides, add beef marrow and onion. Cook, occasionally stirring, for 5–7 minutes or until the onion is soft and translucent but not brown.
- Add rice, reduce heat to low, and cook for 5 minutes, stirring frequently.
- Add wine and about one-third of the stock. Regulate heat so that the mixture is constantly bubbling. Stir occasionally.
- When rice swells and all the liquid has been absorbed, add another third of the stock and regulate heat again. Repeat with the last third of stock; rice should be tender and moist but firm at the end.
- Stir in saffron solution, remaining butter, and cheese. Simmer for 1 minute, stirring frequently.
- Remove from heat and transfer to individual serving bowls. Garnish as desired and serve immediately.

Nutritional Information:

Calories: 255

Protein: 19.1g

Carbohydrates 25.9g

Fat: 10.2g

Cholesterol 83.2mg

Sodium 515.6mg

272. CAPSICUM STUFFED WITH LAMB AND RICE

Preparation Time: 30 minutes

Servings: 4

Ingredients:

- 4 Red or green (bell peppers)
- 1½ tbsp. cooking oil
- 1 small onion (peeled and chopped)
- 1 Garlic (peeled and crushed)
- 240g Minced lamb
- 420g Canned peeled tomatoes
- 1 tsp. Salt
- ½ tsp. Freshly ground black pepper

- 1 tsp. Coriander seeds (crushed)

- 150g Cooked long-grain rice

- 1 tsp. Chopped mint leaves

Directions:

- Use a sharp knife to slice off about 2.5 cm (1 in) from the tops of the capsicums. Carefully remove seeds and pith, then set aside.

- Heat 1 Tbsp. Oil in a medium saucepan over moderate heat. Fry onion and garlic, occasionally stirring, for 5–7 minutes or until the onion is soft and translucent.

- Add lamb and cook, stirring constantly, for 6–8 minutes or until well browned.

- Add tomatoes and can juices, seasoning to taste, and coriander seeds. Cover saucepan, reduce heat to low, and simmer for 30 minutes.

- Add rice and mint. Cook, occasionally stirring, for 5 minutes. Remove from heat.

- Grease a medium baking dish with 1 tsp. Oil. Fill capsicums with lamb mixture, then stand upright in a baking dish.

- Place the dish on the centre shelf and bake in a preheated oven at 190°C (375°F) for 40 minutes or until capsicums are tender.

- Remove from the oven and serve immediately. Garnish with extra mint leaves, if desired.

Nutritional Information:

Calories: 256

Protein: 18.1g

Carbohydrates: 25.9g

Fat: 10.2g

Cholesterol: 83.2mg

Sodium: 515.6mg

273.   ASIAN VEAL AND RICE CASSEROLE

Preparation Time: 20 minutes

Servings: 4

Ingredients:

- 60g Butter

- 4 tbsp. cooking oil

- 900g Boned veal-shoulder (cut into cubes)

- 2 medium-sized Onions (finely peeled and sliced)

- 2 tbsp. Paprika

- 2½ c. Chicken stock

- 4 tbsp. White wine

- Salt to taste

- ½ tsp. Freshly ground black pepper

- Dried thyme Long-grain rice (soaked, washed, and drained)

Directions:

- Melt butter with oil in a large heatproof (flameproof) casserole over moderate heat.

- When foam subsides, add meat and onions. Fry, frequently stirring, for 5–8 minutes or until meat is browned.

- Add all remaining ingredients, except rice, and stir until well mixed. Bring to the boil, then reduce heat to low, cover the casserole and simmer for 11/4 hours.

- Stir in rice, replace the cover and simmer for 20–25 minutes or until rice is tender and has absorbed all the liquid.

- Remove from heat and serve as desired. Sprinkle over extra dried thyme for added aroma.

Nutritional Information:

Calories: 255

Protein: 19.1g

Carbohydrates: 25.9g

Fat: 10.2g

Cholesterol: 83.9mg

Sodium: 515.6mg

274.   PORK CONGEE

Preparation Time: 25 minutes

Servings: 4

Ingredients:

- 500g Minced pork

- 2 tsp. Light soy sauce

- 1 tsp. Ground white pepper

- ½ tsp. Sesame oil

- 2 tsp. Chinese cooking wine (Hua Tiao)

- 1 tsp. Corn flour (corn starch)

- 30g Dried scallops (soaked in 100ml of water)

- 1.5 liters of Water

- 200g Long-grain rice (washed and drained)

Directions:

- Season pork with salt and pepper, then mix in sesame oil, wine, and cornflour. Leave for 20 minutes, refrigerated.

- Meanwhile, steam scallops together with soaking liquid for 10–15 minutes or until soft. Shred scallops, reserve juices, and set aside.

- Combine water and rice in a pot and bring to a boil. Reduce heat and simmer, partially covered, for 45 minutes or until rice is broken up and soft. Stir occasionally to prevent sticking.

- Shape pork into balls and lower into porridge to cook. When pork is cooked, add scallops and juices.

- Cook porridge for another 5 minutes, stirring occasionally.

- Ladle porridge into individual serving bowls. Top with desired amounts of each garnishing ingredient and serve.

Nutritional Information:

Calories: 250

Protein: 16.9g

Carbohydrates: 25.9g

Fat: 10.2g

Cholesterol: 89.2mg

Sodium: 515.6mg

275. CHINESE RICE PUDDING WITH PEAS AND BACON

Preparation Time: 30 minutes

Servings: 4

Ingredients:

- tbsp. Olive oil

- 180g Lean bacon or ham (chopped)

- 60g of Butter

- 1 large onion (peeled and thinly sliced)

- 450g Shelled peas

- 450g Italian rice

- 90ml Dry white wine

- 5 c. of Vegetable or chicken stock

- 1 tsp. Salt

- ½ tsp. Freshly ground black pepper

- 120g of grated Parmesan cheese

Directions:

- Heat oil in a large, heavy saucepan over moderate heat. Add bacon or ham and fry, occasionally stirring, for 5 minutes or until crisp and golden brown. Remove with a slotted spoon and drain on absorbent paper.

- Add half the butter and melt over moderate heat. When foam subsides, add onion and cook, occasionally stirring, for 5–7 minutes or until the onion is soft and translucent but not brown.

- Add peas and rice, reduce heat to low, and cook, frequently stirring, for 5 minutes.

- Add wine and about one-third of the stock. Regulate heat so that the mixture is constantly bubbling. Stir occasionally with a fork.

- When rice swells and liquid has been absorbed, add another third of the stock and regulate heat again. Repeat with remaining stock, and rice should be tender and moist but firm at the end.

- Stir in bacon, remaining butter, seasoning to taste, and cheese. Mix well and simmer for 1 minute, stirring frequently.

- Remove from heat and dish out to serve. Add a sprinkle more of cracked black pepper, if desired.

Nutritional Information:

Calories: 295

Protein: 18.1g

Carbohydrates: 25.9g

Fat: 20.2g

Cholesterol: 83.2mg

Sodium: 515.6mg

276.   BRAISED RICE WITH BOLOGNESE SAUCE

Preparation Time: 30 minutes

Servings: 4

Ingredients:

- 120g Butter

- 1 medium-sized onion (thinly sliced)

- 120g Parma ham (chopped)

- 450g Italian rice

- 6 tbsp. of dry white wine

- 5 c. of Beef stock

- 1 c. of Bolognese sauce

- 30g grated Parmesan cheese

For Garnishing:

- Grated Parmesan cheese

- Cracked black pepper

- Parsley

Directions:

- Melt 90 g (3 oz) butter in a large, heavy saucepan over moderate heat. When foam subsides, add onion, and cook, occasionally stirring, for 5–7 minutes or until the onion is soft and translucent but not brown.

- Add ham and rice, reduce heat to low, and cook, frequently stirring, for 5 minutes.

- Add wine and about one-third of the stock. Regulate heat so that the mixture is constantly bubbling. Stir rice occasionally with a fork.

- When rice swells and all the liquid has been absorbed, add another third of the stock and regulate heat again. Repeat with the last third of stock; rice should be tender and moist but firm at the end.

- Stir in remaining butter, Bolognese sauce, and cheese. Simmer for 1 minute, stirring frequently.

- Remove from heat and divide among individual serving bowls. Garnish as desired and serve immediately.

Nutritional Information:

Calories: 287

Protein: 24.1g

Carbohydrates: 29.9g

Fat: 14.2g

Cholesterol: 73.2mg

Sodium: 515.6mg

"You are what you eat, so eat something sweet."

277. RIZ MELBA (RICE AND PEACH DESSERT)

Preparation Time: 20 minutes

Servings: 4

Ingredients:

- 60g Sugar
- 2½ c. of Milk
- 180g Short-grain rice
- 1 Egg yolk
- 2 Fresh peaches (branched, peeled, and halved)
- 120g Raspberry jam
- 1 tbsp. Double cream
- 60g Almond slivers (lightly toasted)

For the Syrup:

- ½ c. Sugar
- ½ c. Water

Directions:

- Combine sugar, milk, and rice in a medium saucepan. Place over moderate heat and bring to a boil, stirring constantly.

- Reduce heat to low, cover, and simmer for 30–35 minutes or until rice is tender and milk has been absorbed.

- Stir in egg yolk, then remove from heat and set aside to cool completely.

- Meanwhile, prepare the syrup. Combine both ingredients in a medium saucepan. Cook over moderate heat until sugar is dissolved, stirring constantly.

- Increase heat to moderate–high and allow syrup to boil for 4 minutes, without stirring.

- Reduce heat to low and add peach halves, cut sides down and in one layer. Poach for 3–4 minutes or until tender but still retaining shape. Remove with a slotted spoon and leave to cool.

- Stir jam into syrup and cook for 2 minutes, stirring constantly. When the sauce is smooth, remove it from heat and set it aside to cool.

- Stir cream into cooked rice, then divide among 4 individual serving c.. Spoon syrup over and top each glass with one peach half.

- Sprinkle flaked almonds over and refrigerate for 1 hour before serving

Nutritional Information:

Calories: 305

Protein: 19.1g

Carbohydrates: 25.9g

Fat: 20.2g

Cholesterol: 80 mg

Sodium: 515.6mg

278. GINGER AND PUMPKIN TORTA

Preparation Time: 2 hrs

Servings: 9

Ingredients:

For the Crust:

- 3 tbsp. of fresh ginger, grated
- ⅓ c. of sugar
- 5 tbsp. of melted butter, unsalted

For the Filling:

- 1½ c. of pumpkin puree
- 1 c. of milk
- 1 tbsp. of cinnamon, ground
- 3 eggs
- 1 packet of brown sugar
- 1 tsp. of salt

Directions:

- To prepare the crust, mix the ginger, sugar, and butter.
- Bake for 15 minutes.

- Mix the pumpkin and all other ingredients (except milk and egg) to fill.
- Cook on low heat for some minutes.
- Add your milk and egg.
- Mix until you get a smooth consistency.
- Add the filling to your crust and bake for three minutes.

Nutritional Information:

Fat: 1g

Carbs: 32.6g

Fibre: 4g

Calcium: 25 mg

Protein: 3g

279. CREAMY STRAWBERRY TORTA

Preparation Time: 1hr

Servings: 10

Ingredients:

- 10 oz. of cream cheese
- 2 c. of strawberries
- 5 oz. of strawberry Jell-O
- 4 tbsp. of melted butter
- Oreo cookies
- 1 c. of gelatine powder
- 1 c. of sugar

Directions:

- Blend the cookies with the butter for 20 seconds and refrigerate.

- Mix the gelatine powder with water.

- Add the mixture to your strawberries.

- Refrigerate for 40 minutes.

- Add the filling to the crust.

Nutritional Information:

Protein: 5g

Saturates: 10g

Sodium: 250mg

Sugar: 40g

Cholesterol: 44 mg

280. VANILLA DURAZNO

Preparation Time: 1½ hr

Servings: 4

Ingredients:

- ⅛ c. of heavy cream

- ¼ tsp. of salt

- 1 c. of all-purpose flour

- 5 tbsp. of butter, unsalted

- ½ tbsp. of baking powder

For the Filling:

- ½ tsp. of vanilla extract

- 2 peaches

- ½ c. of sugar

Directions:

- Process the baking powder, flour, sugar, and salt topping for 25 seconds.

- Add your butter, and then process some more.

- Pour the mixture into a bowl and add your cream.

- Mix well.

- Refrigerate.

- For the filling, mix your peaches and vanilla extract in a bowl.

- Bake for 40 minutes.

Nutritional Information:

Carbs: 50g

Protein: 5g

Fat: 31g

Sugar: 50.5g

Saturates: 15g

281. RICE-WATER SESAME BALLS

Preparation Time: 40 minutes

Servings: 12

Ingredients:

- 1 c. of sesame seeds, white

- 1 c. of vegetable oil

- 4 c. of rice flour

Directions:

- Boil some water.

- Mix your sugar and rice flour in a bowl.

- Gradually pour the boiled water into the mixture.

- Knead thoroughly to form a dough.

- Cut dough into as many pieces as you desire.

- Form these doughs into balls.

- Coat these balls in your sesame seeds.

- Fry the balls until golden brown on all sides.

Nutritional Information:

Sodium: 25mg

Fat: 7g

Calories: 150

Carbs: 21g

282. RED PÂTE DE HARICOTS

Preparation Time: 30 minutes

Servings: 5

Ingredients:

- ⅔ c. of sugar

- ½ tsp. of salt

- 8 oz. of red beans

Directions:

- Soak your red beans overnight

- The next day, boil with plenty of freshwaters. Keep boiling till the beans go soft.

- Process your red beans to smoothness.

- Mix with sugar and salt.

- Refrigerate.

Nutritional Information:

Cholesterol: 0mg

Calories: 700

Sodium: 620mg

Carbs: 210g

283. VANILLA-COATED WALNUTS

Servings: 7

Preparation Time: 1½ hr

Ingredients:

- 1 c. of sugar

- ⅔ c. of oil

- 2 eggs

- 1 tsp. of baking powder

- 1 tsp. of vanilla extract

- ½ tsp. of salt

- 1 c. of walnuts

Directions:

- The oven should be preheated at 175° F.

- Mix the flour, salt, and baking powder thoroughly.

- Mix the eggs, oil, and vanilla extract.

- Add the flour, salt, and baking powder mixture and mix well.

- Pour the walnuts into the mixture.

- Bake for 45 minutes.

Nutritional Information:

Saturated: 6g

Carbohydrate: 25g

Fat: 11g

Sodium: 48g

284. GOLDEN SESAME

Servings: 3

Preparation Time: 20 minutes

Ingredients:

- 2 c. of sesame seeds

- ½ c. of sugar

Directions:

- Pour the sugar into a pot filled with water.

- Allow boiling for some time.

- Pour in the seeds.

- Stir till they turn golden.

Nutritional Information:

Sugar: 3g

Fat: 60g

Sodium: 15 mg

Potassium: 472 mg

285. WALNUT FRITO EN ACEITE

Preparation Time: 40 minutes

Servings: 12

Ingredients:

- 6 c. of oil

- 1½ c. of walnuts

- ⅛ c. of sugar

Directions:

- Fill a pot with water and boil.

- Pour in your walnuts and cook for 40 seconds.

- Transfer your walnut into a bowl.

- Add sugar.

- Mix properly

- Fry till golden.

Nutritional Information:

Sugar: 1.5 g

Protein: 5g

Fibre: 2g

Fat: 15g

Calories: 125g

286. PINEAPPLE-BANANA CAKE

Preparation Time: 1½ hrs

Servings: 4

Ingredients:

- 1 egg
- ½ tbsp. of butter
- ½ c. of sugar
- ½ tbsp. of vanilla extract
- 8 oz. of pineapple
- 8 oz. of banana

Directions:

- Grate your vanilla extract, pineapple, banana, sugar, butter, and egg together.
- Add some water and mix well.
- Bake for 50 minutes.

Nutritional Information:

Cholesterol: 50mg

Calories: 200

Protein: 2g

Carbs: 40g

287. FRUITY GELATIN

Servings: 7

Preparation Time: 15 minutes

Ingredients:

- 2 oz. of gelatine
- 3 c. of fruit juice

Directions:

- Boil your fruit juice.
- Pour into a bowl.
- Add gelatine.
- Stir well.
- Refrigerate.

Nutritional Information:

Fibre: 1g

Sodium: 10.5mg

Sugar: 25g

288. FORTUNE VANILLA

Preparation Time: 35 minutes

Servings: 6

Ingredients:

- 1 egg
- ½ tsp. of vanilla extract
- ½ c. of flour, all-purpose
- 1 tbsp. of sugar

Directions:

- Heat the oven to 430° F.
- Mix the egg and vanilla.

- Mix your sugar, flour, and salt.

- Combine both mixtures.

- Bake for 10 minutes.

Nutritional Information:

- Protein: 5.6g

- Fibre: 2.5 g

- Fat: 4g

- Carbs:93g

289.   VANILLA GALLETA DE AVENA

Preparation Time: 40 minutes

Servings: 8

Ingredients:

- 4 tsp. of vanilla extract

- 4 c. of oats

- 3 c. of brown sugar, packed

- 2 tbsp. of butter, salted

- 3 eggs

- 3 c. of all-purpose flour

- 1½ tsp. of salt

Directions:

- Your oven should be heated at 355°F.

- Mix the brown sugar, vanilla extract, egg, and butter thoroughly.

- Mix the baking soda, flour, and all-purpose flour in a bowl.

- Add the two mixtures together.

- Pour your oats into the mixture.

- Bake for 20 minutes.

Nutritional Information:

Cholesterol: 0mg

Fat: 6g

Carbs:24g

Calories: 100

290.   BUTTERY VANILLA

Preparation Time: 1hr

Servings: 10

Ingredients:

- 2 tsp. of vanilla extract

- 2 c. of peanut butter

- 1 c. of melted butter

- 1 c. of milk

- 18 oz. of brown sugar, packed

- 1 c. of sugar

Directions:

- Pour your batter into a pan.

- Place the pan on low heat.

- Add your milk and sugar.

- Keep the heat low as you stir. Do this for 3 minutes.

- Turn off the heat and add your vanilla and peanut butter.

- Bake for 30 minutes.

Nutritional Information:

Cholesterol: 20mg

Protein: 4g

Calories: 400

Carbs: 65g

291. CHINESE TARTA DE CREMA PASTELERA

Preparation Time: 1 hr

Servings: 14

Ingredients:

- 2 c. of Milk

- 4 eggs

- ½ c. of sugar

- 2½ tsp. of vanilla extract

Directions:

- Heat the oven at 175°C.

- Mix your egg, milk, sugar, and vanilla.

- Roll out the dough evenly and cut.

- Sprinkle your pastry container with flour and set your dough on it.

- Fill your dough with custard.

- Bake for 40 minutes.

Nutritional Information:

Sodium: 80mg

Fat: 18g

Calories: 300

Protein: 4g

Sugar: 10.5g

Saturates: 5.5g

292. VANILLA PEANUT BUTTER FUDGE

Preparation Time: 1 hour

Serving: 4

Ingredients:

- ½ c. of butter

- 2 ½ c. of brown sugar

- A c. of whole milk

- ½ c. of smooth peanut butter

- ½ tsp. of vanilla extract

- 2 c. of powdered sugar

Directions:

- Allow butter to melt at 100oC, add melted butter into 1 c. of milk, and mix. After mixing, add brown sugar, then mix all together.

- Cook the mixture, leave the mixture to boil for about 2minutes, and continue to mix while cooking. Drop the mixture after boiling.

- Mix the peanut butter and the vanilla extract until it is smooth.

- Get a bowl and put the powdered sugar in the bowl. Add the blended peanut butter and vanilla extract in the same bowl as the confectioner's sugar, then beat well till it becomes smooth.

- After that, pour the mixture into the pan and allow it to cool for 60 minutes. Then chop it into square shapes.

Nutritional Information:

Calories: 92

Protein: 0.8g

Fat: 3.2g

293.   VANILLA OATMEAL COOKIES

Preparation Time: 30 minutes

Serving: 4

Ingredients:

- ½ c. of shortening

- ½ c. of brown sugar, packed or 1 ½ tbsp. molasses c. of white sugar

- 1 large egg

- ½ tsp. of vanilla

- 1 c. of butter

- 1 ½ c. of all-purpose flour

- ½ c. of flaked coconut

- ½ tsp. of baking soda

- 1 ½ c. of rolled oats

- ½ c. raisins

Directions:

- Mix butter, sugar, and shortening altogether in a bowl.

- Add egg, add vanilla, and mix, then put aside.

- Mix all dry ingredients in another bowl after mixing. Add in the coconut.

- Drop each on a cookie sheet that has been sprayed. Continue cooking by baking for 10 minutes.

Nutritional Information:

Calories: 69kal

Protein: 1g

Fats: 4.8g

Carbs: 3.9g

294.   VANILLA FORTUNE COOKIES

Preparation Time: 30 minutes

Serving: 4

Ingredients:

- 1 white Egg
- 1 c. of table sugar
- ½ tsp. of table salt
- 1 c. of all-purpose flour
- 1 tsp. of vanilla extract
- 2 tsp. of hot water
- 1 c. of milk
- ½ c. of fresh lard

Directions:

- Firstly, preheat the oven to about 300F. Then make the dough by adding salt to the flour in a bowl. Measure and add the lard, then mix it all.

- After this, add vanilla extract and hot water, mix it, and make a dough. Cooking further divides the dough into three.

- After dividing dough, cut each divided part into balls and roll until each is thick.

- In each thick roll, cut at least 6 and place it into greased or oiled biscuits tin to shape.

- Beat the eggs and add evaporated milk, milk, and sugar to fill the egg custard.

- Then add custard into each of the biscuit tins but avoid overflowing.

- Bake in the oven until there are signs that the custard is cooked through or for about 25 minutes.

Nutritional Information:

Calories: 35

Protein: 0g

Fat: 0g

Carbs: 7g

295. FRUIT GELATIN

Preparation Time: 20 minutes

Serving: 4

Ingredients:

- 1 package of unflavoured powdered gelatine
- ½ c. of iced water
- 2 tsp. of sugar
- ½ boiling water
- ½ c. of evaporated milk
- 1 ½ tsp. of almond extract
- ½ c. of fresh fruit slices

Directions:

- Pour the gelatine into the cold water and allow it to soften.

- Pick another bowl, put in the sugar, add boiling water, mix vigorously until the sugar dissolves, and add evaporated milk to the mixture.

- Allow to cool slightly and add the almond extract.

- Coming back to the gelatine in cold water, add evaporated milk, stir properly and pour it into a shallow pan, allowing it to firm.

- Cut it into desired shapes and garnish with the fruit slices.

Nutritional Information:

Calories: 134

Protein: 2.6g

Fat: 0g

Carbs: 0g

296. BAKED PINEAPPLE AND BANANA √

Preparation Time: 30 minutes

Serving: 4

Ingredients:

- ½ c. of canned pineapple chunks
- 1 ½ tsp. of butter
- ½ c. of brown sugar
- 1 tbsp. reserved pineapple juice
- ½ tsp. of Chinese rice wine
- 2 bananas
- 1 tbsp. of untoasted sesame seeds

Directions:

- Warm up the oven by preheating the oven to 350F.
- Start by draining the can of pineapple chunks, reserving 1 tbsp. Juice.
- Then add butter and brown sugar together in a bowl.

- The rice wine and pineapple juice should also be added and stirred.
- Taking your baking dish, lay out the bananas and pineapple chunks. Add the brown sugar mixture by spreading it on the bananas and pineapple.
- Bake for about 10 minutes till the fruits are tender. To finish it up, sprinkle it with sesame seeds.

Nutritional Information:

Calories: 84.5

Protein: 1g

Fat: 1.7g

Carbs: 21.6g

297. DEEP-FRIED WALNUT

Preparation Time: 20 minutes

Serving: 2

Ingredient:

- 1 c. of chopped walnut pieces
- ½ c. of sugar
- 2 c. oil for deep-frying

Direction:

- Deeply boil walnut pieces for about 5 minutes to drain all bitter flavour.
- Get a waxed paper and spread sugar on the piece of waxed paper, then roll the walnut in the sugar.

- Place it on a platter or flat plate and leave it overnight to dry.

- Heat the oil. When the oil is hot, add the walnut and deep-fry until golden brown.

- Remove the walnuts and drain.

Nutritional Information:

Calories: 140

Protein: 2g

Fat: 12g

Carbs: 6g

298.   SWEETENED SESAMUM-SEED

Preparation Time: 30 minutes

Serving: 4

Ingredient:

- ½ lb. sugar

- 2 oz. corn-starch

- 1 handful of sesame-seeds

Directions:

- Put at least one bowl of water in an oiled pot and put it on the fire to boil, adding sugar and 2 oz. of corn starch.

- Boil the mixture until the water in the mixture dries completely.

- Allow to cool slightly and roll out on a board sprinkled with sesamum seeds.

- Roll into balls or bars and allow to cool completely.

Nutritional Information:

Calories: 170

Fat: 8g

Protein: 5g

Carbs: 20g

299.   VANILLA WALNUT COOKIES

Preparation Time: 60 minutes

Serving: 4

Ingredient:

- 1 tsp. of baking powder

- 2 c. of flour

- ½ c. of lard

- 1 c. of finely chopped walnuts

- 1 ½ tsp. of vanilla extract

- 1 ½ c. of white sugar

- 2eggs

- 1 egg, lightly beaten

Directions:

- Preheat the oven. Get a bowl, pour the flour into it and add baking powder.

- Cut the lard into the flour and mix properly and tiny balls.

- Then add walnuts, vanilla extract, sugar, and 2 eggs. Mix this mixture properly into the dough till it forms a paste.

- Cut the dough into bits and make it into a ball shape using your hands.

- Put the balls you have made into an oiled baking pan, then brush it with the lightly beaten egg.

- Oven-bake the balls for about 25 minutes.

Nutritional Information:

Calories: 461

Protein: 16g

Fat: 27g

Carbs: 4g

300.   RED BEANS PASTE

Preparation Time: 2 days

Serving: 2

Ingredients:

- 1 c. of dried red beans

- 2 c. of water

- ½ c. of sugar (or to taste)

- 1 ½ tbsp. of oil

Directions:

- Rinse and soak dried beans in water overnight, then drain.

- Boil 2 cups of water, then add the beans and simmer for at least 2 hours till it gets tender.

- After this, drain. Blend the beans and sugar until it is smooth.

- To finish it up, heat the oil in a preheated pot or saucepan, add the blended beans paste and stir-fry until dry.

Nutritional Information:

Calories: 90

Protein: 20g

Fat: 10g

Carbs: 23g

301.   SWEETENED SESAME SEED BALLS

Preparation Time: 60 minutes

Serving: 4

Ingredient:

- ½ c. of brown sugar

- ½ c. boiling water

- 2 c. of glutinous rice flour

- ½ c. sweet red bean paste

- ½ c. white sesame seeds

- 5c. of oil for deep-frying

Directions:

- Boil water and add sugar. Stir continuously till it dissolves. Leave to cool off.

- Pour the glutinous rice flour into a large bowl and make a well in the middle.

- Add your sugar dissolved water into the well and mix with the flour. After mixing the well, you should observe a sticky, caramel-coloured dough at this point.

- Make sure you rub the remaining rice flour on your hands to avoid the dough sticking to them.

- Take the dough and cut into small sizes and shape it into a ball. Then flatten the ball with the palm of your hand, after which you use your thumb to make an indentation in the middle.

- Take 1 tsp. of red beans paste and add it using your hand to shape the paste on the circle.

- Shape the dough by folding it repeatedly and then rolling it back into a ball. Do this to the rest of the dough.

- Then sprinkle the sesame seed on a sheet of foil paper, roll these balls in the seeds.

- Pour 5 cups of oil in a large pot and heat, then deep-fry the sesame balls until they are well cooked, changing colour to golden brown and increasing in size.

Nutritional Information:

Calories: 120

Protein: 2 g

Fat: 1.5 g

302.   VANILLA PEACH COBBLER ✓

Preparation Time: 1 hour

Serving: 4

Ingredient:

- 2 c. of peaches, peeled, pitted, and sliced

- 1 c. of sugar

- ½ c. of flour

- ½ tsp. of baking powder

- ½ tsp. of salt

- 1 c. of margarine

- 1 tsp. of vanilla

- 1 c. of milk

- 1 c. of water

Directions:

- Get a pan and spray using the peaches for lining the pan.

- Get a bowl and put half a c. of sugar, vanilla, add margarine, salt, flour, and baking powder.

- Mix all together until it all blends.

- After which, add the peaches.

- Get another bowl, pour in water, and add half a c. of sugar. After mixing, pour it over the batter.

- Put the batter in the oven and bake for 60 min.

Nutritional Information:

Calories: 190

Protein: 1 g

Fat: 8 g

Carbs: 32 g

303.   CREAMY STRAWBERRY PIE

Preparation Time: 30 minutes

Serving: 4

Ingredient:

- 2 pie crust, pre-baked

- 2 pints of ripe strawberry

- ½ c. of hot water

- 1 ½ package strawberry Jell-O gelatine dessert

- 1 tbsp. corn-starch

- ½ c. of hot water

- ½ c. of cold water

- 1 c. of sugar

- Whipped cream

Directions:

- Pre-bake the crust and leave it to cool.

- Slice the strawberry into a bit and add to the pie crust.

- Get a bowl, put in the Jell-O, add the corn-starch, mix, and add water and sugar.

- Cook the mixture till it starts boiling, mix repeatedly until the boiling is completed.

- After doing this, pour the boiled mixture over the strawberries.

- Place the pie in the refrigerator and leave it to freeze for about four hours.

- To finish it up, add the whipped cream all over.

Nutritional Information:

Calories: 290

Protein: 30.8 g

Fat: 128.7 g

Carbs: 441.2 g

304.   GINGER PUMPKIN PIE

Preparation Time: 2 hours

Serving: 4

Ingredient:

- ½ c. of canned pumpkin

- 1 ½ c. of sweetened condensed milk

- 1 large egg

- ½ c. of firmly packed light brown sugar

- 1 ½ tbsp. sugar

- 1 tsp. of ground cinnamon

- ¼ tsp. salt

- 1 tsp. of ground ginger

- ¼ tsp. Ground nutmeg

- ½ tsp. ground cloves

- 1 pie crust

Directions:

- Pour the pumpkin into a bowl, add all the other ingredients, and beat moderately for about 2 minutes.

- Pour the mixture into the pie crust.

- Bake for half an hour at 425oF.

- Lower the temperature to 35o and bake for the next ½ hour.

- Leave to cool.

Nutritional Information:

Calories: 224

Protein: 4.8 g

Fat: 6.5 g

305.   CHINESE MILK CUSTARD TARTS ✓

Preparation Time: 1 hour 30 mins

Serving: 4

Ingredient:

- 2 c. of plain flour

- 160 g of lard

- 3 tbsp. of hot water

- A pinch of salt

- Ingredient for making custard

- 2 eggs

- ½ c. of sugar

- ½ c. of milk

- ½ drops of yellow food colouring

Directions:

- To prepare the pastry, get a bowl and mix the flour and salt. Rub the lard over the flour till it all looks like breadcrumbs.

- Blend in hot water for the dough to be firm, then knead on a floured surface.

- Pick the dough and roll it into patty tins.

- Make the custard by taking the eggs and beating them with sugar, adding in milk, dropping in two drops of food colouring, and blending them till it becomes smooth.

- Pour the smooth custard into pastry cases.

- Continue cooking by baking for about ten minutes at 475F, then lower the temperature to 425F and bake for ¼ hour.

Nutritional Information:

- Calories: 261

- Fat: 17 g

- Protein: 4 g

Who would have thought that Chinese cuisine would one day have a place in the world's food cultures? Alas, here we are today with cuisine that goes back more than 4000 years ago to dynasties and emperors depicted in colourful mosaics and written about in the literature of a powerful civilization.

Food is a central structure for the Chinese people. Over the years, the hurdles, struggles, and ingenuity have developed and refined cooking styles to suit the living conditions in the region. Today, what looked like a way out practiced globally to taste Chinese flavour using their cooking styles.

This is a beginner's guide to Chinese cooking, and while we have so gracefully added over 300 recipes to make you feel like a 5-star Chinese chef in the middle of your home, there is more to using a wok than you would want to know.

From the days of home cooking until today, Chinese cuisine and cooking styles have been passed down from generation to generation. With innovation and modernity, there are excellent results everywhere. Traditional cuisines have taken on a modern appearance and include delicacies from regions, dynasties, and chef masters from centuries before now.

This book introduces you to cooking Chinese using the wok's most important cooking tool. It does need some professional manoeuvrers, especially the quick hand movements. To get you started on your work, we have added a cleaning routine for your wok to ensure it lasts forever. It's as others say: the longer the wok is in use, the more flavourful the meals cooked in it.

Moving on, we talked about cooking techniques like pickling, fermentation, reprocessing, re-cooking, reheating, and twice cooking, and while we tried to do justice, the Chinese certainly pulled every trick in the book with their techniques. As mentioned, nothing is wasted, so cooking styles ensure every ingredient is allowed to shine as an individual but married with others for a complete experience.

Since you are just beginning, stick with the basics, and you will be a pro in no time. Furthermore, there are 12 chapters of recipes that cover everything Chinese, including dumplings, chicken, duck, beef, vegetarian, and more for you. Chinese cooking has some basic ingredients that must be included in the cuisine. Ingredients like soy sauce, ginger, garlic, scallions, chili, tofu (for vegetarian dishes), and spices are what one is likely to have to start their journey into Chinese cooking.

Printed in Great Britain
by Amazon